The
Reptile & Amphibian
Problem Solver

Practical & Expert Advice
on Keeping Reptiles & Amphibians

Robert Davies
Valerie Davies

Tetra🐾Press
No 16073

Contents

AN ANDROMEDA BOOK

Copyright © 1997
Andromeda Oxford Limited

Planned and produced by
Andromeda Oxford Limited,
11–15 The Vineyard, Abingdon,
Oxfordshire,
England, OX14 3PX

Published in North America by
Tetra Press,
3001 Commerce Street.
Blacksburg, VA 24060

ISBN 1–56465–194–0

Advisory Editor   PROFESSOR MALCOLM PEAKER

Project Editors	Lauren Bourque
	Fiona Gold
Art and Design	Ayala Kingsley
	Chris Munday
	Frankie Wood
Editorial Assistant	Mark McGuinness
Picture Research	
Manager	Claire Turner
Proofreader	Lynne Elson
Indexer	Ann Barrett
Production Manager	Clive Sparling
Publishing Director	Graham Bateman

Managing Editor for Salamander Books
  Anne McDowall

Colour origination by Pendry Litho Ltd.,
  Hove, England
Printed by Imprimerie Pollina S.A.,
  Lucon, France

Cover photo credits: *front* Michael
Fogden/Bruce Coleman, *back* Bill Love.

Introduction

It is difficult to explain the fascination of keeping reptiles and amphibians, collectively known as herptiles. They have had (and still have) a "bad press", often being regarded with superstition, fear and loathing. This is changing, as more people learn to appreciate the great variety of forms these animals take. Some keepers may be drawn to a species for its appearance or habits; others enjoy producing a "little piece of nature" in their living room.

Whatever the reason, the popularity of these creatures has increased rapidly. The past couple of decades has seen more literature published than did the previous hundred years. The availability of specialist equipment, commercial foods and dietary supplements has facilitated the successful keeping and breeding of many species previously considered impossible. In response to environmental threats, the trade in many species is now strictly controlled. Such restrictions can only proliferate with time, which increases the urgency of establishing breeding populations in captivity.

Many species are easy to care for, but problems can arise even for the most experienced keeper. You must give serious consideration to the responsibilities before bringing an animal home. Inadequate preparation causes suffering to animals and leads to disappointment for the owner. The care of reptiles and amphibians (especially their nutrition) is complex; children entrusted with husbandry must be supervised by adults. It is also worth finding an experienced "herptile vet" before you need one urgently.

We have presented information on the basis of questions that have been asked of us (or that we have asked!) during our years of reptile and amphibian husbandry, in our roles as lecturers and writers, and as the authors of the advice column in a specialist magazine. The first section, Starting Out, applies to both reptiles and amphibians. From there, the book is divided into four sections, two each on the two groups; the first of these gives general information about the practical aspects of husbandry, while the second focuses on individual species and their special requirements. We have given the measurements for vivaria as LxWxH, rather than in the old-fashioned form of aquarium gallon sizes. This reflects the wider choice of prefabricated and purpose-built models on the market today.

As keepers and breeders for many years, we have both experienced considerable interest, success and pleasure with these fascinating creatures. We hope this book will help readers to enjoy the same satisfaction.

ROBERT & VALERIE DAVIES

Starting Out

REPTILES AND AMPHIBIANS ARE COLLECTIVELY known as herptiles, or "herps" for short. They are not usually regarded as pets in the sense of animals that provide companionship and affection, although many become tame and their owners swear they have individual personalities. Herptiles are more demanding to keep than cats, dogs and other popular pets, so you should consider the potential problems before you acquire one. "Wanting to keep something different" is not sufficient – the novelty soon wears off. Factors to consider include the space and time needed for the hobby, and whether you can bear the cost: light, heat, food, specialist equipment and its replacement, and possible veterinarians' bills. Before bringing an animal home, make sure you can provide regular supplies of suitable food. Leaping into the hobby without adequate preparation leads to neglected animals and disappointed owners.

Legal Aspects
The trade and keeping of herptiles is controlled by national and international laws (see page 202 for detailed information). These laws vary between (and within) countries and are frequently altered. Most countries have laws to protect their native species and to control the keeping of dangerous animals. In the US, there are federal and state laws, such as a ban on the sale of turtles under 4in (10cm) long. In addition, local laws may prohibit keeping reptiles or amphibians over a specified size, and moving certain species between states is illegal. International trade is governed by CITES – the Convention on the International Trade in Endangered Species). Under CITES, species are grouped according to vulnerability and trade is controlled by a licensing system. The European Union has additional controls to prevent the import of certain species. Furthermore, it is an offence in many countries to allow non-native species to escape into the wild. Given the complexity of the regulations, and the fact that they are frequently amended, it is wiser to become informed than to risk falling foul of the law. There are a number of herpetocultural societies that can supply details of the current laws in your part of the world, and publications are available in the US. Take particular care if you collect from the wild, either at home or abroad.

Scientific Names
Animals with backbones are divided into classes such as mammals, amphibians and reptiles. Classes are further divided into orders, suborders, families, genera, species and subspecies.

Most scientific names have two parts: the first indicates the *genus* (a group containing certain related species); and the second refers to the *species*. Sometimes there is a third name, indicating a *subspecies* – an animal that is slightly different from other members of the species and is found in different areas. For example, the Sinaloan Milksnake has the name *Lampropeltis triangulum sinaloae*. *Lampropeltis* is the genus (including kingsnakes and milksnakes); *triangulum* is the species (milksnake); and *sinaloae* is the subspecies, the Sinaloan form of milksnake. A few scientific names are made up, and others are based on physical characteristics (*Crotaphytus collaris*, Collared Lizard), location or a person's name (*Storeria dekayi*, Dekay's Snake).

Many reptiles have several common names, causing confusion. For example, the Solomon Island Skink, the Monkey-tailed Skink and the Prehensile-tailed Skink are all the same animal: *Corucia zebrata*. There may be different names in other languages. Using the scientific name identifies the species precisely in any language. Common names are used in conjunction with scientific names throughout this book.

◀ *The spectacular Amazon Tree Boa (*Corallus enhydris enhydris*) is not yet available as captive-bred. Specimens may be aggressive and difficult to feed. See page 110.*

Choosing a Species

Before building or buying a vivarium and other equipment, decide which species you want to keep. The choice of animal is yours, but you should consider the following:

Eventual size: Iguanas, large snakes, turtles and some tortoises outgrow their original accommodation and may become difficult to handle.

Temperate or tropical species: Tropical species require extra equipment for heating the vivarium, and will cost more to keep. Species from arid areas do poorly in naturally high humidity.

Feeding requirements: Some people may not like the idea of feeding mammals to reptiles.

Temperament: Many species are docile, but others are well known for their intractability. They may need special handling equipment. Cleaning out the cages can be traumatic.

Single specimen or a pair: If you choose a pair (with a view to future breeding), are they compatible or do they need to be maintained separately except for mating? If the latter, can you provide the additional housing space?

NOTE: Breeding should only be undertaken after serious consideration, beginning with whether you are experienced enough to undertake the care of eggs and young, and whether you are prepared to keep an increased number of specimens. If you do not intend to breed, it is best not to keep pairs, which may mate if left to their own devices. Keep males instead.

Selecting Stock

Two rules apply: never buy on impulse – research and choose carefully; and never buy out of pity – taking on a sick animal brings trouble, expense and disappointment. It also perpetuates poor standards in the trade. Visit several dealers' premises to compare conditions. Look for clean, spacious cages kept at the correct temperature, with clean drinking water. Does the dealer carry a good range of equipment and foods? Are you allowed to examine the animals, and are your questions answered satisfactorily? Buying by telephone or post can also be risky, as the animals may be adversely affected in transit. Ask about guarantees.

Most reptiles and amphibians in the pet trade are still wild-caught. Many people object to this and will only keep captive-bred specimens. If you feel strongly on this issue, it will limit your choice of species. Some species are now labelled "captive-farmed", but both the term and the practice are controversial. For herps bred in captivity, there will probably always be a need for new blood to maintain genetic diversity.

Avoiding Trouble

It is difficult for the inexperienced keeper to spot poor health. Animals that appear healthy may deteriorate within a few days of purchase.

➡️ *Conditions in a pet shop are a key factor in the animals' health. Cages should be clean and large enough to prevent crowding. Careful observation here before purchase will help you to avoid some problems.*

Spend some time observing the animal and, if possible, ask to see it feed. Look for:

Alertness. Be cautious of any specimen that lies motionless in a corner with its eyes closed. (Snakes and some geckos have no eyelids and cannot shut their eyes.) Do not try too hard to provoke a reaction – even a sick animal may move if disturbed. It is normal for many snakes and nocturnal lizards to be sluggish in the daytime. Low temperatures also cause listlessness.

Scars. Look for open wounds, scabs, blisters, swellings, inflamed belly scales and (in turtles and tortoises) cracked shells. Old scars are natural in wild-caught animals. If they have healed cleanly, they are not detrimental to health.

Eyes. Bright and clear, with no discharge, sores, mites or ticks. "Milkiness" due to sloughing should appear on the rest of the body. Turtles or tortoises with closed, swollen eyes are sick.

Emaciation. Lizards and snakes that are dehydrated or have not fed will start to lose the fat from the tail or body. Specimens like this should be avoided. In the worst cases the spine and pelvic bones (where the tail joins the body) become prominent and grooves appear along the animal's tail. Another sign is a sunken belly with loose folds of skin.

However, certain female lizards have loose folds after parturition, and some lizards have a corpulent appearance when full, while the skin appears to loosen between meals. Examples of these are Green Iguanas, collared lizards and chuckwallas. Plated lizards (*Gerrhosaurus* species) should have a fold along the body.

Clean nose and mouth. Discharge or bubbles indicate respiratory disease, which may also cause wheezing (not the same as hissing). Red spots or a cheesy substance in the mouth, often seen with snout damage, indicates mouthrot. Avoid specimens with rubbery or swollen jaws.

Clean cloaca (vent). Large amounts of faeces adhering to the vent could indicate enteritis. Check the cage for loose, watery, slimy, blood-stained or worm-infested droppings.

Sound limbs and tail. Do not buy animals with damaged limbs. Turtles and tortoises should exert a strong push against the hand. Tethering by the limbs while awaiting shipment can cause damage – look for a groove around the legs.

Dealing with a New Arrival

A newly-acquired animal is often stressed. It should be allowed to settle in, not hauled out to be shown off every few minutes. If you already have other animals in the vivarium, quarantine the new specimen until you are sure that it is healthy, and keep careful watch when introducing it. Supply drinking water in a bowl or as a light spray. If the animal is dehydrated, rehydration therapy with electrolytes or probiotics may be required. Food can be offered but may not be eaten. For especially nervous specimens, it may help to cover the front of the cage.

Handling Herps

Sooner or later you will have to handle the new arrival. (Amphibians should only be handled when absolutely necessary; see What is an Amphibian?, pages 140–141.) Wild-caught reptiles may grow more amenable with time, but some remain intractable; younger specimens are easier to tame, but even the most "silly-tame" reptile may bite. Avoid handling before and after feeding, and always use snake tongs – a hungry snake may grab at a moving hand. Wash your hands after handling food, or other snakes or lizards. When handling snakes of uncertain temperament, use grabsticks or snake hooks, or wear strong gloves. The best time is in the morning, when snakes are cool; they enjoy your warm hands. Do not make grabbing

Captive-bred	vs. Wild-caught
Do not reduce wild populations ✓	Reduce wild populations
Are accustomed to an artificial environment, ✓ therefore are less stressed	May be stressed or damaged due to capture, shipping, etc.
Are less likely to be diseased or carrying ✓ parasites	Could be carrying disease and parasites.
	May not adapt to vivarium life – can damage themselves, especially when caught as adults
Should be used to handling – reducing the ✓ danger of biting	May never accept handling – increasing the danger of biting.
Will be accustomed to a captive diet ✓	May refuse to feed, especially those with a specialized diet in the wild.
Are of known age ✓	Are of unknown age – possibly an old specimen with short life expectancy
May be inbred i.e. from related parents	✓ Are unlikely to be inbred

◄— *Even when removing a snake from its vivarium, use both hands to support the whole animal; this will make it feel more secure and amenable to handling.*

◄ *Young turtles are not difficult to handle. They should not be squeezed, as the shell is relatively soft at this age. Beware of nipped fingers – don't drop the animal!*

movements, especially at the head. Never dangle snakes by the tail; support the whole body, moving your hand as the snake moves.

Lizards may shed the tail if it is grabbed, or even if they are startled. Cup small lizards in your palm and place the middle finger under the throat, with the thumb resting (not too tightly) on the nape of the neck. For larger specimens, one hand holds the neck, a finger on each side of the head, while the other fingers and thumb pinion the forelegs – without twisting them up over the back; the other hand holds above or below the animal's body well back against the hindlegs to prevent scratching. Tuck a long tail under the arm.

Hold small terrapins at the rear of the shell using fingers and thumb. Large terrapins and tortoises need a hand on each side of the mid-body – out of reach of claws and away from the jaws, which are at the end of a long neck.

CAUTION: Never attempt to handle a large, powerful reptile alone. Another adult should always be present for safety reasons.

● *How can I tell if a snake has recently eaten?*

... A bulge in its body is a tell-tale sign. Hold the snake and gently run your fingers along its underside. If the belly "gives" and feels concave along its full length, the snake has not eaten for a while.

● *Is the salty deposit around the nostrils of lizards a sign of illness?*

No. Because lizards excrete very little water, undissolved salts are passed through their nostrils.

● *How does starvation show in turtles?*

The soft parts will have retracted well into the shell. Avoid turtles or tortoises if the head flops or is permanently retracted. When handled, a healthy turtle should retract its head quickly and push strongly with the hind legs.

● *Is it wise to buy an animal which is sloughing (shedding its skin)?*

Sloughing the skin is a natural function. If the skin is loose and obviously ready to come off, there is no problem. If the skin is milky however, and sloughing has not begun, the animal may be in poor condition and should be avoided.

● *Are there any problems in buying a gravid female?*

This is not recommended: gravid females which have been imported frequently die before or soon after parturition. Egg retention is a common problem and "live young" are often stillborn.

Reptile Care

Keeping reptiles is more demanding than keeping dogs, cats or other typical pets. Until very recently, their complex requirements meant that reptiles could only be kept by experts. Today the hobby is open to amateurs who can draw on a fund of knowledge and can obtain specialist equipment and foods with minimum inconvenience. This promotes the successful husbandry (and even breeding) of species previously considered impossible to keep in captivity.

For any reptile species to thrive, the conditions in which it is kept must be carefully tailored. Some reptiles are carnivorous, others herbivorous; some require humid conditions, others are desert-dwellers. Nocturnal species do not need much light, whereas diurnal species need natural daylight (or its facsimile, full-spectrum UVB light) to be at their best. All reptiles are poikilothermic ("cold-blooded"). They control their body temperature by moving closer to and farther away from heat as their instinct tells them. For almost all reptiles, it is crucial to provide an environment with a thermal gradient – cool at one end and warm at the other. The vivarium must be large enough to facilitate this. Reptiles that are kept too cool will be sluggish, and overheated ones may literally "cook".

If it is kept in the correct conditions, your reptile should be healthy. Treating a sick reptile is perhaps the most difficult aspect of husbandry. There are very few remedies available, even with a prescription. It is worth finding an experienced "reptile vet" before you need one urgently.

▶ *Green Iguana* (Iguana iguana) *see page 82.*

What is a Reptile?

REPTILES HAVE BEEN AROUND FOR SOME 315 million years and have adapted to almost all habitats except permanently frozen areas. Reptiles are ectothermic (poikilothermic): they maintain their body temperature with external heat rather than by eating. This allows them to live where food is scarce. Heliotherms maintain body warmth by moving in and out of sunlight. Thigmotherms absorb heat from their surroundings.

Reptiles' ectothermic nature and widely differing habitats are important factors to consider. Desert reptiles will perish in a rainforest vivarium and vice versa. Also, conditions in captivity are restricted and should be more moderate than in the wild. Reptiles from cold climates usually hibernate in Winter and wake up in Spring (see Breeding, pages 35–37). Some reptiles give birth to live young, but most lay eggs.

Scaly Ones

Scales are the most distinctive feature of reptiles. One of the main orders is the Squamata, "scaly ones". Scales protect against predators and desiccation. Snake scales are arranged in continuous, even rows along the back and sides; other scales may be keeled, smooth or spiny. Lizard scales may be raised, spiny, platelike, smooth or keeled, and their arrangement is more irregular.

Lizards have the most species and the most varied body shapes. They may be squat and flat to elongated, or in between like lacertids and iguanids – often regarded as "typical" lizards. The limbs may be absent, reduced or well-developed, and may have "adhesive" digits. Tails vary from long and whiplike to short and fat, as well as the specialized prehensile tail of chameleons. Practically all lizards store fat in their tails.

◄ *A gravid female chameleon* (Chamaeleo minor). *Her variable colouring, which repels amorous males, is produced by pigment movement in the chromatophores.*

Reptile Classification

ORDER	COMMON NAME	FAMILIES	GENERA	SPECIES
Chelonia (Testudines, Testudinata)	Turtles, tortoises and terrapins	13	75	244
Squamata (SUBORDER Lacertillia *or* Sauria)	Lizards	16	383	3750
Squamata (SUBORDER Amphisbaenia)	Worm lizards	4	21	140
Squamata (SUBORDER Serpentes *or* Ophidia)	Snakes	11	417	2390

These figures are approximate and are sometimes revised. The other orders, **Rynchocephalia** *(the Tuatara) and* **Crocodilia** *(Crocodiles), have been deliberately omitted as they are not mentioned elsewhere in this book.*

 ▲ *A Brown Water Python* (Liasis fuscus). *Snake skin will expand to accommodate food, eggs or developing young. The smooth regularity of the scales was once thought to make snake skin impervious, but it is not.*

Turtles and snakes are fairly uniform in shape but not in size. Snakes have elongated bodies and lack external ears, eyelids and legs. Their hinged lower jaw allows most species to eat comparatively large prey by extending the jaw downwards to accommodate large objects. The sides of the lower jaw are connected by a ligament that permits independent, alternate movement of each one, enabling the snake to "walk" food down its throat. As snakes lack the breastbone (sternum) that connects the ribs in other animals, the ribs can expand under the flexible skin to permit easy passage of the prey to the gut.

Snakes and most lizards "smell" molecules picked up from the air by the extended tongue and sent to Jacobson's organ in the roof of the mouth. It helps to recognize food, identify mates and track prey. The tongue itself does not sting.

Q & A...

● *Do all reptiles have scales?*

Yes, even turtles – their shells are covered with large scales (scutes). Scales and the rest of the outer skin layer are periodically sloughed (shed), a feature of all reptiles. Reptile scales are a continuous, thick keratinous layer (part of the epidermis), loosely hinged by a thin layer for flexibility. Scales on *Teratoscincus* species (geckos) are separate and detachable like fishes'.

● *Do all reptiles possess Jacobson's organ?*

No, only snakes and lizards. The more frequent the tongue-flicking, the more developed the sense.

● *Why do turtles and tortoises have different shells?*

Most aquatic species have low, streamlined shells for speed or for hiding in mud; most terrestrial species have higher shells for protection against crushing.

● *How do chameleons change colour?*

Chameleons and a few other reptiles have chromatophores (pigment-filled cells) in the lower layer of skin. Nervous activity or hormonal changes may cause the pigment to shift, producing a colour change.

Housing – the Vivarium

THE TYPE, SIZE AND NUMBER OF ANIMALS to be housed, and the space available in your home, will determine your choice of vivarium. Some keepers prefer a standard glass aquarium, but you can buy prefabricated models or build your own. A prefabricated vivarium gives little control over ventilation, but if you are building your own, the ventilation panels can be whatever size you choose. The mesh must be small enough to prevent escape of occupants and food insects, but tough enough to withstand the claws and weight of the animal. Aluminium mesh is soft and easily damaged. Neither it nor zinc should be used

▲ Ready-made vivaria come in several types. A plastic aquarium with lid ventilation and integral light or heat fitting (top) is inexpensive, but is not the best kind of housing – the heat fitting can melt the lid! A simple wooden vivarium (below) is suitable only for a dry habitat; glass (right) may be used for a wet or dry one.

Vivarium Hygiene

A regular routine should include the following:

- Spot-cleaning faeces
- Removing uneaten food and sloughed skins
- Disinfecting furnishings (see below)
- Sterilizing water bowls, a common source of infection
- Providing fresh water daily

Quarantined or sick animals should be dealt with last during the daily routine.

Disinfection

There are proprietary vivarium disinfectants, but a 3% solution of household bleach or a 5% solution of household ammonia is quite adequate. Avoid household disinfectants that are phenol-based. All equipment, especially instruments for cleaning the cage, should be disinfected between use in different cages. Disinfectants must be allowed to work for at least 20 minutes before they are rinsed. Porous materials will need extra soaking and rinsing – baking is effective but may not be possible. After disinfection, cages and materials need thorough rinsing so that the disinfectant does not leach out later and poison the animals. Replace soiled furnishings if possible.

where moisture is present. Metal flyscreen is another possibility, and galvanized mesh is suitable if crickets are not being used as food. Plastic greenhouse shading is useful for ventilation but deteriorates with time, and large snakes and lizards can push through it. Through-flow ventilation is more effective than a grille in the top; where units are stacked side by side, ventilation panels may have to be in the back or the front.

A vivarium must be escape-proof: many reptiles, particularly snakes, can force lids off or squeeze through gaps. Live insects may also escape and become pests in the house. The vivarium must be easy to clean and maintain. Front-opening models may allow animals to dart out, and small specimens or food insects may escape through the gap between the overlapping glass doors. A vivarium with top access is more difficult to clean, but it is more secure. You should be able to reach all the way down to the bottom.

Panels fitted across the front (top and bottom) will mask the lights to prevent glare. A deep lower panel, hinged to allow access to the substrate, allows easy cleaning. It also helps to stop lizards from scrabbling at the glass.

Where a number of reptiles are being kept, rack systems or multiple units are a popular way to make the most of the limited space available. Rack systems consist of one or more individual units in tiers on a rack. Multiple units are simply a large unit divided into several (like bird-cage units). If individual units are heated separately, each layer is progressively hotter. You may need to insulate between the rows or to experiment with different heat sources (see Heating and Lighting, pages 18–19.) Temperature may dictate which row an animal is kept in. Rack systems are often used with clear plastic "sweater boxes" or "shoe boxes", particularly for snakes and their hatchlings. Prefabricated models can be purchased, or you can build them at home.

A HOMEMADE VIVARIUM

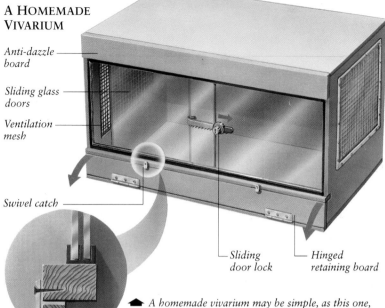

Anti-dazzle board

Sliding glass doors

Ventilation mesh

Swivel catch

Sliding door lock

Hinged retaining board

▲ *A homemade vivarium may be simple, as this one, but it allows you to customize every feature from size to ventilation and the type and position of the doors.*

A glass vivarium must be placed on styrofoam tiles or slabs at least 0.25in (6mm) thick to prevent the base cracking. Once the substrate medium or water has been added, the vivarium may not be moved; it is likely to break.

Making a Divided Vivarium

Some species require two sets of conditions within the same vivarium: for example, the Fat-tailed Gecko (see pages 72–73) requires both an area of dry substrate and an area of damper substrate; and some turtles need both a land area and a pool. You can set up a dual substrate in the vivarium by simply placing the two substrates side by side; using trays makes removal and replacement easy. Alternatively, divide the vivarium at floor level, using a glass strip sealed into place. (If making a pool, the strip must be higher than the water level.) If dividers are fitted, any exposed edges must be ground down to remove sharpness before sticking into place with silicone sealer.

A DIVIDED VIVARIUM

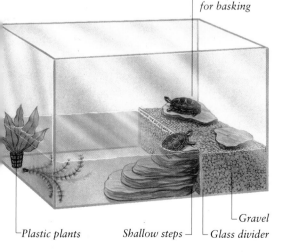

Thin, flat stone for basking

Plastic plants

Shallow steps

Gravel

Glass divider

◄ *Different mini-habitats can be provided in a single vivarium if it is divided using a glass strip sealed into place at floor level with silicone sealer. This will keep separate either two substrates for a terrestrial habitat or land and water for a semi-aquatic habitat.*

◄ *A Box Turtle* (Terrapena ornata) *in an outdoor pool. An elaborate set-up is often not necessary; Box Turtles will be happy with a shallow tray of water.*

Keeping Reptiles Outdoors

Outdoor reptiliaries have been popular for many years. They may be fenced-off compounds, rockery-type gardens surrounded by a brick wall, or mesh structures similar to aviaries. Natural unfiltered sunlight is extremely beneficial to many reptiles, but the design of outdoor enclosures needs very careful thought if they are to be successful. They must be escape-proof and predator-proof; the surrounding wall or fence must be deep enough to prevent burrowing by both inhabitants and potential predators. An overhanging coping of smooth material, or a half-round plastic gutter fixed along the inside of the walls, will stop the reptile(s) climbing out. A mesh cover is required to prevent predation from above (by hawks, cats, dogs etc.). Plenty of shade and deep hiding places should be provided to prevent over-exposure to the sun; reptiles should be able to move to a cooler position. Live foods and plants do not fare well in hot sunlight either.

Many owners of aquatic or semi-aquatic turtles keep them outside in a pool with basking spots or a land area and possibly filtration to keep the water clean. The enclosure must be adequately fenced to prevent wandering – some turtles are quite adept at climbing. Pre-formed plastic and fibreglass pools and filtration systems are available. Butyl rubber pond liners could be damaged by the claws of large turtles.

Your choice of species will be determined by the climate; use common sense. Harsh Winters, poor Summers or heavy rainfall may mean removal indoors, although hardy species such as Snapping Turtles (see pages 124–125) can hibernate outdoors if flood-proof, frost-free hibernation quarters are supplied. (For a discussion of hibernation, see Breeding, pages 34–37.) The enclosure may need to be covered in Winter. Adequate drainage is crucial even in Summer.

● *What materials are suitable for a vivarium?*

... This depends on the degree of humidity required by a particular species. A moist substrate will soon rot plywood and plastic-veneered chipboard, so these two materials are suitable only for dry set-ups that get a light daily spray. Glass, fibreglass and plastics are not affected by moisture, are easy to clean and have no hiding places for parasites and bacteria. All the joins must be sealed with aquarium sealant – NOT kitchen or bathroom sealant, which contains fungicides.

● *Can paint be used in a vivarium ?*

Non-poisonous paints are suitable for a dry vivarium. Yacht varnish contains a molluscicide which might be released.

● *Is there any disadvantage to placing the substrate in a glass or plastic tray?*

Dampness can build up underneath the tray when spraying. In a wooden vivarium where a damp substrate is needed, the lower part of the walls and the base could be lined with plastic laminate, butyl pond liner or glass as long as it is sealed against moisture.

● *Why aren't the basic, inexpensive plastic vivaria recommended for housing?*

They are too small, tend to scratch and discolour quickly, and fitting heat and light is difficult – it is almost impossible to provide a thermal gradient (see Heating and Lighting, pages 18–19), and if the plastic lid becomes too hot, it can melt. They can be used as temporary housing or to house small, nocturnal reptiles that do not require much heat or light and would survive in the heat provided by a small heater mat. Once the plastic is scratched, insects can climb up and escape. The shallower models, often recommended for snakes, do not have lids tight enough to prevent snakes pushing them up. Hatchlings and small snakes can escape through the ventilated lids.

● *Is a greenhouse a suitable home for reptiles?*

Temperatures in greenhouses fluctuate considerably – in hot weather they can become a death trap. A greenhouse in a partially shaded area can be adapted by replacing some of the glass with suitable mesh for ventilation. Even so, it is advisable to monitor maximum and minimum temperatures over a long period before using a greenhouse. A small amount of Winter sunlight can soon raise the temperature above the desired maximum for hibernating reptiles, causing death. Glass filters out vital ultraviolet rays.

● *Are moveable wire cages suitable for reptiles?*

Wire cages on castors are available in the US and are generally used for iguanas. They can be wheeled out into the sun, but it is essential to provide some shade since continuous hot sunlight can be fatal.

● *Are there any problems keeping reptiles outside?*

In addition to temperature control and the need for shade from the sun, feeding can be a problem since live foods can easily hide or escape – use feeding bowls or feed by hand. If reptiles escape, they could be impossible to recapture. It is your responsibility to ensure that they do not escape – and that they cannot easily be set free by mischief-makers. Liberated specimens may not survive in an alien environment; or if they do, they may become pests (see Cane Toad, *Bufo marinus*, on pages 164–165). In some places, particularly in the US, you can be held legally responsible for the escape of a reptile, even if it is harmless; if the reptile injures another person, the consequences will be worse. By and large, the public perception of reptiles is that they are too dangerous to be kept by amateurs. Irresponsible practices that permit the escape of specimens encourage public hysteria, leading to restrictive laws that make the hobby increasingly inaccessible. You MUST make any outdoor accommodation completely secure.

● *Can a reptile be kept in a small cage and allowed out for exercise?*

This is not a good idea. A reptile's quarters should be large enough to permit exercise. Large reptiles allowed to roam the house may attack another pet, or a child. Defecation in the house creates cleaning and hygiene problems. The reptile may also escape via open doors or windows.

● *Are bowls suitable for housing small terrapins?*

Turtle bowls were once popular for housing baby red-eared sliders, but they have been widely criticized for being much too small. Hatchling turtles (in countries where they are still available) need a good area for swimming, water depth twice the height of the turtle's shell, and a stone for basking. If they are kept indoors, a basking lamp and full-spectrum (UVB) fluorescent tube should be suspended over the set-up. A larger aquarium will be needed as the turtle grows.

● *Is it possible to house a number of different reptiles in a community vivarium?*

Yes, if they are carefully chosen for compatibility, but it is best to keep each species separately. This avoids bullying, cannibalism and competition for food.

Heating and Lighting

FAILURE TO KEEP REPTILES IN THE CORRECT temperature range will cause illness and eventually death. Some tropical reptiles need fairly constant temperatures, but others are accustomed to a night-time drop and, in many cases, a cool period in Winter. The vivarium temperature is affected by the ambient (room) temperature. In hot weather, temperatures may soar above the desired level unless the room is air-conditioned; in Winter the room may be warm during the day but cold at night, and the vivarium may need heating overnight. When choosing a spot, avoid radiators and sunlight from windows, which raise the temperature. An overheated vivarium becomes a death trap for its occupants.

Some keepers prefer to have heat and light sources above (outside) the vivarium. Heat and light radiate in through a mesh cover, with a sufficiently narrow gauge that live foods cannot escape through it. Ideally the vivarium should be large enough to produce a thermal gradient, with a cool end and a warm end, so that the inhabitants can thermoregulate (control their body temperature) by moving back and forth between the two ends. A small vivarium soon reaches a uniform temperature and its inmates could literally bake. Put a thermometer at each end of the vivarium for checking the temperature.

◄ *A pig blanket with internal thermostat directs heat upwards. If used under a thick layer of substrate, such heat sources can be damaged by heat building up.*

and tortoises also need a basking lamp. When using whole-room heating, some keepers do not fit individual lighting in each vivarium but rely on the room lighting. However, heat without light can cause diurnal reptiles to become sluggish; additional lighting may be required.

The simplest form of heating is a domestic incandescent light bulb controlled by a thermostat. Although it is relatively "primitive", this method is used successfully for many snakes and lizards, especially for nocturnal and crepuscular

Heating Methods

Heating a vivarium depends on individual circumstances. If you have several vivaria, it may be easier to heat the room and supply supplementary heating in individual cages if necessary. Whole-room heating is often used with snakes, but many lizards

▶ *Ceramic infra-red lamps (left), hot rock (top), heat mat (right). These are "non-visible" heat sources. Diurnal reptiles will need additional lighting, as a dim cage is unnatural and feeding could be inhibited.*

Types of Heater

Ceramic Heaters
No light – infrared rays only. Very hot. Mainly higher wattages. Useful for large vivaria and night-time heating.

Heater Mats
No light – infrared rays only. Useful for night-time heating and "belly heat". Moisture-proof, various wattages and sizes. Can be scratched by claws. Instructions MUST be followed. Can be used outside the vivarium; heat will penetrate most popular materials.

Heater Plates
Similar to mats, usually screwed to top of vivarium. No light – infrared rays only. One side insulated.

Pig Blankets (US)
Similar to heater plates but can be used on floor. 4 sizes/wattages.

Tubular Heaters
Several lengths/wattages, very hot in use, more suited to large vivaria (greenhouse type).

Heat Cables
Useful for thigmotherms, wattage varies with length. Fix firmly to prevent disturbance.

Basking lamps
Available in day and night types, various wattages.

Heat Tapes
Low wattage, often used for hatchling snake boxes on shelf/rack systems.

"Hot Rocks"
Imitation rocks that heat up. Early models criticized for causing burns. Newer models may have a rheostat control; if not, fit one or use a thermostat. Test occasionally with the hand to check heat. Not suitable for large reptiles, possibly useful for nocturnal species. Wattages as low as 4 watts.

Aquarium Heaters and Thermostats
May be needed for terrapin tanks if the basking light is insufficient to heat the water. Can also be used to heat a vivarium pool. Will need some protection to prevent accidents.

lizards. A spotlamp bulb is ideal; it concentrates heat and light for basking. It is fairly easy to purchase metal vivarium lids with a hole for the light bulb holder, a ventilation panel and a sliding glass aperture to fit most standard aquaria. Many other heating appliances are available.

Powerful heat sources must have a guard to prevent contact with animals. Snakes will often coil round a bulb, especially if it is fixed to a wall rather than the roof. Guards can be purchased for ceramic heaters – for other types it may be necessary to construct them. A number of companies (mainly in the US) supply hood modules that contain various combinations of heat and light appliances for use with glass aquaria. Most of them have reflectors to maximize heat and light. Before buying one, check to see if thermostatic control can be used to prevent overheating.

Temperature Control
It is possible to buy different types of control systems ranging from simple on/off thermostats to modules that can be expanded to include day and night settings, alarm systems, maximum and minimum temperature readouts, synchronized lighting, simulated dawn and dusk periods, and so on. Such systems can even be used with computer monitoring. Most modern thermostats are extremely accurate and are placed outside the vivarium, using a probe to detect temperature inside. To guard against the danger of thermostat

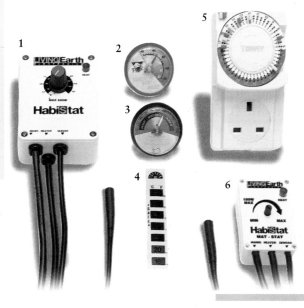

▸ *A range of simple temperature controls: (1) dimming thermostat, with sensor, for basking lamps, (2) stick-on temperature gauge, (3) stick-on humidity gauge, (4) stick-on LCD thermometer, (5) 24-hour timer, (6) temperature thermostat for non-light-emitting sources.*

failure in the "ON" position, a recent innovation is a thermal protector that shuts off the power if the thermostat fails. At least one thermostat model now has a high-level cutout, which could be useful. Night temperature is important and should be checked regularly.

Cheap thermometers are often inaccurate, but modern digital models with an external probe, specially designed for use in a vivarium, are more accurate. They are readily available from reptile dealers. Maximum/minimum thermometers are very useful for monitoring temperature change over a longer period.

Lighting

In the wild, when reptiles bask, they absorb ultraviolet (UV) light – one of the components of sunlight. It is vital to diurnal reptiles, though their precise requirements are not known. The invention of full-spectrum fluorescent tubes (bulbs in the US), containing the same components as sunlight, has made a dramatic difference with many species previously considered too difficult to be kept. UV light must enter the cage through mesh or be provided inside it; its rays do not pass through glass. Recent research suggests that some reptiles can see UV light.

There are three kinds of UV light. UVA is believed to increase appetite, stimulate activity and induce mating in reptiles. UVB plays a role in the synthesis of vitamin D3, which in turn assists the metabolism of calcium. Some experts argue that vitamin D3 supplements (with appropriate amounts of calcium and phosphorus) are an adequate substitute for UV light, but experiments show that reptiles deprived of UV light suffer

Points to Remember

- In a large vivarium two low-power heat sources are better than one powerful source, but ensure that there is a thermal gradient.
- Position the heat source carefully to prevent a fire. Keep clear of furnishings and bear in mind the nature of the vivarium material.
- Ceramic bulb-holders are safer and last longer than other types.
- The heater must be adequate for the size of vivarium, also taking into account the ambient temperature.
- Fit all heaters with thermostats. Even the smallest heater can cause overheating.
- In theory, infrared heat sources (mats or plates) do not warm the air, only the surface on which the rays fall, but air temperature may rise from convection as the surfaces warm up. Animals lying on the mats or plates can cause a build-up of heat. Only low wattage models are suitable for "belly heat".
- Unless you are a competent amateur, always have new installations fitted or checked by a qualified electrician.

poor health even with dietary supplements. Lizards kept outside in natural sunlight do not usually need supplements except calcium. UVC light is extremely dangerous to all living things.

Not all UV radiation promotes the synthesis of vitamin D3. Before purchase, check products for wavelengths of 260–315nm in the UVB range. Some products are claimed to be "full-spectrum" or "suitable for reptiles" but lack the UV component. As far as is known, basking lamps for reptiles do not produce UV light, although they

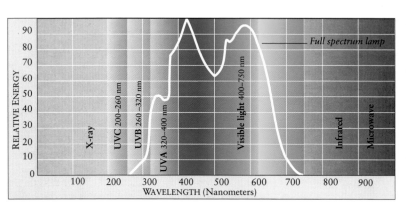

The wavelengths of natural light are measured in nanometers (nm). Ultraviolet is the part of the spectrum between 400nm–320nm (UVA) and between 320nm–285nm (UVB). UVC is very dangerous to living organisms. Above 700nm is infrared light. Full-spectrum light includes both visible and ultraviolet light – UVA and UVB, which are crucial to reptile health.

Vivaria with fluorescent full-spectrum lamps and ordinary tungsten bulbs. Red and blue reflective flood lamps (below) provide spot heating at a range of temperatures and can be useful for night heating.

may be labelled "full-spectrum". If possible, ask for a spectrum analysis for the tubes and bulbs from the manufacturer and compare them. Certain tubes are available with different UV strengths for different reptiles. The choice for any vivarium depends on the species kept, and where it comes from. If in doubt, contact others who keep the same species successfully and ask for details of their lighting regime, especially the photoperiod. Using a tube with an incorrect strength could be harmful. The photoperiod can be controlled by a timer. Replace tubes every 6–12 months for maximum efficiency. Effective distance is said to be 12in (30cm) but UV can also be reflected off surfaces.

Safety Precautions

Strong infrared or UV sources (sunlamps, for example) can cause burns or cataracts. Use only tubes designed for vivaria. The vivarium should have hiding places or shaded spots. Avoid staring at UV sources for lengthy periods – fit a panel (see Housing, pages 14–15) or anti-dazzle board. When fitting tubes, pay attention to warnings on the package. Aquarium fluorescent control units with moisture-proof caps on leads are preferable; batten-type units are susceptible to moisture. Fluorescent tubes cannot be thermostatically controlled. They will continue to produce heat even when the heat source has cut out or dimmed. Finally, do not spray electrical fittings, especially when they are hot!

● *Which is the best type of thermostat to use with bulbs?*

... On/off types produce alternate periods of light and dark, which are unnatural and potentially stressful for the vivarium inhabitants. Dimmer thermostats dim the bulb as the set temperature is reached. Some on/off thermostats are not designed for use with lightbulbs.

● *Do all reptiles need ultraviolet light?*

Only diurnal ones absolutely require it. Rodent-eating snakes and nocturnal or crepuscular lizards seem to do quite well without it, although dietary supplements should be provided for the lizards to compensate for the missing vitamin D3. However, when a UV source is made available, some nocturnal species will come out and bask for short periods in the daytime. They appear to benefit from this extra light.

● *Are any other lights needed in addition to fluorescent tubes?*

Ordinary bulbs produce visible and infrared light, which provides warmth for basking reptiles and raises the body temperature. Blacklights, which produce mainly UVA (very little UVB), are very popular, but they emit little visible light and need to be used alongside "white" light. Blacklight seems to inhibit feeding in some species by altering the colour of the food.

● *Where should the light be positioned?*

Both the spotlamp and full-spectrum UVB fluorescent tube should be positioned over spots which are suitable for basking, so that the inhabitants have the benefit of both kinds of light.

Furnishing the Vivarium

A TASTEFULLY FURNISHED VIVARIUM LOOKS very attractive, but practical considerations must be taken into account. Because of the time involved in maintenance, some keepers may prefer to provide only a basic setup – newspaper substrate, a hide box and possibly a log or stone for basking. This facilitates cleaning, locating eggs and removing sick or dead creatures. Some reptiles (especially snakes) thrive and even breed in such quarters. For other species, the clinical approach may not fulfil their needs, whereas a more elaborate vivarium enhances the quality of life. There is a theory, difficult to prove scientifically, that lizards in particular gain some psychological benefit from the visual disruption caused by furnishings – in other words, when they have a number of things to look at, they do not "know" that they are in a restricted space. At the very least, a well-furnished vivarium provides exercise and hiding places. The keeper may also prefer a naturalistic layout that has more aesthetic appeal.

Natural or Artificial Materials?

Natural materials (plants, branches, soil, sand and moss) look better in the vivarium, but they present a number of hygiene problems. In addition to these commonly available products, most dealers offer a range of cork bark, driftwood, vine roots and sand-blasted woods in a variety of interesting shapes to add more natural detail.

Artificial items can seem incongruous but are much easier to clean. Branches (the non-resinous type), soil and moss may harbour their own ecosystems of pests; while some pests may be eaten by the reptiles, others may multiply uncontrollably. Branches and logs can be stripped and scrubbed to avoid the problem, but this makes them less attractive and possibly too smooth for climbing. Soil and sand can be sterilized by heating, and moss can be thoroughly washed, but this removes nutrients and often kills the moss. Rockwork eventually becomes soiled and needs frequent scrubbing; the porous types such as tufa are particularly difficult to clean. It is probably easier to discard and replace some natural materials than to try to clean them.

PLANTS IN THE VIVARIUM

Plants are an attractive and natural way of furnishing the vivarium, and they have long been popular for certain species. The vivarium should be set up well before any animals are introduced so that the plants are established and any necessary replacements have been made. It must be tall enough to accommodate the plants – check the ultimate height before installing them. Surround the pots with stones to keep them securely in place. In a shallow substrate, pots can be disguised with curved pieces of cork bark.

The use of living plants may present certain problems. Herbivores eat plants, large reptiles might damage them with their body weight, and burrowing animals uproot them. Watering the plants increases humidity in the vivarium, so it is better not to use live plants with desert reptiles; use plastic plants.

1

2

3

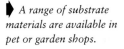

▶ *A range of substrate materials are available in pet or garden shops.*

Substrate Materials

MATERIAL	ADVANTAGES	DISADVANTAGES
Newspaper	Cheap, dust-free, absorbent. Easy to replace. Useful for quarantine cages.	Unattractive, wrinkles when wet. Animals can be trapped underneath. Not suitable for fossorial species. Live foods may hide underneath. Reptiles tend to crumple it.
Carpet (washable) **Artificial Turf Astroturf**	Some degree of absorbency. Easily cut to size. Washable, neat.	Unnatural appearance, unsuitable for fossorial species. Hard to spot-clean, soon becomes soiled. Carpet may have loose threads which choke or entangle animals.
Aquarium Gravel* (available in various sizes)	May look "natural". Can be washed for re-use. Can prevent oviposition in wrong place. Useful for drainage.	Heavy – difficult to replace. Not absorbent. Needs thorough sterilizing and rinsing before re-use.
Sand* (various types, some dust-free sands are available including bird sand/play sand)	Natural look, easily spot-cleaned. Useful for fossorial species from arid areas.	Some types turn dusty, large amounts inconvenient to replace. Not re-usable. Compact when damp – avoid ordinary building sand – totally unsuitable. Also avoid very sharp gritty types.
Loam Leaf Litter* Chopped (milled) **Sphagnum Moss Potting Soil**	Natural appearance, moisture retentive. Useful for fossorial species with slight humidity requirements. Useful for planted set-ups.	May need sterilizing to kill off insects. Overwetting causes compaction.
Peat*	Natural appearance, light-weight (dry). Moisture-retentive.	When damp it is acidic and compacts. Very dusty when dry. Not really to be recommended.
**Chipped Bark* ** ** (various sizes)	Looks attractive. Pleasant smell.	May contain splinters and insects. Not very absorbent (large). Difficult to spot clean. Not suitable for fossorial species.
**Hardwood Chips * ** **	Attractive appearance, slightly absorbent. Can be spot-cleaned.	May contain splinters or sharp pieces. Not suitable for fossorial species. Large amounts inconvenient to replace.
**Alfalfa Pellets ** ** (mainly used for iguanas)	Claimed to be harmless if ingested. Fairly absorbent. Can be spot-cleaned when dry.	Expensive to use in large quantities. Crumbles when wet, becomes dusty.
**Dust-free Wood Shavings ** ** (mainly for snakes)	Attractive appearance and pleasant smell. Absorbent, can be spot-cleaned.	Seldom totally dust-free.
**Corncob Granules ** **	Attractive, can be spot-cleaned.	Could possibly be ingested. Not suitable for fossorial species.

* Ingestion of particles could cause impaction in the gut. **Develops mould if moisture is present.

1 *Sphagnum moss*
2 *Chipped bark*
3 *Potting compost*
4 *Corncob granules*
5 *Sand*
6 *Gravel (large)*
7 *Gravel (small)*

A Green Anole (Anolis carolinensis) *in a planted vivarium. Plants are functional as well as decorative; some reptiles drink from leaves rather than bowls.*

Houseplants will probably have been treated with pesticides at some point, so it is advisable to spray them thoroughly with water and change the top layer of soil before use.

Plants in the vivarium need light even if the vivarium's occupants do not. The light in the vivarium may be inadequate, causing the plants to grow spindly or die; certain plants may be invasive and choke or shade others. Plants that do not thrive should be removed. Leaving them in their pots facilitates removal, whereas those planted directly in the substrate will become a tangled mass of roots which will be difficult to remove when refurbishing.

A carefully furnished vivarium, with thoughtful planning and some application of artistic ability, can be a delight to the eye. However, it is vital to remember that only healthy, parasite-free reptiles should be introduced – preferably after a quarantine period – otherwise the whole system could require sterilizing and possibly replacing.

CONSTRUCTING HABITATS

A reptile habitat can be anything from an arid desert to a rainforest, with numerous variations in between. When furnishing any vivarium, apart from the basic clinical type, the particular needs of the intended occupants should be studied and a habitat constructed accordingly. The main variables to consider are: temperature, degree of moisture, suitability of materials, layout and, for arboreal reptiles, height. There is probably more scope in furnishing lizard habitats than those meant for snakes and tortoises. Arboreal snakes can have a naturalistic set-up, but tortoises will flatten elaborate systems.

A Dry Habitat

Reptiles from arid areas are suited to a dry set-up with a loose, sandy substrate, furnished with rocky outcrops, small stumps or logs. Daytime temperatures should be high, and there should be no moisture apart from a small water bowl.

Collared Lizards (Crotaphytus collaris) *in a dry habitat. The furnishings are minimal but attractive. (This is in a pet store, and the vivarium is overcrowded.)*

(This same habitat with a lower maximum temperature, a larger water bowl and one or two plants with low moisture requirements would also suit lizards from more temperate climates.) Water bowls should be placed on a flat stone to prevent upset if the substrate is disturbed.

However, a small "pocket" of moist substrate is needed in the breeding season; and certain species from arid regions need to be able to burrow into a slightly moist layer to protect their skin. This can be difficult to achieve without increasing the air humidity. Burying a box of moist (not wet) substrate material is one solution. The box will need an entrance in one end to provide access and must be checked frequently to test the moisture level. Many snakes need a dry woodland habitat; for these, the sandy substrate can be changed to loam or leaf litter.

A Low-Humidity Habitat

A loose substrate of loam, leaf litter, chopped sphagnum moss or other moisture-retentive (but non-mould-forming) materials suits fossorial species and even some arboreal species that need just a slight degree of humidity. Living plants are useful and decorative in such a system. Adequate ventilation is important – the humidity should be quite low, otherwise the vivarium simulates a rainforest. Permanently wet conditions should be avoided. The ideal for many reptiles is that the

● *What are the benefits of using live plants?*

... Live plants will provide shade, cover, climbing facilities and humidity for reptiles that need these. In a properly designed vivarium it may be possible to create a permanent balanced set-up in which the animals' waste is recycled through the soil and used by the plants – this is only possible if the system is not overloaded by too many inhabitants or by overly large ones.

● *What are the benefits of using artificial plants?*

Artificial plants can brighten up a bare vivarium and provide shade. They are also washable and can be used where living plants are not suitable. Small bunches can be fastened to walls, or sprigs siliconed into drill holes in a cork or wooden base that is buried just under the substrate. In a dry vivarium, a few (undyed) "everlasting" flowers will create a more attractive scene. Pine cones, ornamental gourds and other natural items give a decorative effect.

● *How can I stop branches and rockwork falling over?*

Branches must be fixed firmly – if possible, they should be screwed to the sides of the vivarium. In a glass vivarium the branches will need to be shaped so that they are stable. Rockwork formations can be glued together with silicone sealer. Leave a few caves or crevices for hiding places. All rocks should be firmly bedded on the base of the vivarium to prevent them from sinking into the substrate and partially trapping or even burying the occupants.

substrate is almost dry by nightfall. Some experimentation will be needed to achieve just the right balance. One solution is to fix a divider across the vivarium base and have two different degrees of dampness in the substrate (see Housing, pages 14–15). Fossorial species often show a preference for one side or the other.

A Moist Rainforest Habitat

Increasing humidity creates suitable conditions for rainforest reptiles or those from moist temperate regions. The moisture-retentive substrate should be sprayed daily, but ventilation is still required to prevent sodden conditions; many rainforest reptiles do well in less than their natural humidity. Many common houseplants will thrive in the humid atmosphere.

A pool or waterfall contributes to humidity and enhances the landscape. The pool can be anything from a litter tray to an area of the vivarium sectioned off with a glass panel sealed into place. Deeper permanent pools need some form of filtration, either an aquarium canister filter or undergravel filtration as used in an aquarium. Frequent water changes are advisable even with filtration. A pump must be accessible for servicing, and the chamber needs a close-fitting lid.

If moss is used as a substrate, it should be changed regularly, especially if mould develops. A more permanent substrate can be constructed

by first adding a layer of large pea gravel 1in (2.5cm) deep, followed by a layer of aquarium activated carbon 1in (2.5cm) deep; add potting soil to the required depth and follow this with a 1in (2.5cm) layer of medium aquarium gravel topped with a covering of moss. Bury any potted plants in the soil before adding the top layers of gravel and moss, delaying the final layer so that plants can be moved or replaced if they are not thriving. A plastic aquarium gravel tidy can be spread on the soil to prevent the gravel from sinking into the soil. This system should work well as long as it is not overloaded by too many occupants. Spot-cleaning helps, but faeces tend to wash down through the gravel, where they are converted into nitrates by soil organisms.

▲ *Semi-aquatic turtles such as the European Pond Turtle (Emys orbicularis) need to be able to dry out completely on dry rocks.*

◀ *A waterfall can be made from cork bark, driftwood or a pile of stones. The water tube is hooked over the top of the fall.*

WATERFALL CONSTRUCTION

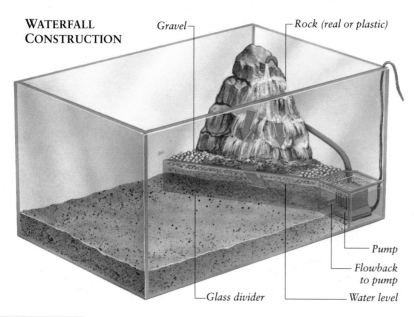

Gravel

Rock (real or plastic)

Pump

Flowback to pump

Water level

Glass divider

Tortoise Habitats

Tortoises kept indoors require spacious quarters. Species from arid regions need a sandy substrate, forest species a mixture of loam, leaf litter and small chopped or shredded bark. Furnishings must not be too elaborate, but the substrate can be landscaped with slopes to break the monotony. Living plants will probably be eaten unless positioned well out of the way. Plastic plants can be used instead; they provide a shady spot for forest tortoises. Other requirements are a hide box, basking lamp and fluorescent (UV) tube. Hard surfaces may damage the plastron but some flat stones or slates here and there will help keep the animal's claws worn down. Rocks for climbing should not be too large; they may impede movement across the vivarium floor, and a tortoise may fall off, injuring itself.

For a discussion of semi-aquatic or aquatic habitats for turtles, see Housing, pages 16–17. The remarks above can be applied to the land area of a divided vivarium or outdoor enclosure. A pool should be sizeable to provide exercise and to prevent pollution. It is important to have dry rocks projecting out of the water, to allow the turtles to climb out and dry off when needed.

Points to Remember

- The type, size and number of animals to be housed will dictate the type of materials, the layout and the frequency with which the vivarium must be cleaned or refurbished.
- Too many animals will overload the system and cause hygiene problems.
- Humidity requirements bar the use of certain materials,
- Fossorial reptiles need a particular type of substrate for burrowing, and burrowing or digging can upset other aspects of the decor.
- Large, heavy animals require robust furnishings, as they will soon wreck a delicately or elaborately furnished vivarium.
- Arboreal species need branches or plants.
- Plants are not normally recommended for herbivorous species.
- Local availability of materials will affect choice, but many dealers now stock a variety of natural and artificial materials for vivarium furnishing.

➤ *Trans-pecos Rat Snakes* (Elaphe subocularis) *need dry conditions, so dried natural materials may be used for aesthetic effect without contributing humidity.*

Foods and Feeding

REPTILE CARE HAS BECOME MUCH EASIER with the availability of commercially-produced reptile foods. A range of such foods, from live insects to frozen and even canned and pelleted foods, can be purchased from pet stores or by post. It is advisable to research a food supply before acquiring a new animal.

Reptiles can be divided into groups based on their feeding requirements. Many snakes eat mammals, ranging from pinkies (baby mice) to rabbits according to the size of the snake, while others prefer birds, lizards, other snakes, insects, worms, slugs, frogs and fish. A few are specialist feeders, taking a single type of food such as birds'

eggs, snails or salamanders. The real specialist cannot usually be weaned onto other foods and should not be kept unless a regular food supply is available. Many lizards eat live insects and a range of other invertebrates. Some large lizards will take mammals such as mice, rats and fish. There are also herbivorous and omnivorous species. Turtle species vary from herbivorous to carnivorous – some will take both types of food in varying degrees.

Although many species adapt readily, introducing an unfamiliar diet can cause problems. Snakes – with the exception of egg-eaters – eat live animals. Some people find this disturbing,

A Stump-tailed Skink (Tiliqua rugosa) *eating a variety of foods. As with other omnivores, too much animal protein causes obesity, which shortens lifespan.*

An African Egg-eating Snake (Dasypeltis scabra) *after swallowing a bird egg. The snake crushes the egg shell and regurgitates it as a compact pellet.*

but most snakes can get used to eating dead animals (thawed from the freezer), especially if movement is simulated by wiggling the food with forceps. As well as being more acceptable to many keepers, dead animals are also safer; live mammals left with snakes for more than a short time may damage or kill them.

Since the captive diet is artificial, dietary deficiencies are common in reptiles, particularly in lizards and turtles. Many of the foods used by keepers are low in calcium and high in phosphorus. This can lead to metabolic bone diseases (MBD) such as calcium deficiency or calcium and phosphorus imbalance. Other vitamins and minerals may also be missing from the diet. The ideal ratio of calcium to phosphorus (Ca:P) for reptiles is usually set at between 1.5:1 and 2:1. The higher level (2:1) is for young animals and breeding females. A calcium supplement is often needed to achieve this, and multivitamin supplements formulated for reptiles are widely available. Liquid multivitamins do not contain calcium, but this can be supplied separately as cuttlefish bone (either powdered or in small chunks) or calcium carbonate powder. Vitamin supplements intended for mammals are unsuitable for reptiles and should not be used. Some manufacturers offer different formulations for specific purposes: supplements for young or gravid reptiles are high in calcium; and supplements for tortoises are high in vitamins A, C and E.

Wild Insects

Searching the hedgerows and collecting insects in the garden used to be a popular method of supplying live foods, but nowadays keepers are concerned about pollution with pesticides, and creatures from ponds can pass on parasites to aquatic reptiles. If you are sure there is no contamination, and you can spare the time to collect them, wild insects can be used as food. Potentially harmful insects, such as bees, wasps and bombardier beetles, should be avoided. Reject anything you cannot identify. Smooth (not hairy) caterpillars, spiders, bush crickets, grasshoppers, craneflies and green aphids can all be used. Leave slugs, snails and earthworms (*Lumbricus terrestris*) in clean moss for 2 or 3 days to clean out their gut – feed them on lettuce or other vegetables with calcium added. Some slugs and worms may be rejected. Avoid brandling worms.

Feeding Herbivores

Herbivorous lizards are often given too much protein in their diet. Many such species will eat beef, chicken, rodents, insects and pet foods, but although a small amount of animal protein may be beneficial for young specimens, it can cause kidney damage in older animals. For true herbivores, such as Green Iguanas, a maximum of 15% protein for youngsters and 5% for older animals is advised, preferably as plant protein. Plant foods for herbivores (lizards and tortoises) should only be gathered from sites where no pesticides have been used, so that they are known to be free from pollution. Some suitable plants are: dandelion, sow thistle, clover, plantain, nasturtium and rose flowers. Chopping the plants into small pieces and mixing them together will prevent the animal from selecting one large piece of its preferred food and eating nothing else; this ensures that it takes a variety of foods and benefits from a wide range of nutrients.

Plant protein sources such as peas and beans can be given fresh or thawed from frozen. Sprouting lentils, chickpeas, aduki beans, mung beans, and alfalfa are all suitable. Apart from alfalfa, these protein foods tend to be low in calcium but rich in vitamins, and should be used in combination with high-calcium plants or a calcium supplement. Alfalfa, watercress, broccoli tops and carrots are all rich in calcium, though the content may vary according to growing conditions (old carrots are said to have a higher calcium content than young ones). Foods with a good Ca:P ratio include yellow melon, raisins, oranges, and dates. Most household fruit and vegetables – but not rhubarb – can be offered, chopped small, with any of the items above.

It is likely that some foods will be repeatedly refused. If the animals pick and choose, withhold food for a day or so and try again. Not all plant foods are suitable – some contain phytic acid or oxalic acid, which binds with calcium and prevents the animal from using it. Wheat bran (used to feed Mealworms), spinach, Swiss chard, beetroot and oats should only be given to herbivores in small amounts as part of a varied diet. Spinach, with its high levels of tannin, binds protein, affects digestive enzymes and reduces the availability of vitamin B12 and iron. Large amounts of tannin can damage the liver, so it is better to avoid using spinach. Oxalates (from oxalic acid found in rhubarb leaves and spinach) can be dangerous: large amounts produce convulsions, and lower levels can cause poor bone formation and kidney stones.

Soy beans, peanuts and plants of the Brassica family – including cabbage, cauliflower and kale – are goitrogenic (low in iodine) and should only form a small percentage of the diet. If more than a little of these is used, add 2mg per week of ground kelp tablets as a dietary supplement.

A Tokay Gecko (Gekko gecko) *eating a locust. As with other crepuscular or nocturnal species, dusted foods should be introduced in late evening, as the longer they remain uneaten the more supplements they lose.*

Commercially-produced Insects

Black Field Cricket (*Grillus bimaculatus*)
Brown House Cricket (*Acheta domesticus*)
Available in black, brown and a silent form (does not chirp). A good basic food for insectivores. A range of sizes. Store at 26–28°C (79–82°F).

Desert Locust (*Schistocerea gregaria*)
Migratory Locust (*Locusta migratoria*)
A good basic food in a range of sizes. More expensive than crickets. May nibble plants if not eaten immediately. Store at 26°C (79°F).

Waxmoth larvae – "Waxworms"
(*Galleria melonella*)
Readily taken but can be fattening – use sparingly. Large numbers may not be digested properly. Adult moths are attractive to many small lizards. Store at 12–15°C (55–60°F).

Tebos (*Chilecomadia moorei*)
Orange, soft-bodied moth larvae. Comments as for waxmoth larvae. Store at 8–10°C (45–50°F).

Mealworms (*Tenebrio molitor*)
Often condemned for causing intestinal upsets because of tough outer skin. Occasional use will add variety. Too many will cause obesity. Adult beetles rejected by most herps. Store at 9°C (48°F).

Buffalo Worms (*Alphitobius diaperinus*)
Small beetle larvae. Comments as for mealworms; beetles more palatable to some species. Store at 10–15°C (50–60°F).

King or Supergiant "Mealworms"
(*Zoophobas morio*)
Not actually Mealworms, but comments as for Mealworms. Useful for larger lizards, but they can bite smaller animals. Store at 15–20°C (60–68°F).

Fruit flies (*Drosophila* species)
"Wingless" and winged but flightless varieties available. Useful first food for some small species, including young chameleons, but more substantial food is soon needed. Only available as starter cultures; you have to breed your own. Store at 26°C (79°F).

Storage and Preparation of Foods

Some storage facilities are needed to ensure a regular supply of food. Dealers of live food usually supply instructions, but the following general rules apply. Crickets require an escape-proof container, which needs heating in cool conditions, and adequate ventilation – they will die in damp conditions. An old aquarium fitted with a vivarium lid and a light bulb is suitable. Crickets also need food and water (see "gut loading" in Q&A section, page 33). Keep Mealworms, King Mealworms, Buffalo Worms, Waxworms and Tebos in well-ventilated containers at the correct temperature to prevent pupation (see the chart opposite). Locusts need a ventilated container as well as food and water. Live foods must be stored hygienically to minimize the risk of infecting animals. Clean insect containers and rodent breeding cages regularly. Treat frozen foods as if for humans and chop vegetables on a clean surface. Do not give animals old or rotten fruit and vegetables – or food that is too big for them. Serve food for herbivorous lizards in a bowl. Use a shallower bowl for tortoises. In both cases, place the bowl on a flat stone to prevent substrate particles adhering to the food and being ingested; many herbivorous species pull their food away from the bowl. Outdoors, bury bowls in the substrate (for terrestrial species) or place them at various leve' (for arboreal species).

LIVE FOOD

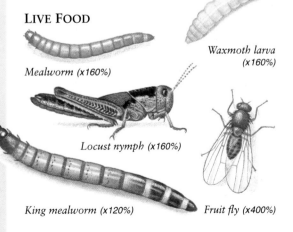

Mealworm (x160%)

Waxmoth larva (x160%)

Locust nymph (x160%)

King mealworm (x120%)

Fruit fly (x400%)

Live foods must be chosen on the basis of appropriate size. Do not offer more than the reptile will eat; uneaten food should not be left in the cage.

Convenience Foods

Pellets for small aquatic turtles have been available for many years and can be useful, although some animals refuse them. More recently, pellet and canned foods have been developed for iguanas, and tinned foods for tegus, monitors, land tortoises and box turtles. The latest products are "sausages" for snakes, geckos and skinks.

Convenience foods save time and are easy to store, but long-term assessment of their suitability is still in progress. Early tests on some iguana foods suggested that they may be too high in protein, having been developed for iguanas that were farmed for food. Manufacturers of convenience foods claim that they are scientifically formulated. They are expensive, however, especially if imported. Some reptiles will not accept such foods unless scented with their normal food (particularly in the case of the snake "sausage").

Although convenient, cat and dog foods must not be fed in excess, especially to herbivorous species; the levels of vitamins A and D, fat and animal protein are all too high. Excess vitamins can lead to over-absorption of calcium and result in mineralization of soft tissues in the body.

Excess calcium is rarely a problem unless there is also too much vitamin D3 or overexposure to UV light. A vitamin A deficiency causes eye trouble, particularly in young turtles, but too much can produce severe skin trouble.

Fussy Eaters

Captive-bred reptiles do not usually pose feeding problems. When specimens need encouragement to eat, try offering a variety of foods. If a snake will not adapt to rodents, scenting them with its natural prey is often successful. You can keep a disease-free frozen lizard, lizard's eggs or a chick for this purpose.

Snakes that will not feed may need assisted feeding or force-feeding. These methods should be used only by experienced keepers once other causes of refusal to feed have been eliminated. Gently prise open the snake's jaws and place the food in its mouth – if the food is not taken voluntarily, it may have to be forced farther down until the swallowing reflex commences. Newly-hatched snakes that refuse their food can be "pinky-pumped"; a pinky pump macerates a pink mouse by pressure and forces it into the snake. This should be done only by experienced keepers. Larger pumps can be used for bigger snakes. Pumps must be lubricated with water or surgical jelly before use. Such methods may sound drastic but they save lives.

Drinking Water

Some reptiles hardly drink at all in the wild, apart from occasionally lapping dew. In captivity, some species will not drink from a bowl, but lap water that has been sprayed on leaves or walls. (Use a gentle spray – a powerful jet can be fatal.) Herbivorous species may not drink very much in the wild, as their food contains water. However, a bowl of water should be supplied for tortoises and lizards from arid regions, who need to drink to compensate for the absence of moist burrowing places. Water from the mains should be filtered and stand for 24 hours to dechlorinate it. Some keepers prefer to use bottled water.

◀ *Pelleted foods: for iguanas, fruit or vegetable varieties (left); for aquatic animals, floating foodsticks (right). If these are refused, a more natural diet should be used.*

Q&A

● *Can frozen foods be thawed in a microwave?*

A... No. Frozen foods should be allowed to thaw naturally. They must be completely thawed before use, and never refrozen. Frozen fish needs to stand at 30°C (86°F) for several minutes after thawing, to destroy thiaminase, an enzyme that attacks B vitamins. One method of thawing fish, pink mice or rats is soaking in tepid water.

● *How much vitamin supplement do reptiles need?*

Exact requirements are not known, but supplements usually come with a recommendation. Vitamin and mineral requirements of older animals are less than those of younger specimens or gravid females. Overdoses can be toxic – do not exceed the recommended dose.

● *How do I supply vitamin and calcium supplements?*

To dust an insect, place it in a container or polythene bag with the supplement and swirl it round until it is coated. (Pre-chilling crickets makes them easier to handle.) For herbivores, the supplement is sprinkled on the food or mixed up with it. Many lizards, turtles and tortoises readily eat small pieces of cuttlefish bone, and certain lizards will lick supplements mixed with honey and fruit. Sick animals may need liquid multivitamins administered by dropper or injection.

◀ *African Spurred Tortoises* (Geochelone sulcata) *eating salad. These large herbivores need substantial amounts of food, but variety is important. Their diet must be high in calcium for healthy shell growth.*

● *What is "gut loading"?*

Feeding live foods on a nutritious diet just before using them, so that the reptiles benefit from the insects' gut contents and need fewer multivitamin supplements. Feed crickets, Mealworms and Buffalo Worms on fish flake food, powdered milk, crushed trout pellets or rodent pellets with multivitamin powder and ground cuttlebone. For moisture, use apples or carrots – not potatoes. "Boost" locusts with alfalfa hay or watercress. Proprietary gut-loading foods are available.

● *Can I offer uneaten food to another animal?*

No. Although it is wasteful to throw food away, it is very much safer to do so.

● *Are uneaten (live) crickets a threat to the vivarium?*

Avoid having large numbers of live insects in the vivarium – they can damage the occupants and nibble eggs. If you have only a few animals, you can feed them using forceps until they have had enough. Some keepers chill crickets and nip the "jumping" legs with forceps, to keep them in the food bowl until they have been eaten. This practice is often condemned as cruel.

Breeding

THERE ARE TWO REPRODUCTION METHODS in reptiles: egg-laying (oviparous species) and live-bearing (ovoviviparous species); in the latter, fully-formed young develop inside a membrane within the female, sustained by a yolk. (Strictly speaking, some livebearing reptiles are viviparous: they give birth to fully-formed young that have developed in the female without a membrane and been sustained by her.) Snakes and lizards may be either egg-layers or livebearers, but all turtles and tortoises lay eggs. According to the species, eggs have a hard shell or a softer "parchment" shell that absorbs moisture and increases in size during incubation.

Sexing Reptiles

Determining the sex of reptiles can be difficult, especially for the novice. Not all species exhibit distinct physical differences between the sexes. Those that do are said to be sexually dimorphic. Where the difference is one of colour, the term "sexually dichromatic" is used. This is common in lizards, rare in chelonians, and extremely rare in snakes. Because juvenile lizards often resemble females in their colouring, they can be difficult to sex before maturity. Sexing by appearance is somewhat easier if there are several specimens to compare. The sex of some species may need to be confirmed by observing behaviour. Finally, for some species, physical examination is needed.

Popping and Probing

These techniques can be used to sex snakes and some lizards. "Popping" is the use of gentle pressure from the thumb behind the cloaca; it produces an eversion of the hemipenes in the male. It works best on juveniles – adults are difficult to "pop". "Probing" is when a lubricated probe is placed in the cloaca pointing towards the tail tip, and gently rotated until it penetrates as far as possible. Penetration is much shorter in females than in males, as the probe measures the length of the inverted hemipenes in males. The depth of

External Sex Characteristics

Snakes
Sexual dimorphism is only slight. The tail is often longer in males and thicker at the base (due to the hemipenes). Males may have slimmer bodies than females. Male boas and pythons have longer anal spurs than females.

Turtles and Tortoises
In terrestrial tortoises, the size of males and females varies according to species. Aquatic males are often smaller, and the males' plastron is often concave. The tail is longer in males and thicker at the base. The male's cloaca is further from the shell than that of the female. Certain male turtles (especially sliders) have elongated claws on the forelegs.

Lizards
Males are usually larger and more heavily built, with larger heads and thicker tails; females may have a plumper body shape. The swelling of the hemipenes is often distinct. Males are usually more colourful than females, especially in the breeding season or when threatened. In some species, males and females are different colours. Males tend to have horns, crests, casques, nasal appendages, gular pouches and tarsal spurs. If females have similar features they may be reduced or vestigial. Enlarged pre-anal scales, post-anal scales, pre-anal pores and femoral pores are more prominent in males or absent in females. (Not all species have these features.)

penetration is measured against the subcaudal scales on the snake's tail – for many species, the depth of penetration (calculated as a number of subcaudal scales) is documented. Probing is done with a lubricated stainless-steel sexing probe. The choice of diameter varies with the species. Petroleum jelly and surgical jelly are frequently used to lubricate the probe, but it is possible that

▶ *Granite Spiny Lizards* (Sceloporus orcutti) *show marked sexual dichromatism. The female's bands are more distinct, but the male is more brightly coloured.*

Sexing Mediterranean Tortoises (Testudo graeca).
*Looking at the underside of the shell to compare them,
the female (on the left) has a less developed tail. The
longer, thicker tail of the male (on the right) enables him
to curl it underneath the female's in the act of mating.*

they may act as spermicides. For this reason, they
should not be used close to mating. Physiologic
saline is recommended as a safer alternative.

CAUTION: Do not use popping or probing on
autotomous lizards, as they will probably shed
their tail. Both techniques should be used with
great care, as permanent damage can result. It is
advisable to ask an experienced keeper for help.

Breeding Cycles

Reptiles from temperate regions tend to be seasonal breeders, stimulated to mate in the Spring
by rising temperature and longer periods of
daylight. In tropical areas, breeding may occur
throughout the year, or it may be triggered by a
rainy season after a dry period. Most reptiles
breed every year in maturity, but there are some
exceptions. Imported reptiles may retain breeding patterns from the wild, sometimes taking
several years to adjust to the different seasons.

Winter Hibernation

Hibernation (or brumation, also known as Winter cooling) is necessary for most temperate
species if they are to breed successfully. Providing the correct temperature for hibernation can
be a problem – if captive breeding is rare, this
information may not be documented. Reptiles
from warmer subtropical regions generally need
a slight drop in temperature for a short period;
those from equatorial areas are used to a fairly

constant temperature throughout the year and do not require hibernation. With hardy species, full hibernation in captivity should not last for the same length of time as it does in the wild.

Reptiles intended for hibernation must be in perfect health. Many species will automatically decrease their food intake as Winter approaches, having already built up fat reserves to sustain them through the cool period. Maintain normal temperatures and photoperiod while withholding food for 2–3 weeks to allow the animal's gut to empty. During the following 2 weeks, gradually decrease the temperature and photoperiod.

◀ *Green Anole Lizards* (Anolis carolinensis) *in mating embrace. Seizing the female's neck to restrain her is a common feature in many lizards and some snakes.*

Once the temperature has been reduced, the animal should be placed in a ventilated, rodent-proof and ant-proof plastic container filled with sphagnum moss. The moss may need to be misted slightly for certain species (though it should not be wet). Store the container in a room, garage, shed or loft, where lower temperatures can be maintained. Some form of thermostatically-controlled room heater may be needed to ensure that the temperature does not fall too much. Controlling the maximum temperature is more difficult, and some keepers resort to using refrigerators, chilled food cabinets or cooling systems. Specimens undergoing full hibernation should be completely shielded from daylight, which would disturb them if the temperature rose slightly. If, however, the reptile buries itself for hibernation, as is done by some tortoises, the amount of light does not matter.

Inspect the animals weekly. When hibernation is over, gradually reverse the whole process: return the animal to the vivarium; increase the photoperiod and temperature to normal levels over a period of 2 weeks; and resume feeding.

Stimulating Breeding Behaviour

In the vivarium, the breeding season can be determined by controlling the lighting and heating. Reptiles from warmer or tropical climates may need other stimuli, such as separation and reintroduction of the sexes, extra spraying, or (for rainforest species) simulated rain in a rain chamber. This should be similar to the type used for amphibians (see Breeding in Amphibian Care, pages 154–155) but with an efficient drain to prevent flooding. In some species the presence of several males triggers mating behaviour, but it could also lead to injury in combat.

Where the sexes are kept together, mating will occur if and when conditions are suitable. If kept separately, introduce males and females when the time is thought to be right. For reptiles that have hibernated, Spring is the obvious time; others mate at different times during the year.

Readiness to mate is often indicated by restlessness (males and females), loss of appetite (mainly in males), and intensification of colour (some male lizards). Mating is also preceded by ritualized behaviour by males, such as nodding, push-ups, butting and stroking. In many reptile species, the female is held by the neck while the male inserts one or other of his hemipenes inside her cloaca. Some damage to the neck is normal, but if the female appears unreceptive then the pair should be separated before serious damage results. Females do not remain receptive for very long – perhaps for only a few days. If this chance is missed, breeding will not be successful.

● *Is there any difference between hibernation and Winter cooling?*

… In true hibernation the animal's body temperature is so low its metabolism is just "ticking over". In this case darkness is beneficial. In Winter cooling, the temperature drop is not as extreme, the animal is merely sluggish, and a photoperiod is desirable. This state is sometimes distinguished by the name "brumation".

● *Can Winter treatment be skipped?*

It is recommended for animals that hibernate or that live in climates with a distinct cold season. Similar conditions should be provided in captivity.

● *If I only want to keep a single specimen, does it matter if it's a male or a female, and can I "borrow" someone else's reptile if I want to try breeding?*

Sharing ownership of a pair is quite common as it reduces the amount of space needed. Many keepers begin by keeping a single specimen. In this case it is better to keep a male, as some solitary females develop infertile eggs, which can cause problems.

● *How long do eggs take to hatch?*

The incubation period varies between species and also depends on temperature. Within a clutch there can be a significant delay between the first and last hatching. Do not raise the temperature to speed up incubation; this can cause deformities or even kill the embryos.

● *Is it true that reptile eggs should never be turned?*

In general, the eggs are quite tough. When removing them for incubation, however, they must be kept in the position in which they were laid, otherwise they may not hatch. Some keepers mark the tops with a pencil.

● *Do all eggs need moisture?*

No, only parchment-shelled eggs. Hard-shelled eggs can be incubated on a bed of dry, coarse sand.

● *What should I do with incubating eggs that go bad?*

Inspect eggs every few days and remove any that show signs of fungus or decay – unless they are adhering to others, in which case they should be left. Eggs that discolour slightly may still be good.

● *Do I need to keep breeding records?*

Keeping records of parentage helps avoid inbreeding. You can also collect information about hibernation temperatures and duration, date of mating, length of gestation or incubation, incubation temperatures and size of hatchlings or neonates. This can be invaluable.

Male snakes should be introduced into the female's cage, which holds the scent produced by her musk glands. Female lizards should be placed with the male because – as in the wild – he will want to mate with females who intrude into his territory. Multiple matings are usually advantageous and often produce more fertile eggs or live young. The pair can either be left together or reintroduced daily for several days until the female refuses further matings. Once gravid, the female will probably eat more for a while, but her appetite decreases as parturition approaches. She will also spend longer basking, possibly because of the need to metabolize calcium or to speed up the embryos' development.

Raising Young from Eggs

Egg-layers need a suitable place to lay, usually an area of moist (not sodden) substrate, free from obstructions such as stones. The site must be large enough for the animal concerned, and some cover – a plant or log – may be useful for privacy. A box of moist vermiculite is suitable for snakes, but lizards will scatter the contents when digging. Some geckos will stick eggs on branches or vivarium walls, or may simply secrete them in a concealed spot – in loose substrate or even in the soil of plant pots. After burying the eggs, lizards usually tamp down the substrate with little or no trace of disturbance. You will have to observe the gravid females carefully to know when they have laid; loose folds of skin along the body are a good sign. If no suitable site is found, for whatever reason, eggs may be retained or deposited haphazardly about the vivarium; in the latter case they must be removed quickly to prevent them drying out.

It is extremely difficult to provide the correct conditions for eggs to hatch where they have been laid in a vivarium, so it is standard practice for the keeper to remove them for incubation. Purpose-built reptile incubators can be purchased, but some keepers build their own, or use a spare vivarium. In some cases, simply leaving the eggs in a warm room can be sufficient, since the required incubation temperatures vary from species to species. The temperature of the eggs should be carefully controlled; in certain reptiles incubation temperature is known to determine

Reproductive Problems

Failure to Mate
- Inadequate stimuli
- Animals too young or too old
- Animals in poor health
- Obesity or malnourishment
- Wrong season or time of year
- Incorrect temperature, humidity or photoperiod
- Egg retention from previous clutch (females)

Failure to Produce Eggs or Young
- Immature specimens
- Inadequate hibernation period at unsuitable temperatures
- Sperm damaged by toxins (disinfectants, insecticides)
- Injury to hemipenes (males)
- Excessive breeding (females)
- Small cages leading to ineffective mating
- Colour morphs from different regions may be incompatible

in a cluster and should not be separated. Bury the whole clutch, with part of the topmost egg showing. The weight of the container should then be recorded. Check it regularly and add tepid water if necessary to maintain the original weight.

Care of the Young

If young hatch with remnants of the yolk sac still attached, they should be left in the hatching box. Remove the hatchlings when the yolk is absorbed or becomes detached. Liveborn young should be removed from their mothers as soon as possible to prevent damage or cannibalism.

Babies of both types should be housed in small cages where they can find their food easily. They should be kept apart to prevent squabbling or intimidation. If hatchlings are raised communally, individuals that are not eating or thriving should be housed in separate quarters; removing them only long enough to feed them can cause regurgitation when they are returned to the community. The maximum temperatures should be slightly lower than those for adults. Take care to avoid dehydration, especially in species that require humidity.

Offer food small enough to prevent choking. Although some baby lizards and chelonians eat on the first day, others may survive on absorbed nutrients for a few days. Baby snakes will not feed until they have sloughed at least once, usually about 7 days after hatching or birth. In some cases they may go without food for 2 or even 3 months, sloughing several times before feeding. As long as they are producing faeces, they are still using up their store of nutrients, so do not resort to force-feeding (see Foods and Feeding, pages 32–33) too quickly. For the first few weeks, some hatchling snakes only accept food scented with a preferred food item. Caution is needed with snakes in case several try to eat the same food item. Cannibalism is not unknown in these circumstances. This is a good reason why many keepers prefer to house young snakes separately in small ventilated containers.

the sex of the hatchlings. Temperature-regulated sex determination (TSD) can be useful to the keeper who wishes to breed more of one particular sex. Generally, eggs are incubated at a constant temperature, but successful hatchings and larger young have often resulted from dropping the temperature overnight.

Eggs for incubation should be removed carefully and placed in a plastic box with a few small ventilation holes. The box should contain moist vermiculite at a depth which varies from 2–6in (5–15cm), depending on the size of the eggs. Other materials are sometimes used, but vermiculite is sterile and absorbent. The exact ratio of moisture to vermiculite is debatable – 1:1 by weight is widely used but slightly less water (0.8:1) is preferable, especially for lizard eggs. Too much water can cause the eggs to burst; too little causes desiccation. Place the eggs carefully in depressions in the vermiculite, with about a third of each egg above the surface. Certain geckos tend to produce eggs in pairs, and these should be incubated together. Snakes' eggs are often laid

Health and Disease

IF A SPECIMEN IS SICK, EXPERT DIAGNOSIS AND treatment by a veterinary surgeon will probably be needed. (In Britain, it is illegal for an unqualified person to treat someone else's reptile, apart from a few basic treatments as described·in this section.) Not all vets have experience of reptile diseases; it is worth finding one before you need one urgently. Other keepers or members of your local herpetological society may be able to recommend one. Diagnosis is easier if the owner has kept basic records such as date of acquisition, temperature range, photoperiod, feeding and dates of mating and parturition.

What You Can Do

Reptile keepers have access to only a limited range of proprietary medicines, such as povidone iodine, hydrogen peroxide, eye ointment and eyewash – all available from the local pharmacy. Antibiotics suitable for reptiles are only available on prescription (leftover human antibiotics are useless and can be dangerous). Antibiotics can deplete levels of some vitamins, notably vitamin K, so a multivitamin course may be prescribed. Do not use medicines meant for cats and dogs.

Treat minor wounds promptly with povidone iodine or hydrogen peroxide solution. Check treated wounds carefully for any deterioration. Bites and broken legs can be sustained during fights or mating, but broken legs may also be due to calcium deficiency. Severe burns can arise from contact with heat sources, and tortoises may suffer cracked shells from falls or attack by dogs. All of these need veterinary attention.

External Parasites

Bloodsucking parasites, ticks and mites are commonly seen on reptiles. Many dealers treat their animals, but some parasites may be missed and they multiply quickly. Parasites carry disease; heavy infestation can cause debilitation, refusal to feed, sloughing, skin problems – even death. A course of antibiotics is usually advisable.

◄ *A Roughtail Gecko* (Cyrtopodion scabrum) *with red mite infestation. Even if only one is spotted, there are bound to be others; appropriate steps must be taken.*

More than 250 types of mite can infest reptiles. Common snake mites are small, black creatures that can be seen moving on the snake, embedded between the scales, clustered around the eyes, or in the gular fold under the chin. When a snake coils up in the water bowl, mites may be visible in the water. Lizard mites are usually red to orange and are smaller than snake mites. They have more places to hide – between toes, in folds of skin, ear openings, armpits and groins. Small scabs or encrustations between scales, or dry white flecks on the body, indicate mite activity.

Infested specimens should be handled over a sheet or a bowl of water, to keep dislodged mites out of the vivarium. A tepid bath for 30 minutes a day will remove some mites, but not those on the reptile's head. (Beware: prolonged regular soaking can cause skin problems.) Clusters of mites or individuals can be picked off using sticky tape or a cotton bud dipped in puppy or kitten insect spray. Diluted eyewash sometimes dislodges them from around the eyes. Use the following treatments with care, as some substances used to kill mites are also fatal to reptiles if improperly used:

(i) Use a cloth to wipe a light film of puppy or kitten insect spray along the animal's body – leave for 1 minute and rinse off with tepid running water. Avoid eyes, nostrils and mouth.

(ii) Dichlorvos fly strip is often used, but may have side effects. These strips produce a vapour that permeates the vivarium. A 0.25in (6mm) piece cut along the full strip will treat 10ft^3 (0.28m^3) of vivarium. Put the piece in a container with a perforated lid to avoid contact. Place it in a cage with normal ventilation for 3 hours a day, 3 times weekly for up to 3 weeks.

Ticks are larger than mites and stand out from the reptile's body when full of blood. Immature ticks are harder to detect; they often burrow down between the scales. They are common on imported reptiles, but many dealers remove them. They also carry disease. Removal by hand is easiest – grasp the tick with forceps and pull out slowly. (Dabbing with surgical spirit or rotating the tick can sometimes aid removal.) Treat the site with povidone iodine, hydrogen peroxide solution or antibiotic ointment.

Internal Parasites

Single-celled protozoans such as amoebae and flagellates are so common in reptiles that many are thought to be natural. However, certain types can be dangerous, especially to a stressed animal. The most common method of infection is via the faeces of an infected animal. Prevent this with proper vivarium hygiene and quarantine. Reptiles can be resistant to pathogenic protozoans but pass them on to others; this is one argument against mixing animals from different regions. Symptoms vary: diarrhoea, regurgitation and blood or mucus in the faeces. Debilitation, emaciation and death follow. Faecal analysis is needed to identify the organism(s) responsible, and delaying treatment is usually fatal. The vet will probably prescribe metronidazole. Following protozoan infections, and after antibiotic treatment, live yoghurt or a probiotic is helpful in restoring normal organisms to the gut.

The protozoan parasite Cryptosporidiosis is transmitted in faeces. One major symptom is a firm mid-body swelling, but this may develop at a late stage. Early symptoms include: refusal to feed, lethargy, regurgitation of food, bronchial trouble and weight loss. Expert diagnosis is required, usually through faecal examination.

● *What are the first signs of illness?*

The warning signs are lethargy and refusal to feed. Some animals may keep their eyes closed. Eliminate other reasons for refusal to feed: incorrect temperature range; unfamiliar surroundings; bullying or intimidation; food that is unfamiliar, too large, or offered at the wrong time of day; dehydration; pregnancy (females); breeding condition (males).

● *How safe is a dichlorvos vapour strip?*

Safety depends on appropriate use. You must remove water during treatment; when replacing, use a small bowl to prevent snakes coiling up in it. Change the substrate at least every 2 days and keep the vivarium clean. After the final treatment, thoroughly disinfect and rinse the vivarium and fixtures to kill any remaining mite eggs, which will not be affected by the strip. Dichlorvos is an organo-phosphate; do not handle without disposable gloves. Keep away from children and pets. Do not try to treat several cages by hanging a single strip in the room; the vapour will not penetrate all the cages equally, and it eventually produces a dangerous build-up in some cages. Too large a piece of strip will be damaging or fatal to the occupants.

● *How do I check for worms?*

Examine droppings for eggs, larvae and small worms. Tapeworm eggs resemble cucumber seeds. Flukes look like small flattened leeches and are found in the mouth, cloaca or faeces. Bloody droppings may indicate hookworms, which are invisible to the naked eye. Lungworms can cause pneumonia-like symptoms – a sputum sample will show eggs and larvae.

● *How do I detect retained eggs?*

A large number of eggs will appear as bulges along the female's flanks. She will probably remain on the floor, unable to move. Fewer eggs can be difficult to detect. If the animal is used to handling, gentle pressure may reveal the eggs. This method can be difficult in chelonians because of the shell, and in those lizards that inflate the body when they are handled.

▲ *A Red Rat or Corn Snake* (Elaphe guttata guttata) *sloughing. Young growing snakes slough more often than adults. Sloughing also precedes mating and laying.*

Fortunately this parasite is not common outside large zoo collections, but strict hygiene is necessary. Heat is needed to kill the oocysts (eggs). Euthanasia is usually recommended for infected animals. (It may be illegal for you to make this decision without expert advice.)

Several hundred species of worm can infest reptiles. Most of these live in the intestine, but some, especially in the larval stage, can migrate through tissues. This often causes secondary bacterial infection. Worms compete with the host for food and cause debilitation, particularly in stressed animals. Heavy infestation can obstruct the intestine, respiratory tracts or other organs. Some forms destroy tissues and organs inside the host, and tiny worms can infect the bloodstream.

Wild reptiles invariably carry worms. Moderate numbers are often tolerated but eventually can cause trouble. Some types, including flukes

and tapeworms, have an indirect life cycle – that is, they need an intermediate host. Infestations occur when a reptile eats something that is infested. This does not normally occur in captive conditions because the intermediate host is missing. Other worms have a direct life cycle and can be ingested with contaminated food or water. Wild-caught live foods can be a source of worms and other parasites. Freezing for several days usually kills them. The larvae of hookworms, lungworms and some others can gain access by actually penetrating the skin of the host animal. Fenbendazole will kill some worm species but is ineffective against others.

Sloughing

Healthy reptiles slough without any trouble. Snakes take several days and the skin should come off in a single piece. Lizards slough piece by piece, but it is a quicker process. Incomplete sloughing is frequently due to dry conditions. To soften the dead skin, spray lightly with water or place the animal in a ventilated box of wet moss or paper towel for a few hours. With snakes, wrapping them in damp cloth and allowing them to slide through a few times is also effective. Bits of skin that are not removed can become infected. In lizards, pay particular attention to the feet and ear openings, and in snakes, to the brille and tail tip. Sloughing snakes often coil up in the water dish, which must be large enough to prevent water slopping over. Unlike lizards, snakes do not normally feed while sloughing.

Reproductive Problems

Dystocia (egg retention or egg binding) is more common in turtles and tortoises than in other reptiles, although it can occur in snakes and lizards. Anything from one egg to a whole clutch can be retained. The eggs then become necrotic or rupture inside the female, with fatal results.

Dystocia should be treated by a vet, who may prescribe oxytocin to induce contractions. If a blockage is responsible, a caesarean section will be needed, but it is not usually possible to use this procedure on small reptiles. It may be worth asking the vet about aspiration – a technique to be used only by experienced professionals.

Causes of Dystocia (Egg Retention)

- Large, misshapen or fused eggs
- Impaction of ingested substrate material, causing a blockage
- Delay in oviposition due to the lack of suitable oviposition site
- Obstructions in the nesting medium, causing the female to abandon digging
- Disturbance by the keeper or other animals
- An abnormally large number of eggs
- Twisted oviducts
- Age or illness in the female
- Obesity, especially in snakes
- Infection of the reproductive tract

Mating when eggs are already present can cause ruptured eggs. Male turtles can be particularly aggressive sexually, so gravid females should be kept away from them. Rupturing causes damage to the oviduct and subsequent infection, requiring urgent treatment by a vet. Rough handling by the keeper or cage mates may also damage eggs inside lizards and snakes.

Prolapses of the hemipenes (males) and the oviducts (females) may also occur. Skilled treatment is needed immediately, as desiccation and damage can result. As a first-aid treatment, you should lubricate the prolapsed organ with surgical jelly and wrap a wet bandage around it before consulting a vet.

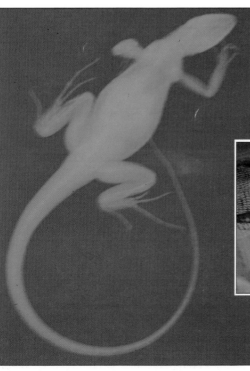

◀▲ *An operation to remove eggs (above) from an eggbound Green Iguana (Iguana iguana). An X-ray (left) shows eggs inside. This is the surest way of detecting retained eggs; consult a vet if you suspect this condition.*

COMMON BACTERIAL DISEASES

Abscesses

Symptoms: Internal and external abscesses, often on head or limbs. Usually start as small swellings but fill up with cheese-like material.
Comments: Caused by skin damage, feeding damage from mice and ticks, incorrect diet or too-moist housing. There are 2 types, which need different treatment; a vet will advise.

Mouthrot (Infective Ulcerative Stomatitis)

Symptoms: Small haemorrhages in the mouth that produce a cheesy substance – jaws and mouth start to rot. Head becomes swollen.
Comments: Common in snakes after abrasion or splitting of snout against glass.

Blister Disease (Scale Rot; Necrotic Dermatitis)

Symptoms: Small fluid-filled blisters, often on belly, followed by ulceration and inflammation.
Comments: Caused by damp and dirt. Improve living conditions and start antibiotic treatment.

Respiratory Diseases

Symptoms: Reptiles cannot cough, so infected mucus bubbles from nose, mouth and eyes. Aquatic reptiles may lose balance in the water.
Comments: Often caused by low temperatures and damp vivarium conditions. Similar symptoms are caused by lack of vitamin A or even lungworm.

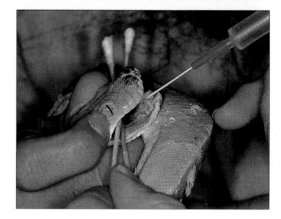

▲ *A Green Tree Python* (Morelia viridis) *being treated by a vet for respiratory problems. This could have several causes; skilled diagnosis is a must.*

Salmonellosis

Symptoms: Acute enteritis, septicemia (causing ulcers), pneumonia. Droppings may be dark green, tinged with blood and mucus.
Comments: Reptiles can carry and excrete salmonella bacteria while remaining unaffected.

Shell Rot (Ulcerative Shell Disease)

Symptoms: Shell becomes eroded or ulcerated.
Comments: Lesions vary from less than 1mm to several cm. More common in aquatic turtles than terrestrial species. Vets use povidone iodine or potassium permanganate solution. Serious cases should be covered with epoxy resin and fibreglass patches after cleaning.

▶ *A Green Iguana*
(Iguana iguana) *with necrotic dermatitis. As first aid, wash with a mild germicidal soap.*

Bacterial Diseases

Diagnosis is very difficult, even for an experienced keeper, and must be left to a professional. Many conditions produce similar symptoms: gastrointestinal upset, anorexia, lethargy. Common ailments are caused by omnipresent bacteria. Some are pathogenic, some opportunists. Bacteria thrive wherever dirty conditions exist, so the importance of strict hygiene cannot be overemphasized (see Housing, page 14). External infections in small areas may respond to a povidone iodine or hydrogen peroxide solution, but most infections will require antibiotic treatment. Sick animals should always be isolated and kept at the upper limit of their temperature range, especially if they are receiving any antibiotics for this condition.

Fungal Infections

Aquatic and semiaquatic turtles can develop a cotton-like growth on their limbs caused by fungal infection, which often invades small wounds or scratches. Humid conditions and dirty water encourage it to spread. In turtles, mild cases may clear up if the animal is given dry basking facilities, preferably in sunlight, for 2 or 3 days. If not, then veterinary treatment will be needed. Living conditions must be improved, with particular attention being paid to water quality.

Dietary Deficiencies

The most common diet-related illness is Metabolic Bone Disease (MBD), a term that covers several bone diseases including rickets. MBD is most common in herbivorous species, particularly in tortoises and Green Iguanas (*Iguana iguana*), but it can occur in other lizards. It is uncommon in mammal-eating snakes because of their complete diet. Affected animals may feed well and look plump, especially around the hindlegs, so that MBD is usually well advanced by the time it becomes apparent. The most common causes are inadequate calcium and excessive phosphorus. Do not simply feed the animal extra vitamins, as this can be dangerous; without adequate calcium, vitamin D will aggravate some problems and cause others. Delaying treatment can cause deformities and death; if you suspect MBD, consult your vet immediately.

Personal Hygiene

Like other animals, reptiles carry disease organisms that can be passed on to humans, but cases of infection are rare. Although salmonella outbreaks in the US have been attributed to captive reptiles, humans are at greater risk from other domestic animals. Cage hygiene, coupled with strict personal hygiene, should prevent illness. Always wash your hands with an anti-bacterial handwash after servicing equipment or handling reptiles. Wear disposable gloves while cleaning cages and, if necessary, a face mask to stop you inhaling dust. Scratches or bites should be treated immediately with antiseptic. Young children should only be allowed to handle animals under supervision, followed by handwashing as for adults. Any mouth contact should be prevented.

A Green Iguana (Iguana iguana) *showing the limb swelling associated with Metabolic Bone Disease. Some forms respond to treatment if not too advanced, but prevention – through correct diet – is better than cure.*

Symptoms of Metabolic Bone Disease

- Twitching limbs
- Swollen limbs
- Broken bones (mainly legs)
- Paralysis of hind limbs
- Soft, deformed lower jaw
- Difficulty in walking
- Unusual walk
- Deformity of the spine
- Lower lip tightened in a "grin"
- Soft or deformed shell (tortoises and turtles)

Reptile Species

When people think of keeping reptiles, they often think automatically of large, powerful species such as pythons and Green Iguanas – which also tend to be the controversial ones. However, there are plenty of others to choose from if space in your home is restricted, or if controversy is not part of the attraction. Exotic species have their own appeal, but legal restrictions and depleted wild populations mean that the commonplace may soon become rare.

The vast majority of reptiles are simply not found in the pet trade (nor should they be). The ones presented in this section have been chosen because they are readily available. This often means that they are bred in captivity and there is a more established body of information about their husbandry. Many are suitable for beginners, while others will require more experience. There are deliberate omissions: monitor lizards, the largest pythons, venomous snakes and members of the order Crocodilia, which tend to be subject to much stricter regulations. These species are for experts only.

A note on terminology: Semi-aquatic chelonian species are referred to throughout this book as turtles. They have traditionally been known as terrapins, especially in British usage.

▶ *Eastern Box Turtle* (Terrapene carolina) *see page 130.*

Agamids FAMILY: AGAMIDAE

THIS FAMILY OF LIZARDS IS FOUND ACROSS southern Asia, Australia and Africa, and it contains some 30–40 genera with more than 300 species. The males of many species are spectacularly coloured; colour change also occurs in some breeding females. The habitats of the family are diverse. Some species are native to tropical rainforest, such as Water Dragons (see pages 54–55); the others presented in this section are all from hot, arid climates. All the members of Agamidae are diurnal and mainly terrestrial, though rock-dwellers and arboreal species also exist. Most are oviparous, but a few Asian species are viviparous. Loss and regeneration of the tail (autotomy) is not seen in any Agamidae.

AGAMAS

Agama species. This diverse group of 60 lizard species is widespread across eastern Europe, Asia and Africa. Some species are occasionally placed in the genus *Laudakia*. Agamas are primarily ground-dwellers, but a few species, such as Blue-headed Agamas (*Agama atricollis*, also known as Tree Agamas) are semi-arboreal; other species may climb also. All agamas are very active and require plenty of space. Various sub-species are found mainly in arid areas along the edges of forests, in rocky areas and mountain regions. Agamas are frequently imported, but some are known for not thriving in captivity – although others, such as the Blue-headed Agamas and Desert Dragons (*A. stellio*), have proved more adaptable. The smaller members of the genus may reach a length of 10in (25cm). Desert Dragons typically grow to 13–14in long (33–36cm), and the 15–16in (38–41cm) long Blue-headed Agama is usually the largest specimen.

Even during the breeding season, Blue-headed females remain olive-coloured, with black marbling and a dark shoulder spot, while males have a blue back, bright blue throat, green-blue head and a broad yellow-green vertebral stripe as well as the shoulder spot. Males also possess 2 or 3

◄ *A male Blue-headed Agama* (Agama atricollis) *is conspicuous in its native habitat. Wild-caught adults are nervous and take time to adjust. New imports usually carry parasites and must be treated immediately.*

rows of 10–12 pre-anal pores. Desert Dragons can be grey to almost black with light yellow to orange spots. Males possess 2 rows of pre-anal pores, a median line of enlarged scales on the abdomen and somewhat larger heads.

Both Blue-headed Agamas and Desert Dragons have proved to be successful subjects for captive breeding. Mating usually takes place a few weeks after the Winter cooling has ended and normal temperatures resumed. Supply a box of damp sand 18in (45cm) deep for egg deposition. The gravid female will need some means of gaining access to the box, such as a ramp.

About 30–45 days after mating, females of both species deposit their soft-shelled eggs. An overnight drop in temperature by 5°C (10–12°F) prolongs the incubation period by 2–4 weeks, and it also seems to produce larger, more robust hatchlings. The temperament of agamid hatchlings varies. Desert Dragons soon become tame, but if hatchlings of Blue-headed Agamas feel threatened, they throw open their mouths and are not reluctant to bite. However, with some patience on the keeper's part, even Blue-headed juveniles will learn to accept feeding by hand.

● *Can agamas be kept in groups?*

For Blue-headed Agamas, Desert Dragons and Toad-headed Agamids, it is generally advisable to keep a pair or trio, as males can be aggressive. Some other species live in groups governed by hierarchies, but a very large vivarium would be needed.

● *Are all agamas completely insectivorous?*

Some species may take sweet fruits and other plant material – it is worth trying to see if they are accepted. Occasionally they may accept pink mice, but these should be a limited part of the diet.

● *What conditions do hatchling agamas need?*

After hatching, remove the young to a vivarium measuring 24x12x18in (60x30x45cm) and furnished similar to that of the adults. Temperatures should be 2°C (4°F) lower, and full-spectrum (UVB) light is essential. Hatchlings will readily accept small, vitamin-dusted livefoods. Desert Dragon hatchlings are particularly voracious feeders.

● *Are agama bites venomous?*

In their native habits, the popular belief is that these lizards are venomous, but this is not the case.

Vivarium Conditions
Blue-headed Agama, Desert Dragon and Toad-headed Agamids

VIVARIUM SIZE   Min for a pair or trio

Blue-headed Agama	36x18x30in (90x45x76cm)
Desert Dragon	36x18x18in (90x45x45cm)
Toad-headed Agamids	36x12x12in (90x30x30cm)

SUBSTRATE   Dust-free sand

Toad-headed Agamids	3–4in (8–10cm) deep
Others	2.5in (5cm) deep

HABITAT Firmly bedded rocks and stumps. Cork bark caves. Spray rocks lightly in morning. Small water dish for all except Toad-headed Agamids. Blue-headed Agamas also need sturdy climbing branches and slightly more moisture.

TEMPERATURE High percentage full-spectrum (UVB) light and a basking lamp.

Toad-headed Agamids 30–35°C (86–95°F) at cool end, 40°C (104°F) at hot spot; 15°C (60°F) at night. Photoperiod: 12 hours.

Others 28–30°C (82–86°F) at cool end, 37–38°C (98–100°F) at hot spot; 20–23°C (68–74°F) at night. Photoperiod: 14 hours.

WINTER COOLING

Blue-headed Agama 10–12°C (50–54°F) for 8 weeks. Photoperiod: normal daylight hours.

Desert Dragon 15–18°C (60–65°F) for 8 weeks. Photoperiod: normal daylight hours.

Toad-headed Agamids 9°C (48°F) 12 weeks. Photoperiod: normal daylight hours.

FEEDING Most live foods (see Foods and Feeding, pages 30–31), dusted with supplements.

INCUBATION   In moist vermiculite

Blue-headed Agama 3–4 annual clutches of 7–12 eggs. Incubate for 90 days at 30°C (86°F).

Desert Dragon 2 annual clutches of 7–12 eggs. Incubate for 70–80 days at 30°C (86°F).

Toad-headed Agamids 4–5 annual clutches of 2–6 eggs. Incubate for 50–70 days at 28–30°C (82–86°F) during day, 21°C (70°F) at night.

▲ *Toad-headed Agamids* (Phrynocephalus mystaceus) *display an open mouth in threat. Toad-heads are large enough to give a sharp nip to a keeper, but rarely do so.*

TOAD-HEADED AGAMIDS

Phrynocephalus helioscopus and *P. mystaceus.* These small to medium Asian species are also known variously as Sungazing Agamids, Bearded Toad-heads and Sungazing Lizards. *P. helioscopus* is found from central Asia to Mongolia; *P. mystaceus* from central Asia to northern Iran and Afghanistan. Their native habitat is in sandy deserts and rocky steppes. *P. helioscopus* is the smaller, growing only to a length of 3in (8cm); *P. mystaceus* can reach a length of 10in (25cm).

P. helioscopus resembles a miniature horned lizard (*Phrynosoma;* see pages 92–93) with its squat shape, short, broad head, very short spines and thin short tail. The colour is grey with darker markings and a light blue spot on each shoulder in both sexes. *P. mystaceus* is a sandy brown colour. Also squat, it extends a spiny flap on each side of the mouth when threatened, which makes

the mouth seem larger. Both species should be kept in pairs or trios, but because of the great difference in their sizes, they should not be mixed. Spiders are a favourite food of both.

Male Toad-heads can be recognized by the wider tail base and swellings underneath. Both species are egg-layers. For egg deposition, provide a box of damp sand 3in (8cm) deep for *P. helioscopus* and 6in (15cm) deep for *P. mystaceus.* Lack of a suitable oviposition site may result in dystocia (see Health and Disease, pages 42–43). The vivarium must be well ventilated to prevent any build-up of humidity. Babies need a maximum temperature 3–4°C (5–7°F) lower than adults to prevent desiccation (drying out).

DABB LIZARD

Uromastyx acanthinurus. Sometimes known as the Mastigure Lizard or the African Spiny-tailed Agamid, this species belongs to a genus found across northeastern Africa and the Middle East. The maximum length for adults is 18in (45cm). Dabbs' habitat is arid, desert or rocky areas. The

Vivarium Conditions
Dabb Lizard

Vivarium size   Min 72x24x24in (184x60x 60cm) for a pair or trio.

Substrate Dust-free sand, min 5in (12.5cm) deep

Habitat Heavy, immovable rocks with 1 near hot spot for basking. 2 or 3 cork bark shelters. Spray lightly daily but avoid overwetting. Ventilate well.

Temperature 25°C (77°F) at cool end, 45–50°C (113–122°F) at hot spot; 20°C (68°F) at night. Photoperiod: 14 hours. Provide high-percentage full-spectrum (UVB) light and a basking lamp.

Winter cooling 20°C (68°F) during day; 60°F (15°C) at night for 8 weeks. Photoperiod: 8 hours.

Feeding Herbivorous and varied (see Foods and Feeding, pages 29–30). Vegetables, edible flowers, sprouted pulses and fruits, chopped small and mixed well. Also insects, no more than 10% of diet. Dust food with vitamin supplements twice a week, extra calcium 3 times a week. Avoid animal fats and proteins.

Incubation   1 annual clutch of up to 20 eggs. Incubate for 85–95 days at 30–33°C (86–89°F) in moist vermiculite with 80–85% air humidity.

● *Can living plants be used with Toad-heads and Dabb Lizards?*

... No. A dry atmosphere is essential, and live plants increase the humidity. Dabbs would also tend to dig up or eat the plants.

● *Are Toad-heads suited to an outdoor enclosure?*

Yes, if summers are hot and dry with a temperature drop at night, and if winters are sufficiently cool. Areas with high summer humidity would not be suitable.

● *Are Dabb Lizards amenable to handling?*

Babies tame easily, but wild-caught adults may thrash about – the spiny tail can cause lacerations. Even adults usually become tamer eventually.

● *Can Dabbs be fed on commercial iguana diets?*

These may be used to supplement the diet, but should not comprise more than 10%. If dry foods are used, they must be soaked to provide moisture.

● *Will Dabbs eat seeds?*

They have been known to eat millet and dehusked sunflower seeds, split peas and lentils. The latter two are better soaked first to provide moisture and prevent them swelling inside the lizard.

● *Will my Dabb Lizard need food and water during the Winter cooling period?*

Cooling must be gradual (see information on hibernation in Breeding, pages 35–37), and the appetite should decrease accordingly. Spray the lizards lightly on the head once a day, but make sure that the substrate is not dampened.

body is heavy and has a short tail with rows of spiny scales arranged in whorls. The colouring varies from dark grey to brown when cool; when warm, red, yellow or green appears on the dorsal surface, and the remaining areas may turn black. In the wild Dabb Lizards dig tunnels to escape the heat of the day and to keep warm at night. They are adapted to dry conditions and obtain adequate moisture from their food. Low temperatures can inhibit digestion, and lack of light causes sluggishness. Too much protein or fat causes obesity, kidney and liver problems.

Adult male Dabbs are larger and have more prominent femoral pores, often with comb-like waxy secretions. Hemipenile swellings are obvious in breeding males, which develop brighter colours. Females may also colour up, often causing them to be confused with males. Males may coexist reasonably well, but aggression occurs in the breeding season when in warm, bright conditions, especially natural sunlight outdoors. The best grouping is a single male with 2 or 3 females. Mating occurs after Winter cooling.

◆ *A hatchling Dabb Lizard* (Uromastyx acanthinurus). *Chasing live crickets provides exercise for these lizards, which can easily become obese.*

Bearded Dragon

FAMILY: AGAMIDAE
SPECIES: POGONA VITTICEPS

WITH ADULTS REACHING A TOTAL LENGTH of 22–23in (57–58cm), the Bearded Dragon is one of the largest of the 31 species of the genus *Pogona*. The "beard" is a pouch under the throat that inflates in response to threat. Bearded Dragons are also known as Inland Dragons for their native habitat in eastern continental Australia. They are diurnal and spend long periods basking and climbing logs and stumps. Their colours range from tan, brown and grey to green, "pastel" and desert colours: gold, orange and red. Selective-breeding programmes for captive specimens, especially those in the US, emphasize coloured morphs. There are also hybrids called "vittikins" – crosses between *P. vitticeps* and the smaller Rankin's Bearded Dragon (*P. brevis*).

Mature males have larger, broader heads than the females and display a jet-black throat during courtship or threat. Males also have enlarged

▲ *A red morph Bearded Dragon* (Pogona vitticeps). *Males are highly territorial and may not feed if they are intimidated by another male in too small a space.*

femoral and pre-anal pores. Another characteristic in adults is the cloacal opening. If the flap of skin covering the vent is gently pulled back, that of the male is wider or longer. Hatchlings can be sexed by the "popping" method (see Breeding, pages 34–35). In juveniles the sexes look similar.

Hierarchies and Alpha Males

Groups of Bearded Dragons quickly form hierarchies after hatching. Larger, heavier juveniles always feed first; rearing in small groups minimizes any bullying. Among adults, a dominant (alpha) male emerges. He establishes a territory and defends it against other males. His position also gives him the right to mate with a female.

● *Are Bearded Dragons tameable?*

Despite their appearance, they quickly become tame, because they are usually obtained as hatchlings. They will feed from your hand whenever possible. Although the spines look sharp, they are quite soft.

● *Are they a good choice for beginners?*

Yes. In addition to their temperament, they do not require highly specialized conditions or diet. Their size is ideal: not too big (requiring a huge vivarium) or too small (easily lost if let loose in the house).

● *How often should Bearded Dragons be fed?*

Adults can be fed 4 or 5 times a week, juveniles daily. Hatchlings – especially if several are raised together – need 2–3 feeds a day, with extra for "snacking". This ensures that smaller, weaker hatchlings get enough food and are not intimidated by dominant siblings. After 4 weeks, reduce to a daily feed until they are 6–8 months old; then begin feeding as for adults.

● *Can they be reared on beef and pink mice?*

Juvenile Bearded Dragons readily eat raw meat, and a high-protein diet will initially help them to put on growth and bulk. However, over time this diet will produce abnormally fat bodies, which may prove fatal. Pink mice as part of a varied diet can be used occasionally, but do not use beef; it is low in calcium and high in phosphorus (see Foods and Feeding, pages 28–29).

● *When are Bearded Dragons mature?*

This depends on size rather than age. Well-fed dragons attain their full size in 6–8 months. Those on leaner rations may take 12–14 months.

▲ *A group of young Bearded Dragons* (Pogona vitticeps). *If raised solely on insects, they may later refuse plant material and miss valuable nutrients.*

Bearded Dragons need a cool period (from the beginning of December in the northern hemisphere) to stimulate breeding. Mating may take place without the keeper's knowledge if a pair are kept together, so it is better to separate the sexes for the cool period. It is particularly important that the females are well fed after the cool period ends. Introduce the female about 3 weeks after normal conditions are restored, and provide damp sand for egg deposition. Some 45–60 days after mating, the female lays about 20 eggs in an excavated chamber.

Other species requiring similar conditions are *P. barbata*, *P. nullarbor* and *P. henrylawsoni*. All three are also known as Bearded Dragons.

Vivarium Conditions

Vivarium size	60x24x18in (150x60x45cm)
Substrate	Dust-free sand

Habitat Grapevine logs and cork bark for shelter. Put basking rocks directly in the beam of a spotlight. Supply a small water dish.

Temperature 28°C (82°F) at cool end, 40–43°C (104–110°F) at hot spot; 21–24°C (70–75°F) at night. Photoperiod: 14 hours. Provide full-spectrum (UVB) light and a basking lamp.

Winter cooling 7–8 weeks. 17–18°C (63–65°F) at cool end, 24–26°C (75–80°F) at hot spot. 15°C (60°F) at night. Photoperiod: 10 hours.

Feeding Insects (crickets, locusts, waxworms, mealworms); vegetables and fruits including: chopped apple, orange, peppers, broccoli, endive, grated squashes, carrots and courgettes (zucchini), watercress, chinese leaves (bak choi), dandelion and nasturtium leaves and flowers. Chop food small and mix well; dust with multivitamin and calcium supplements. Leave small pieces of cuttlefish bone on a lid. Provide clean water daily.

Incubation 60–75 days in a moist vermiculite substrate at 30°C (86°F), with 10% air humidity (see Breeding, pages 38–39). The whole clutch may hatch within 24 hours, or hatching may be spread over 6–8 days. New hatchlings measure 4–4.5in (10–11cm). When they are active (after a few hours), remove to their own vivarium with conditions as for adults. Juvenile Bearded Dragons may be reared in small groups.

Water Dragons

FAMILY: AGAMIDAE
SPECIES: PHYSIGNATHUS COCINCINUS

THESE TROPICAL LIZARDS, NATIVE TO PARTS of China and most of southeast Asia, are also known as Green Water Dragons, Chinese Water Dragons and Asian Water Dragons. Their total length of about 36in (90cm) makes them a popular alternative to iguanas, which can grow to double this size and require considerable space.

Water Dragons are bright green with darker rings on the tail. Youngsters have a blue hue on the shoulders and light green diagonal body stripes. The body scales are very finely textured, giving them the appearance of smooth fabric. The larger scales on the lower jaw and throat are lighter in colour, and in some mature males this area is pink. Specimens that are obtained as hatchlings or young juveniles soon become hand tame, but wild-caught adults rarely accept the

▶ *Water Dragons* (Physignathus cocincinus) *are mainly insectivorous and carnivorous, but some will accept soft fruit, which provides valuable extra nutrients.*

limitations imposed by living in a vivarium. They frequently injure their snouts by throwing themselves against the glass.

Water Dragons are arboreal and semi-aquatic, so they require climbing branches and a pool for bathing and drinking. A water bowl can be provided but may not be used. Many ordinary houseplants will thrive in the humidity of the vivarium, but they should be positioned well out of the dragons' way – the plants could be fastened to the wall, for instance. Dragons are similarly destructive of stocked pools; any fish in the pool with them will probably be eaten.

The Courtship Chase

Maturity is reached at 2 to 3 years old. During the Winter cooling period, it is advisable to separate adult males from females. When vivarium temperatures are returned to normal, increase the humidity slightly and reintroduce the female to the male. The male courts the female by chasing her around the vivarium, stopping to bob his head. When she is receptive, he mounts, grasping the nape of her neck in his mouth.

The gestation period lasts between 2 and 3 months. During this time, the female's appetite diminishes. For egg deposition, provide a box measuring 18x18x12in (45x45x30cm) and fill it with substrate material, or simply pile this volume of substrate in a corner of the vivarium. The female will dig 1 or more nests about 12in (30cm) deep. After laying her eggs, she fills in the hole and tramps down the ground. Watch carefully to see where the eggs are deposited so that you can remove them for incubation.

Incubating eggs will almost triple in size and some natural discolouration may occur. New hatchlings measure some 1–2 in (3.5–5 cm) from snout to vent, and about 6in (15cm) from the snout to the tip of the tail. Transfer to a small vivarium and give them the same conditions as the adults. Hatchlings and juveniles should be fed insects daily. Large foods are not suitable.

Other species requiring similar vivarium conditions to *P. cocincinus* are the Brown Water Dragon *(P. leseurii)* and the Northern Water Dragon *(P. temporalis)*, both of which are native to New Guinea and some parts of Australia.

● *Are there any particular problems with wild-caught specimens?*

... When inspecting wild-caught dragons for purchase, pay special attention to the snout and mouth. It is not unusual for specimens to have damaged themselves against their cages in the distress following capture.

● *Can a number of Water Dragons be kept together?*

Yes, if the vivarium is large enough: males may not be particularly aggressive toward each other if they have plenty of space and separate basking facilities. However, it is usually better to house one male with one or more females.

● *I have a female that bobs her head like a courting male. What does it mean?*

Headbobbing is a sign of status, and a female may use this signal to show dominance over other females. In reply, a subordinate female will wave a foreleg to make signs of appeasement.

● *How can I tell the sex of my Water Dragons?*

Mature males tend to be bigger and more brightly coloured than the females. A male will also have a larger head, a larger crest and more prominent femoral pores (the line of small circular pores on the underside of each thigh).

● *My dragons defecate in their water pool. Is this abnormal, and will it contaminate the water?*

This is typical Water Dragon behaviour – but because they also drink from the pool, you will need to change the water frequently. However, because the dragons tend not to defecate on the substrate, at least you will not need to change that as regularly.

Vivarium Conditions

Vivarium size Min 48x30x36in (120x75x90cm) for a pair.

Substrate Mixed potting compost, leaf litter and sphagnum moss, 4in (10cm) deep.

Habitat Branches for climbing; pool for drinking and bathing.

Temperature 30°C (86°F) at cool end, 35°C (95°F) at hot spot; 24°C (75°F) at night. Photoperiod: 14 hours. Provide a full-spectrum (UVB) light and basking lamp.

Humidity 75–85%. Spray daily.

Winter cooling 3°C (5°F) lower than normal temperatures for 8 weeks. Photoperiod: 11 hours.

Feeding Insects supplemented with large earthworms, large snails, morios, occasional defrosted rat pups and day-old chicks. Some individuals may accept soft fruit. Feed adults only 3 to 4 times a week to prevent obesity.

Incubation 1–2 annual clutches of 8–12 eggs. Incubate for 75–90 days at 30°C (86°F) in moist vermiculite, covered with a layer of damp sphagnum moss. Maintain nearly 100% humidity by misting the moss.

Southern Alligator Lizard and European Slow Worm FAMILY: ANGUIDAE

THE 60–70 MEMBER SPECIES OF THE FAMILY Anguidae are found mainly in the temperate and subtropical regions of South America, North America and southeast Asia. Some have 4 legs, but others may be legless or have reduced limbs.

SOUTHERN ALLIGATOR LIZARD

Gerrhonotus multicarinatus. This diurnal lizard from the west coast of the US is easy to keep. Its native habitat is mainly oak woods with open areas and plenty of cover. It cannot tolerate extreme heat. The body (reaching a total length of 16in/40cm) has lateral folds; the long tail, although partly prehensile, is fragile and easily shed. Colouring is variable, brown to grey or yellow with dark crossbands interspersed with white spots. The belly may have dark stripes or broken lines, and the eyes are pale yellow. When handled, wild specimens will writhe and smear faeces, and males may extrude the hemipenes.

Mating usually occurs in Spring. Females excavate an oviposition chamber and guard the eggs. Males are distinguished by hemipenile swellings at around 9–10 months. Young are more secretive than adults and require hiding places. They may be raised communally until fighting occurs.

EUROPEAN SLOW WORM

Anguis fragilis. These legless lizards are found throughout Europe, as far east as the Urals and in southwestern Asia and northwestern Africa. Generally crepuscular, Slow Worms can sometimes be seen basking, especially in late Spring. They also like to burrow under flat, sun-warmed

---

Vivarium Conditions
Southern Alligator Lizard and European Slow Worm

VIVARIUM SIZE

Southern Alligator Lizard   Min 36x18x24in (90x 45x60cm) for a pair or trio.

European Slow Worm   Min 24x12x12in (60x 30x30cm) for a pair.

SUBSTRATE

Southern Alligator Lizard   Sandy loam and leaf mould, 2in (5cm) deep, divided into a dry and moderately damp section (see Housing, pages 14–15, and Fat-tailed Gecko, page 73).

European Slow Worm   Soft, sandy or peaty soil mixed with crushed dead leaves, topped with moss.

HABITAT

Southern Alligator Lizard   Hides and sturdy branches. Live plants optional. Small water dish.

European Slow Worm   Thin, flat stones, roofing slates or cork bark for hides.

TEMPERATURE

Southern Alligator Lizard   22°C (72°F) at cool end, 30°C (86°F) at hot spot; 15°C (60°F) at night.

Photoperiod: 12 hours. Full-spectrum (UVB) light and basking lamp.

European Slow Worm   15°C (60°F) at cool end, 27°C (80°F) at hot spot; 13–18°C (56–64°F) at night. Photoperiod: 12–14 hours.

WINTER COOLING   Normal daylight hours

Southern Alligator Lizard   9–10°C (48°–50°F) for 8–12 weeks.

European Slow Worm   5°C (41°F) for 12 weeks.

FEEDING

Southern Alligator Lizard   Dusted insects, cuttlefish bone pieces. Thawed mice once every 2 weeks.

European Slow Worm   Slugs, earthworms, cranefly larvae, spiders, small snails.

INCUBATION

Southern Alligator Lizard   Egg-layer. 1 annual clutch of 12–20 eggs. Incubate for 40–50 days at 27–29°C (80–84°F) in moist vermiculite (0.8:1).

European Slow Worm   Livebearer. Gestation: about 4 months. Produce litter of 5–12 young.

European Slow Worms (Anguis fragilis) *are large legless lizards with gentle dispositions. They tame quickly and will accept food offered on forceps.*

Q&A

● *How can I tell if my Southern Alligator Lizard is male or female?*

... Males have broader heads and swellings at the tail base. It may help to compare several specimens. If any fight, they are probably males. An experienced keeper can evert the hemipenes by "popping" (see Breeding, pages 34–35).

● *Can Alligator Lizard eggs be left with the mother?*

Artificial incubation is preferable because it is a more controlled situation than the vivarium. The mother may try to bite when the keeper removes the eggs.

● *Should young Alligator Lizards be cooled for their first winter?*

No. They should be kept active at normal temperatures to encourage growth.

● *My Slow Worm has lost its tail. Will it grow back?*

Yes. The species name (*fragilis*) refers to the ease with which these lizards throw their tails when attacked – a trait shared by other members of the family Anguidae. Regrown tails, shorter than the original, are often seen in wild-caught specimens.

● *Can Slow Worms be kept outdoors?*

Yes. An outdoor enclosure is suitable as long as it has appropriate substrate, sufficient hiding places and hibernation chambers that are frost- and flood-proof.

stones. In the wild, their habitat includes hedge-rows, open woodland and scrubland, areas with ground cover, railway embankments and sometimes gardens. Slow Worms grow up to 16–18in (40–45cm) in length and can live 50 years in captivity, though there is no way of discovering the age of a wild-caught adult specimen.

The tiny scales resemble highly polished skin. Adult males are a uniform colour (usually brown or copper) on the dorsum and sides; the underside is grey with darker mottling. Some males have blue spots. Females have a heavier body and smaller head, sometimes with a mid-dorsal stripe and darker sides; the underside is usually black. Slow Worms are ovo-viviparous, mating in April, May and June in the northern hemisphere. Males fight during the breeding period, so it is advisable to keep them apart. Litters are born from late August to October, depending on temperatures. The young are usually born in a membrane and break free. At birth they measure 2.5–4in (6–10cm). The dorsal surface is pale gold, silvery or pale yellow; undersides are black. Rear the hatchlings away from the adults and supply large quantities of suitably small food.

Chameleons   FAMILY: CHAMAELEONIDAE

ONCE REGARDED AS ALMOST IMPOSSIBLE to keep in captivity, chameleons are now among the most popular pet reptiles. Unfortunately, they are popular "impulse buys" and many do not survive long. Minimum handling and disturbance are the keys to initial success. In time, many specimens will take food from fingers or forceps and will climb onto the keeper's hand. Animals newly imported from the wild are often in poor condition, with internal parasites, /and stressed from overcrowding and dehydration. Captive-bred animals make much better pets, especially for the inexperienced owner.

All species are superbly adapted to an arboreal existence with their prehensile tails, grasping feet, rotating eyes and extensible tongues. Prising them away from their perch is very stressful, and their claws and tail may be damaged if they cling. Many species will release their hold and drop to the floor if feeling threatened, and the keeper must be aware of this when handling them. Although they are slow-moving, many species can make a sudden dash or even a short leap if they do not wish to be picked up. Most chameleons drink by lapping water from their surroundings, so daily spraying is essential. Drip systems can be used if the vivarium is properly drained, but drinking from a waterfall should be discouraged as the water may be contaminated with droppings or dead insects. A few individuals will learn to eat or drink from a dish.

Dramatic Colour Change

Chameleons are camouflaged to fit in with their native habitats, but colour changes are based on temperature and emotional state, not surroundings. Such changes are more marked in some species, and in the males rather than the females, although gravid females may exhibit dramatic colouring if approached by an amorous male. Captive-bred males of some species tend to be less colourful than wild-caught ones, a fact also observed in Dwarf Chameleons (*Bradypodion thamnobates*). Keepers should never provoke colour change – it is very stressful for the animal.

Most chameleons are solitary animals. They are better housed separately and out of sight of others except for mating. Males are antagonistic, especially in restricted quarters. Intimidation can be purely visual: the sight of another chameleon often inhibits feeding or provokes competitive

▶ *A stout-bodied Panther Chameleon* (Chamaeleo pardalis) *clings to a branch with its tail and back feet. Never try to prise one from its perch.*

colour changes. Even pairs should be housed in separate cages except at breeding time. Female chameleons may retain unfertilized eggs if they are not mated. This can be fatal. Do not keep any females unless you will breed them. If you wish to keep only one chameleon, choose a male.

Rearing the Young

Sexual maturity usually occurs at 6 months, but as with many reptiles, size (rather than age) is the crucial factor. Baby chameleons should be removed from their parents early and reared separately at slightly lower temperatures. If you rear them communally, make sure there is plenty of space. Use small ventilated containers with climbing perches, some foliage, but no substrate. Containers must be kept clean. Full-spectrum (UVB) tubes fitted with reflector hoods can be suspended over them. Feed babies on large fruit-flies, green aphids and dusted hatchling crickets.

PANTHER CHAMELEON

Chamaeleo pardalis. Native to Madagascar, this species is sometimes also classified as *Furcifer pardalis.* Much of its native habitat is being destroyed, but it seems adaptable and has moved into plantations and near human settlements.

Panther Chameleons (Chamaeleo pardalis) *have a characteristic pale lateral line. In this blue male from Nosy Bé, the lateral line turns white as the body colour intensifies in response to threat or mating conditions. In green males, the lateral line turns pale blue.*

● Do I need to feed chameleons that are kept outdoors?

... Keeping them outdoors cannot guarantee an adequate supply of insects. Additional feeding is usually necessary. A number of feeding stations should be provided for this purpose (see Foods and Feeding, page 31).

● Do all eggs in a clutch hatch at the same time?

In some cases eggs hatch within a few days of each other. However, with Panther Chameleons there have been differences of 4–12 weeks even with identical conditions. Do not discard healthy-looking eggs, regardless of how long they have been incubating.

● How often are female Panther Chameleons receptive for mating?

Normally 11–17 days after oviposition, but some specimens have become receptive only 9 days later. These females tend to have a gestation period of only 19–21 days (their eggs incubating and hatching normally). The pink colouring is the best guide.

Panther Chameleons breed very successfully in captivity and are widely available in the United States, Britain and Europe. It is one of the larger species; males are 20–22in (51–56cm) long, and females 13in (33cm) long. Basic coloration of males tends to be green with orange-brown markings, although there are regional variations including a blue form with varying red markings. All have a pale, broken lateral line. Males also have distinct hemipenile swellings (often apparent from the age of 6 weeks in juveniles). When threatened or pursuing a female, males intensify their colours considerably – some specimens become completely orange with a pale blue lateral line.

Females are usually brown with pale lateral spots, but in the breeding season this changes. A receptive female assumes an almost uniform pink coloration. At this point she can be introduced into the male's quarters. She may initially assume her threat coloration (dark brown with a salmon-coloured broken lateral line), extend her throat pouch and threaten the male with her flattened body and gaping mouth. If properly receptive, when the male approaches she will resume the pink coloration, raise her tail and allow the male to mate. Unreceptive females will intensify their usual colour, constantly move, lie flat on the branch or descend to the floor, attempting to break away. If this happens the female should be removed to avoid a struggle. Four or five matings are advisable to ensure that all the eggs are fertile. Females are generally receptive for 5–7 days. However, sperm retention from a previous mating occasionally occurs, producing fertile eggs. For oviposition, place a mixture of moist potting soil and sand in the female's cage, either as a mound or in a plastic box. A 13in (33cm) female needs at least an equal depth of material to burrow into. "Trial" digs may be made before eggs are deposited. If no suitable site is available, eggs may be retained.

▶ *Male Jackson's Chameleons* (Chamaleo jacksonii) *have three distinctive horns. The eyes rotate to look in two directions, giving excellent all-around vision.*

Vivarium Conditions
Panther, Jackson's, Mountain and Elliot's Chameleons

VIVARIUM SIZE   Use box cages or glass tanks.

Elliot's Chameleon   Min 24x18x24in (60x45x60cm)

Others   Min 36x24x36in (92x60x92cm) for mature male; slightly smaller for female.

SUBSTRATE   Potting soil covered with fairly compacted moss. Newspaper can also be used for Panther Chameleons.

HABITAT   Fixed walkway of dead branches for basking spots and access to all parts of vivarium. Branches should not be too thick for grasping foot. Living plants such as Weeping Fig (*Ficus benjamina*) give cover, lapping surfaces and assist humidity. Do not use dense or large-leafed plants.

TEMPERATURE   Full-spectrum (UVB) light and a basking lamp are needed.

Panther Chameleon   27°C (80°F) at cool end, 32°C (90°F) at hot spot; 18°C (65°F) at night. Photoperiod: 13–14 hours.

Jackson's Chameleon   24°C (75°F) at cool end, 28°C (82°F) at hot spot; min 10°C (50°F) at night. Photoperiod: 12–14 hours.

Elliot's Chameleon   25.5–26.5°C (78–80°F) at cool end, 29.5°C (85°F) at hot spot; 15°C (60°F) at night. Overnight drop of at least 5–6°C (10°F) for montane species. Photoperiod: 14 hours.

Mountain Chameleon   21°C (70°F) at cool end, 25°C (78°F) at hot spot; minimum 10°C (50°F) at night. Photoperiod: 12–14 hours.

HUMIDITY   Spray once daily for drinking, more frequently to maintain humidity.

Panther Chameleon   50–60%

Jackson's and Elliot's Chameleons   70–90%

Mountain Chameleon   85%. Substrate should be kept wet but ventilated at side with fine mesh.

WINTER COOLING   Not necessary except for Panther Chameleons which need a slightly cooler day and 15°C (60°F) at night for 6–8 weeks. Photoperiod: 11 hours.

FEEDING   Live insects and invertebrates dusted with supplements. Some individuals develop food preferences. Panther Chameleons adapt easily to eating from a bowl.

JACKSON'S CHAMELEON

Chamaeleo jacksonii. Also known as the Three-horned Chameleon, this species is a native of Kenya and Tanzania. Kenya banned exports in 1981 but the subspecies *C. j. xantholophus* is still widely available in the United States, where it was released in Hawaii (Oahu and Maui) in the 1970s and proceeded to thrive. Some specimens descended from the Hawaiian imports have reached Europe. The Tanzanian subspecies *C. j. merumontana* is very rarely seen in the pet trade, and subspecies *C. j. jacksonii* cannot be legally exported at all. Occasionally the egg-laying three-horned species Johnston's Chameleon

▶ *Newborn Jackson's Chameleons* (Chamaeleo jacksonii). *If reared communally, horizontal space is more important than vertical to prevent bullying.*

(*C. johnstoni*) is mistaken for the livebearer Jackson's Chameleon, but there are colour and various other differences. Jackson's Chameleons do very well when kept outdoors.

Jackson's Chameleon is one of the medium-sized species, with males averaging a length of 10in (25.4cm) excluding the horns. Males also have a thicker tail base. Female *C. j. xantholophus* may have no horns, or greatly reduced horns; the other two subspecies may have one horn. Male horns are weapons; males should not be kept together. They should also be kept separately from the females except for mating. Receptive females tend to turn a uniform green-grey. Those that are not receptive show a contrasting pattern. They may hiss, sway and even bite, in which case they should be removed from the male's cage. Dominant hatchlings intimidate the weaker from higher vantage points. Ensure plenty of horizontal rather than vertical space.

▲ *Male (left) and female (right) Elliot's Chameleons (Chamaeleo ellioti). This species loves to bask and can be kept outside as long as shade is available.*

Breeding Conditions

PANTHER CHAMELEON	Egg-layer
Clutch size	4 annual clutches of 25–30 eggs
Incubation	180–390 days at constant 27°C (80°F) in clear, plastic hatching box with a few ventilation holes and 2in (5cm) moist vermiculite. Some breeders recommend 28–56 days at 18°C (65°F) followed by 25°C (78°F) during day and 21°C (70°F) at night.
JACKSON'S CHAMELEON	Livebearer
Gestation	5–10 months. Spray the vivarium lightly with water just before birth to prevent membrane drying out too soon.
Litter size	Up to 50 young dropped in sacs
ELLIOT'S CHAMELEON	Livebearer
Gestation	3–4 months
Litter size	Up to 14 young dropped in sacs; fluid in sacs absorbs the shock.
MOUNTAIN CHAMELEON	Egg-layer
Clutch size	4 annual clutches of 8 eggs
Incubation	98 days at 25–26.6°C (77–79°F) during day; 15°C (60°F) at night. Alternatively, some breeders incubate for 112–119 days at 24°C (75°F) during day; 15°C (60°F) at night. For either method, use a hatching box prepared as for Panther Chameleons above.

ELLIOT'S CHAMELEON

Chamaeleo ellioti. Widespread in eastern Africa and surviving at a range of altitudes, Elliot's Chameleon may be kept outdoors when conditions are suitable. The taxonomy of its group is still unresolved, and it is easily confused with *C. bitaeniatus* and *C. rudis*. Elliot's Chameleon can be distinguished from the others by a dorsal crest with spines of equal length, whereas the other two species have crests with unequal spines. The males of all three species grow to about 6–7in (15–17cm) long, though occasionally some individuals may grow larger.

In comparison with the females, male Elliot's Chameleons have a slimmer body, thicker tail base and brighter coloration, often light green with yellow–orange rays on the face and similar colours on the sides. Females have a plumper,

deeper body. The females' colouring tends to be brown/fawn with darker markings, often dark triangles, alongside the spine. Several colour forms exist for males and females. Pairs may cohabit amicably, but a period of separation will often induce mating when they are paired up again. Gravid females are better kept individually. They bask for long periods, often twisting the body to expose their undersides to full-spectrum (UVB) tubes. A perch on a branch some 2in (5cm) away from the tubes is ideal.

MOUNTAIN CHAMELEON

Chamaeleo montium. Also known as the Sailfin Chameleon, this species is a native of Cameroon, where it lives at altitudes of 1650–3960ft (500–1200m). It is related to other Cameroon mountain species such as *C. pfefferi, C. quadricornis, C. cristatus* and *C. wiedershami.*

Male Mountain Chameleons are impressive animals, with two horns, dorsal crests along their backs, and tail crests. They can grow to almost 10in (25cm) long, while the females are typically much smaller. Females have two conical scales in place of horns, and they lack the dorsal crest. When threatened or courting, the males exhibit contrasting colours such as white spots on top of the head. Both males and females have enlarged scales on each side of their bodies that can also display contrasting colours.

● *What size mesh should be used for an outside enclosure?*

... 0.25in (6mm) is needed to keep out mice and other pests while allowing in flies, on which the chameleons will feed. Note: this is not secure in all circumstances. Neonates can escape through this size mesh, and gravid females should be confined when parturition is near.

● *Will Jackson's Chameleons eat pink mice?*

Some medium to large chameleons will take pinkies, but they should not be given more than once a week.

● *Are male Elliot's Chameleons compatible?*

Males should be kept separately unless the vivarium is large and well-planted. Continuous threat displays and aggressive encounters are stressful.

● *Is it possible to sex baby Elliot's Chameleons?*

Yes. In bright sunlight 3-week-old males tend to have the same colouring as adult males. This is the easiest and most reliable way to tell baby Elliots apart.

▲ *A female Mountain Chameleon* (Chamaeleo montium) *lacks horns and the raised crest along the back and tail which males have.*

Mountain Chameleons are better kept singly, as both males and females are intolerant of their own as well as the opposite sex. Unreceptive and gravid females turn dark in the presence of males. Each animal retreats to a corner and may refuse to feed. Females should be introduced to the males' quarters only for mating and then removed. Sperm storage is common among all Cameroon species, but precise data for the individual species is not yet known. It is advisable to attempt a mating after a clutch in case the female has no stored sperm. Females other than *C. montium* usually repel the male's advances after the first clutch has been produced.

When they reach 2 weeks old, Baby Mountain Chameleons can be sexed very accurately by the beginnings of the dorsal crest and horns in the males. Hatchlings become sexually mature when they are between 7 and 12 months of age.

▲ *A Leaf-tailed Chameleon* (Brookesia perarmata) *blends in among the leaves on the forest floor. Though mainly terrestrial, they climb at night.*

LEAF CHAMELEONS

Brookesia and *Rhampholeon* species. In contrast to their tree-dwelling relatives, the various leaf chameleons, including stump-tailed and ground chameleons, are all ground-dwellers. *Brookesia* is native to Madagascar, and *Rhampholeon* is found in the region from Cameroon to eastern Africa. These dwarf chameleons, with their cryptic coloration and relative inactivity, are often ignored in favour of larger and more brightly coloured species. Advantages are that they may be kept in small vivaria, and recreating their forest floor habitat offers an opportunity for an attractive naturalistic display. *Brookesia* ranges in size from 1.3in (3.3cm) up to 4in (10cm) long.

Rhampholeon ranges from 1.3in (3.3cm) to 3in (8cm) long. Both species are mainly brown to match the forest floor; colour changes are more or less restricted to lighter browns, although some *Brookesia* species can show bright colours when excited. All leaf chameleons have tails that are only slightly prehensile; small spines and tubercules are another common feature.

In the wild *B. stumpfii* and *B. thieli* aestivate (become inactive) in hot, dry conditions and hibernate in cool weather by burrowing into dead leaves. Duplicating these conditions in a vivarium requires experience and should not be attempted by novice keepers.

Rhampholeon males have a thicker tail along much of their length and a larger rostral process, while *Brookesia* males exhibit a small swelling of the hemipenes. Coloration of males and females differs during mating, with the males tending to change from a uniform brown to a lighter shade with dark patches, with traces of other colours. *Rhampholeon* males also exhibit red tubercules on their orbital crests. All leaf chameleons are oviparous. The tiny eggs are not buried in the wild but are barely concealed under dead leaves, where they are in danger of being chewed by crickets. The young need small food – springtails, fruitflies, aphids and such. Like other baby chameleons, they should be reared separately.

Vivarium Conditions
Leaf Chameleons

VIVARIUM SIZE Min 24x12x12in (60x30x30cm)

SUBSTRATE Loamy soil with leaf litter

HABITAT Low walkways of slender twigs needed for night climbing. Small plants provide shade and hides.

TEMPERATURE Leaf chameleons seldom bask unless very cold, but a thermal gradient is important to prevent overheating. Provide low-percentage full-spectrum (UVB) light and a small basking lamp. Photoperiod: 12–14 hours.

Rhampholeon 21–25°C (70–77°F) at cool end; 14–15°C (58–60°F) at night.

Brookesia For *B. stumpfii* and *B. thieli* 25–27°C (77–80°F), for *B. superciliaris* max 25°C (77°F) during day; 20°C (68°F) at night for both.

HUMIDITY Spray regularly, 85–90% humidity, with some ventilation to prevent stagnant air.

WINTER COOLING 13–14°C (55–58°F) for 6 weeks. Photoperiod: 8–10 hours.

FEEDING Small insects including springtails. Cultured foods should be dusted with vitamins. Some specimens will drink from bromeliad axils and take small pieces of cuttlefish bone from a lid.

INCUBATION 3–4 annual clutches of 2–4 eggs. Incubate 35–55 days at a constant temperature of 23°C (73°F) in moist vermiculite.

● *Is the Mountain Chameleon a suitable species for outside?*

... Yes, with careful attention. Extremes of heat and cold should be avoided – in cooler climates they should be taken indoors before the first frost. Prolonged dull or wet weather also requires removal to suitable heat and light sources, otherwise the animals may become torpid.

● *Why does my Mountain Chameleon burrow?*

If kept too hot (more than 25°C/77°F), a male may try to burrow in the substrate. Both sexes bask only for short periods, often to one side of the heat lamp, but will then spend much of the day close to the full-spectrum tube.

● *Can male leaf chameleons be kept together?*

No. Even in a large vivarium it is advisable to keep only one male with one or two females.

● *Is it true that* Brookesia *species "buzz" when picked up?*

"Buzzing" has been observed in several species, especially females of *B. thieli* when approached by unwelcome suitors. They may produce the noise when picked up. Many species go rigid when disturbed. *Rhampholeon kersteni* also produces vibrations.

● *How long do leaf chameleons live?*

Usually not much longer than 2 years. The young are mature at 4–5 months.

● *How often should the vivarium be sprayed?*

For Cameroon chameleons (Mountain and leaf), 2 or 3 sprays daily to maintain humidity may be needed; or the substrate can have water added. A daily drink is important for all chameleons. Sprayed water often evaporates before it has been lapped. A drink from a syringe, if acceptable, ensures enough intake.

Giant Plated and Flat Lizards

FAMILY: CORDYLIDAE

THESE ATTRACTIVE LIZARDS ARE NATIVE TO southern Africa. Plated lizards tend to be more solitary than Flat Lizards, which are often found in large congregations among rocky outcrops. A dominant male Flat Lizard will usually have a "harem" of several females which he defends fiercely against any intruders or competitors.

GIANT PLATED LIZARD

Gerrhosaurus validus. Without sufficiently large quarters, it is best not to keep these 27in (70cm) long lizards. Specimens in the trade are almost always wild-caught imports from Mozambique; captive breeding is rare, possibly due to the space required. Like other plated lizards, Giants have large dorsal scales placed in regular rows, under-laid by bony plates (osteoderms) that reduce flexibility. A fold of skin along each side of their heavy body allows expansion and movement.

▲ *A Giant Plated Lizard* (Gerrhosaurus validus) *does not climb well, but hides in crevices and inflates its body for protection against predators. Other Plated Lizard species bury themselves in the sand instead.*

Vivarium Conditions
Giant Plated Lizard and Flat Lizard

VIVARIUM SIZE

Giant Plated Lizard   Min 48x24x18in (122x60x 45cm) for a pair. Larger is better.

Flat Lizard   30x12x15in (75x30x18cm) for a pair or trio of adults is adequate.

SUBSTRATE   Dry and sandy, 2in (5cm) deep

HABITAT   Semi-arid with rocky outcrops, raised for basking, and hiding places at cool end. Artificial plants for decoration. Furnishings must be sturdy for large lizards. Provide a small water dish and a light daily spray.

TEMPERATURE   Full-spectrum (UVB) light and basking lamp are needed.

Giant Plated Lizard   28°C (82°F) at cool end, up to 35°C (95°F) at hot spot; 20°C (68°F) at night. Photoperiod: 14 hours.

Flat Lizard   29°C (84°F) at cool end, 32–38°C (90–100°F) at hot spot; 18°C (64°F) at night. Photoperiod: 14 hours.

WINTER COOLING   Normal daylight hours

Giant Plated Lizard   18–20°C (64–68°F) for 6 weeks

Flat Lizard   12–13°C (54–55°F) for 6 weeks

FEEDING

Giant Plated Lizard   Omnivorous and as varied as possible. Insects, mice and termites; plant material, especially fruit. Provide vitamin and calcium supplements. Captive specimens have accepted canned reptile foods.

Flat Lizard   Most insects and invertebrates. Try dandelions, nasturtiums and other edible flowers, also sweet fruit and vegetables. Small pieces of cuttlefish bone for calcium supplements.

INCUBATION   In moist vermiculite

Giant Plated Lizard   1 annual clutch of 6 eggs. Incubate for 75–83 days at 30°C (86°F) with 90% air humidity.

Flat Lizard 1–2 annual clutches of 2 eggs. Incubate for 75–90 days at 25.5–26.5°C (78–80°F).

The colour is mainly dark brown, with small light dots which may form longitudinal stripes.

Giant Plated Lizards are not easy to sex. Both sexes have femoral pores, but breeding males develop pink-to-purple colouring on the chin, throat and cheeks. Males are better kept separately, especially in the breeding season. Serious efforts should be made to breed these lizards; importing them merely as pets is a waste. Large quarters, a varied diet, appropriate heating and lighting and winter cooling will all help. Rain in the native habitat may provide added breeding stimulus. Further research is needed into this and other aspects of plated lizard breeding.

Other species requiring similar treatment are the Rough-scaled Plated Lizard (*G. major*) – these males have more prominent femoral pores, making them easier to sex, but captive breeding is rare; the Yellow-throated Plated Lizard (*G. flavigularis*); and the Black-lined Plated Lizard (*G. nigrolineatus*). The latter 2 are smaller, slimmer and more colourful. All are widely available.

 A Flat Lizard (Platysaurus intermedius) *among rocks, its favoured hiding and basking place.*

FLAT LIZARD

Platysaurus intermedius. This lizard adapts particularly well to vivarium life and can live 14 years or more if given proper treatment. Males grow to 7–11in (18–28cm) long and are territorial, especially in the breeding season. When newly imported, specimens tend to be quite skittish and dash for cover, but they become calmer.

Male Flat Lizards are easily recognizable by their contrasting colours, which vary according to species. The tail is usually orange to yellow, with the brightest colours on the underside of the throat and belly. The head colour also varies. Colours tend to intensify in the breeding season. Females and juveniles are black with three light stripes along the dorsum, occasionally with light spots. Supply a damp area of substrate for egg deposition (see Breeding, pages 38–39) – a small amount of loam or leaf mould can be mixed in. Eggs are often deposited in crevices as in the wild. Normally they are produced in November to December, but females imported into the northern hemisphere produce theirs between June and July. Newly imported females may be gravid and should not be cooled until eggs have been produced and the females have been well fed. Several females often use the same site. Raise the young at slightly lower temperatures than the adults. Other species requiring similar treatment are the Emperor Flat Lizard (*P. imperator*), the largest and most brightly coloured member of the genus, and a few insectivorous species of *Cordylus* such as *C. warreni* and *C. jonesi*.

Q&A

● *How amenable to handling are Giant Plated Lizards?*

... Although large lizards have a powerful bite, they generally become tame quickly, especially the younger specimens.

● *Are Giant Plated Lizards difficult to keep?*

No. If their need for space can be adequately met, and if they are in good condition when purchased, they are relatively easy to maintain.

● *Should Flat Lizard males be kept separately?*

Yes, if the vivarium is small. However, 2 males and 4 females may live fairly peacefully in a large vivarium with plenty of crevices for cover.

Geckos FAMILY: GEKKONIDAE

ONE OF THE LARGEST LIZARD FAMILIES, with some 700 species, is the gecko family. Ranging in length from 1in (2.5cm) to more than 2ft (0.6m), geckos are found from the tropics to temperate regions, from sea level to 13,000ft (4000m). Their habitat may be rainforest, desert – or a house; geckos are expert insect-catchers.

Geckos have highly sensitive skin, which has tiny scales of varying textures and is shed several times a year. The tail stores nutrients and can instantly split off from the gecko's body to distract predators. This practice, called autotomy, does not occur in all geckos, and some species shed more easily than others. A new tail grows within several weeks, but it is never as good as the old. Never pick up a gecko by the tail – it may break off! Many geckos also have adhesive pads on their feet which allow them to climb straight up smooth surfaces. Those without pads often have small claws to help them climb. Two species have webbed feet (rear only, or front and rear), that seem to act as "snowshoes" on the sand.

Most geckos are nocturnal or crepuscular – a lifestyle reflected in their subtle coloration and their vertically-slit pupils. Their preferred range of ambient (room) temperature is from 20–30°C (68–86°F). Moving back and forth from a cool spot to a warm spot allows them to maintain the temperature that suits them. Most do not require full-spectrum lighting, although they do bask occasionally if light is available. All geckos have good eyesight and relatively good hearing; they can communicate with a variety of sounds. The ear is visible on the head, above and behind the jaw.

Secretive and Aggressive

Geckos are secretive and need plenty of hiding places. Squeezing into tight spaces helps them to feel secure. Climbers and gliders also need plenty of room for exercise; use a vivarium that is taller than it is long. For ground-dwellers, lower and longer is better. A larger vivarium makes it easier to maintain both a thermal gradient (see Heating and Lighting, pages 18–19) and peaceful coexistence. Adult males should not be kept together; the ideal grouping is 1 male to 1 or more females. Except during the breeding season, a pair may ignore each other. It is not always easy to tell one sex from the other, but some males have broader heads, and most have prominent femoral or cloacal pores which the females lack. The hemipenes of the male fit into cavities in the tail base, which is relatively thick.

◄ *A Big-headed Gecko* (Paroedura pictus) *can move fast in spite of its build.*

● *Does temperature influence the sex of hatchlings?*

... At least one report claims that 28°C (82°F) produces female Big-headed hatchlings and 32°C (90°F) produces males. There are similar claims of temperature-related sex determination (TSD – see Breeding, page 38–39) in other reptiles, including other geckos, but further research is needed.

● *What can be done if female Big-headed Geckos are obviously suffering from overproduction?*

Give them vitamin D3 and soluble calcium orally, and consult a veterinary surgeon for further help. Adjusting the temperature may also reduce their productivity (see Breeding, pages 36–37).

● *Does it make a difference where the cork bark shelter is located for desert geckos?*

Yes. Even for desert species, the shelter should be placed away from the hot spot to prevent overheating.

◆ *A desert gecko* (Stenodactylus petrii) *has typically nocturnal, narrow vertical pupils that widen at night to help it locate its insect prey. Geckos also hear well.*

Geckos will not breed if they are not kept under the correct conditions. Courtship consists of the male calling to a female, waving his head and tail, and eventually approaching to smell and taste her. If she accepts him, he straddles her back and inserts one of his hemipenes into her cloaca. Most geckos are oviparous – they lay eggs, usually 2 to 4 weeks after mating. Eggs should be removed for incubation and the hatchlings reared separately from adults, which may eat them. Hatchlings require tiny food, such as aphids, hatchling crickets and fruit flies.

BIG-HEADED GECKO

Paroedura pictus. These 5.5in (14cm) long nocturnal geckos inhabit dry forest, scrubland and rocky areas of western and southern Madagascar. Although they have broad heads and stout bodies, they are fast and agile. Their colouring is light with brown markings. Some are striped, others banded; the latter also have a dark and light phase based on background coloration. The adhesive lamellae on adult toes are rather weak, and adults prefer a mainly terrestrial existence. They do not seem able to climb smooth surfaces. Males have hemipenile swelling under the tail.

Big-headed Geckos can be too prolific for their own good. Females may produce more than 30 eggs in a season. Overproduction causes calcium depletion, which shows as quivering fits (tetany), swollen limbs and soft eggs in later clutches, even after calcium supplements have been given. The females may die as a result of this depletion.

Eggs are buried in the substrate and should be removed for incubation. Hatchlings are an attractive light-fawn colour which fades after a few weeks. They have adhesive toes and are expert climbers. Rearing individually prevents bullying. Hatchlings reach maturity at 9 to 12 months, depending on diet. Females have been known to breed at 5 months, but cannot withstand intensive egg production and often die. At 5 months, geckos should be sexed and separated to prevent mating until at least 9 months old.

DESERT GECKOS

Stenodactylus species. The 8 to 12 species of this genus, also known as sand geckos and ground geckos, are distributed from northwest Africa to southwest Asia. Their taxonomy is uncertain; keepers tend to use the generic name. The information here is based on *S. sleveni* and *S. stenodactylus* but other species require similar treatment. Imported species available in the pet trade tend to be either *S. stenodactylus* or *S. petrii*.

Desert geckos are nocturnal and small, around 3in (6cm) long, with small smooth scales, rounded heads, bulbous eyes and protuberant nostrils

that give their snouts an upturned appearance. Autotomy occurs easily, and regrown tails are common. Desert geckos' colouring is variable: small, dark markings and occasionally white flecks on a light fawn to sand background. These geckos lack adhesive lamellae, and climb only on small rock piles. They seldom take water.

Desert geckos are relatively easy to keep and are frequently bred. Mature males exhibit two swellings just posterior to the cloaca. The eggs are hard-shelled and are covered with a mound of sand after deposition. Once they are hatched, the young can be raised in a small vivarium under a similar regime to that of the adults.

LEOPARD GECKO
Eublepharis macularius. This semi-desert, rock-climbing gecko is one of the most widely captive-bred lizards and is often recommended for beginners. Baby Leopard Geckos become very tame and eventually grow to reach a length of 8–10in (20–25cm). The body has numbers of raised tubercules but the skin has an almost velvety feel. Fat is stored in the plump tail. The dorsum has a background in varying shades of yellow, with white on the tail. In addition, the head, back and legs are marked with small, dark spots. Modern selective breeding has produced forms (morphs) with a deeper yellow background colouring.

The distinctively-marked Leopard Gecko (Eublepharis macularius) *is popular and easy to keep, but it rarely comes out of hiding during the day.*

Leopard Geckos are ground dwellers and do not climb. Although they are crepuscular to nocturnal and do not need full-spectrum light, they bask for short periods if it is provided. Rocky terraces and caves for shelter can be constructed; ensure that all rockwork is firmly bedded.

These geckos should be kept either as a pair or as a colony of one male to several females. Males are more heavily built, with a broader head, a V-shaped row of pre-anal pores and 2 small hemi-penile swellings. Some keepers do not impose a cool period, but others find breeding success increases if there is a 2-month reduction. Leathery eggs are produced about 6 weeks after mating. Supply a deposition site consisting of moist sand or sand and peat. Hatchling Leopard Geckos look different from adults: they are yellow with black and mauve bars which change to spots. After 1 week the tubercules begin to grow. A few days after hatching the young accept insect fare. They can be kept slightly more humid than the adults for the first few weeks. Use paper towel for substrate. The Banded Gecko (*Coleonyx variegatus*) requires similar treatment, with Winter cooling at 10°C (50°F) for 2–3 months.

Vivarium Conditions
Big-headed, Desert, Leopard, Fan-footed and Fat-tailed Geckos

VIVARIUM SIZE

Fan-footed Gecko 30x15x30in (75x38x75cm) for a pair. The height is necessary for active climbers.

Others Min 24x12x15in (60x38x30cm) for a pair or trio of adults.

SUBSTRATE

Fat-tailed Gecko A moisture-retentive substrate (sprayed daily) placed next to dry dust-free sand 1in (2.5cm) deep; or a divided vivarium with both.

Others Dry dust-free sand: 2–4in (5–10cm) deep for Leopard Geckos (or an artificial, carpet-type, substrate); 1in (2.5cm) deep for other species.

HABITAT
Rocks and branches for climbing; rock caves or cork bark for shelter, located away from hot spot. Plants suited to dry conditions, such as succulents, may be used but must not contribute to humidity. Leave plants in pots, ensure rocks are firmly bedded. Ventilate well. Supply small water dish. Lightly spray rocks in evening for lapping.

TEMPERATURE

Big-headed Gecko 26°C (79°F) at cool end, 33°C (92°F) at hot spot; 24°C (75°F) at night. Photoperiod: 12 hours.

Desert Geckos 30°C (86°F) at cool end, 33–35°C (92–95°F) at hot spot; minimum 20°C (68°F) at night. Photoperiod: 12–14 hours.

Leopard and Fat-tailed Geckos 25.5°C (78°F) at cool end, 30°C (86°F) at hot spot; 21°C (70°F) at night. Photoperiod: 14 hours.

Fan-footed Gecko 25°C (77°F) at cool end, 35°C (95°F) at hot spot; 20°C (68°F) at night. Photoperiod: 12–14 hours. Provide full-spectrum (UVB) light and a basking lamp.

WINTER COOLING

Big-headed Gecko Max 25°C (77°F) during day; 20°C (68°F) at night for 8–9 weeks. Photoperiod: 7–8 hours.

Desert Geckos 13–15°C (55–60°F) for 6–8 weeks. Normal daylight hours.

Leopard Gecko 24°C (75°F) during day; 18°C (64°F) at night for 8 weeks. Photoperiod: 8–9 hours.

Fan-footed Gecko 10°C (50°F) for 8 weeks with normal daylight hours or 6 hours of artificial light if necessary.

Fat-tailed Gecko Max 24°C (75°F) during day; 15–18°C (60–65°F) at night for 8 weeks. Photoperiod: 8 hours. Withhold daily spraying to dry out vivarium, but provide a small water dish.

FEEDING
A variety of vitamin-dusted insects and arthropods. Supply small pieces of cuttlefish bone for calcium supplements, which are especially important for females.

FAN-FOOTED GECKO

Ptyodactylus hasselquistii. Sometimes called the Fan-fingered Gecko, this small species is fairly easy to care for, and it has been a popular choice among amateur gecko keepers for many years. Its native habitat is hot, dry, rocky areas with a geographical range from northern Africa through the Middle East to southwestern Asia. Fan-foots are found in stone walls, dry river embankments and even near human settlements, at altitudes up to 6000ft (1800m).

The Fan-foot's body is slightly flattened, often with a fold of skin along each side. Its comparatively large head sits atop spindly limbs, giving a total length of 5.5in (14cm). The colouring of

▶ *Large fan-shaped digits give the Fan-footed Gecko* (Ptyodactylus hasselquistii) *its name. Many geckos have names based on descriptions of their digits.*

Fan-footed Geckos is variable, usually grey-brown with light and dark spots or marks and sometimes with a dark stripe from the nostrils through the eyes. The common name is derived from the enlarged, fan-like toes which bear adhesive lamellae like those of many other geckos.

Fan-foots are climbers and need vertical space. They will climb both walls and furnishings such as rocks, branches or cork bark. Although partly nocturnal, Fan-foots will often be seen basking in the day if full-spectrum light as available. They normally feed around dusk and are particularly fond of flying insects such as moths.

Breeding Conditions

BIG-HEADED GECKO

Clutch size	15–20 annual clutches of 2 eggs (from a single mating).
Incubation	55–60 days at around 28°C (82°F) in a small, clear, ventilated plastic box with 0.5in (1.2cm) of dry sand.

DESERT GECKOS

Clutch size	6 annual clutches of 2 eggs at monthly intervals.
Incubation	60 days at 30°C (86°F) during day; 25.5°C (78°F) at night, in a small plastic box (as for the Big-headed Gecko, above) placed at the cool end of the vivarium. An incubator can be used instead if desired.

LEOPARD GECKO

Clutch size	5–6 annual clutches of 2 eggs produced 6 weeks after mating.
Incubation	55–65 days at 26–33°C (79–91.5°F) in moist vermiculite.

FAN-FOOTED GECKO

Clutch size	4–5 annual clutches of 2 eggs produced at 2–4 week intervals.
Incubation	90–100 days at 20–25°C (68–77°F) on a dry medium. You may need to remove the laying surface with the eggs.

FAT-TAILED GECKO

Clutch size	5–6 annual clutches of 2 eggs produced at monthly intervals.
Incubation	60–70 days at 29–32°C (84–90°F) in a mixture of vermiculite and perlite with water (1:1 ratio; see Breeding, pages 38–39).

Fan-footed Geckos should be kept in pairs. Males are especially territorial, but both sexes of a breeding pair will attack any intruders into their territory. Males are identifiable by the swellings under the tail base. After mating, the females lay soft adhesive eggs which they manipulate to make them adhere together before they stick them to the laying surface. This may be a crevice or a cork bark cave, or any other secluded spot in the vivarium. It may be difficult to remove the eggs without removing the laying surface as well; this is perfectly all right, as the eggs may be incubated on the laying medium. You must ensure that the incubation medium itself is almost completely dry.

Once they are hatched, the young Fan-foots may be reared in the same conditions as adults and given food of the appropriate size. Although Fan-footed Geckos are often reported to be tolerant of the young, it is better to raise hatchlings in their own vivarium to prevent bullying or cannibalism by adults.

Other species requiring similar treatment are Bibron's Gecko (*Pachydactylus bibroni*) – its maximum daytime temperature should be 32°C (90°F); also, the Moorish Gecko (*Tarentola mauritanica*); the Turkish Gecko (*Hemidactylus turcicus*); and Kotschy's Gecko (*Cyrtodactylus kotschyi*). The eggs of the three latter species may be buried or laid in crevices.

FAT-TAILED GECKO

Hemitheconyx caudicinctus. This West African species is similar in appearance to the Leopard Gecko and is becoming increasingly popular with hobbyists. Its common name is derived from the tail, which should be noticeably plump and bulbous; a shrunken tail indicates lack of food. Fat-tails have moveable eyelids but lack adhesive lamellae. Their basic colouring consists of alternating broad, transverse bands of rich chocolate brown and light brown. One form has a light, longitudinal stripe, and it tends to be more sought after in the pet trade. Selective breeding, mainly in the US, has produced a colour known as "tangerine" because the lighter bands are suffused with peach and the darker bands have an orange hue. Most specimens in the trade are wild-caught from Ghana.

◆ *The Fat-tailed Gecko* (Hemitheconyx caudicinctus), *closely related to the Leopard Gecko, is a ground-dweller and a very poor climber.*

One special requirement of Fat-tailed Geckos is the need for both a damp and a dry environment – they need more moisture than Leopard Geckos. This can be achieved by using a physically divided vivarium if it is small (see Housing, pages 14–15) or by placing the two different substrates side by side. Overlay the damp area with sphagnum moss and spray daily to provide moisture, except in the cooling period. Set up shelters in two or more places. Fat-tailed Geckos are terrestrial and do not require climbing facilities, only hiding or burrowing sites. They occasionally bask in the daytime. Trios of Fat-tailed Geckos can be kept, but pairs seem to breed better.

Male Fat-tails are sexed by the broader head, slightly larger size and the two swellings under the tail. Eggs are visible through the pale skin on the belly of gravid females. Food intake by a gravid female reduces rapidly several days before oviposition. The eggs are laid under a cork bark shelter where there is a trace of dampness. The sex of hatchlings can be influenced by temperature: lower temperatures seem to produce mostly females, higher temperatures mostly males.

● *Do both eggs of the Leopard Gecko hatch at the same time?*

... The eggs usually hatch within 30–36 hours of each other. The young take between 2 and 4 hours to emerge.

● *At what age do Fan-footed Geckos mature?*

Unlike some gecko species, which mature early, Fan-foots take 18–24 months to become fully adult.

● *What does it mean if my Fan-foot croaks?*

If caught up or attacked they can make a croaking sound, which is also produced by males to proclaim their territory.

● *Why do Fat-tails move their tails when disturbed?*

This is a threat response and is seen in other gecko species. The tail vibrates more quickly when feeding, probably to distract would-be predators from the head.

● *How readily do Fat-tails become tame?*

Wild-caught specimens do not like being handled and will nip the keeper's fingers. Captive-bred babies usually become amenable as they grow.

● *Do baby Fat-tails differ from adults in appearance?*

Up to 6 months, the pattern and coloration are different; hatchlings have a yellow-green ground colour with U-shaped patches of grey and brown.

TOKAY GECKO

Gekko gecko. These attractively-coloured 12in (30cm) long geckos have been popular in the hobby for many years in spite of their reputation for biting the keeper, and they are widely available. Relatively few captive-bred specimens are offered for sale; most are imported from their native southern and southeastern Asia. Large and well-built, Tokay Geckos are blue-grey with small rust-coloured and white spots by day, turning a pale blue at night. The large yellow eyes have narrow, vertical black irises and lack eyelids, as on most geckos. Tokays' common name is derived from a distinctive sound ("to-kay") made by males to attract mates or threaten other males. This noise may also indicate protest at being handled. Females are also vocal but produce different sounds. The tail in both sexes breaks off readily if grabbed.

All Tokays are aggressive and need plenty of space. The most compatible pairing is one male to 2 or 3 females. Slabs of cork bark against the vivarium walls will provide climbing facilities

▲ *A large head is characteristic of several geckos including the Tokay Gecko (Gekko gecko). The ear opening can be seen behind and above the jaw.*

Breeding Conditions

TOKAY GECKO

Clutch size	3–4 annual clutches of 2 eggs
Incubation	120 days at 28–30°C (82–86°F) in moist vermiculite. 60% air humidity.

LEAF-TAILED GECKOS   Captive breeding of *Uroplatus* species is rare at present.

Clutch size	3 annual clutches of 2 eggs
Incubation	90–95 days at 25.5–26.5°C (78–80°F) in moist vermiculite.

FLYING GECKO

Clutch size	2–3 annual clutches of 2 eggs produced throughout the year.
Incubation	65–80 days at 26–28°C (79–82°F) Leave eggs on the laying surface and remove to a clear plastic box with a layer of foam and a few air holes. Maintain humidity of 65–70%.

and hiding places. Tokays spend much of their resting time squeezed behind bark, adhering to the wall. They will not drink from a bowl; the vivarium must be sprayed every evening.

Male can be distinguished from females by their larger size and a row of prominent pre-anal pores. Babies become tame with regular handling. The young should not be housed with adults – there is always the potential for cannibalism. Given the correct diet and conditions, the young are sexually mature at about one year. Males should be separated at 6 months, or even earlier if aggression occurs.

LEAF-TAILED GECKOS

Uroplatus species. Also known as the Flat-tailed geckos, these various Madagascar species were not available through pet stores until recently. The 12in (30cm)-long *U. fimbriatus* is the largest and best-known. Individual species have no generally accepted common names.

These lizards are regarded with superstition by many Malagasy. They are nocturnal, with large heads, and the eyes have narrow vertical pupils. Tree-dwelling leaf-tails such as *U. fimbriatus*, *U. henkeli*, *U. allaudi* and *U. sikorae* have fringe-like flaps of skin which provide effective camouflage against a background of tree bark. This is further enhanced by the coloration. *U. sikorae* has lichen-like markings on the dorsum. *U. ebenaui* and *U. phantasticus* tend to use the lower

● *Are Tokay Geckos difficult to handle?*

... They can give a substantial bite – not deep (they will barely break human skin), but they hang on fiercely. Minimum handling is advised. Wear gloves during maintenance.

● *How do I incubate Tokay Gecko eggs that are stuck to a large piece of cork bark?*

The bark may be carefully cut or sawn and the piece with eggs on placed in an incubation box.

● *Are bites from leaf-tails serious?*

The capacious mouth contains large numbers of very small teeth, so it looks ferocious when opened. A bite may startle the keeper but it is not serious. Take care not to drop the animal.

● *Do leaf-tails become tame?*

They can become used to the keeper to the point of accepting food from forceps, but they do not like handling. Like all arboreal creatures, leaf-tails feel more secure with their feet in contact with branches.

● *If eggs are left undiscovered in the vivarium, will adults attack the hatchlings?*

Generally they do not, but it is always a possibility and hatchlings should be removed. Adults often eat the empty eggs shells, which provide calcium.

➤ *A Leaf-tailed gecko (Uroplatus phantasticus) has inconspicuous colouring that can be adjusted for extra camouflage against the bark of trees.*

Vivarium Conditions
Tokay, Leaf-tailed and Flying Geckos

VIVARIUM SIZE

Leaf-tailed Geckos   Min 36x24x36in (90x60x 90cm) for a pair of the larger species (*U. fimbriatus*).

Others   Min 30x15x30in (75x38x75cm) for a pair

SUBSTRATE   Moisture-retentive. Leaf-tailed geckos require a moist mixture of loam, leaf mould, moss and leaf litter.

HABITAT   Vertical or angled slabs of cork bark and branches, easily removable to help find eggs. Plants help maintain humidity. Small water dish.

TEMPERATURE

Tokay Gecko   25.5°C (78°F) at cool end, 29–32°C (85–90°F) at hot spot; 21–22°C (70–72°F) at night. Photoperiod: 14 hours.

Leaf-tailed Geckos   *U. fimbriatus* 24°C (75°F) at cool end, 29°C (84°F) at hot spot; 22°C (72°F) at night. *U. henkeli* 20/30°C (68/86°F) day, 20°C (68°F) night. *U. lineatus* 24/29°C (75/84°F) day, 24°C (75°F) night. *U. ebenaui* and *U. phantasticus*

20/26.5°C (68/80°F) day, 20°C (68°F) night. *U. sikorae* 19/24°C (66/75°F) day, 20°C (68°F) night. Photoperiod: 12 hours. Low-percentage (UVB) light optional for occasional daytime basking.

Flying Gecko   28°C (82°F) at cool end, 32°C (90°F) at hot spot; 21–25°C (70–78°F) at night. Photoperiod: 12 hours.

HUMIDITY

Tokay Gecko   50–65%. Spray daily.

Leaf-tailed Geckos   85%. Spray once or more a day as required. Adequate ventilation of the vivarium is needed to prevent mould and rot.

Flying Gecko   65%. Spray in late evening.

WINTER COOLING   Only for leaf-tailed gecko species *U. henkeli*, *U. ebenaui* and *U. phantasticus*: 19–20°C (66–68°F) for 6 weeks. Reduce spraying.

FEEDING   Dusted insects and cuttlefish bone. Leaf-tailed geckos need vitamin supplements only once a week, with calcium 3 times week.

---

bushes at night and spend the day on the forest floor among dead leaves. They lack the fringes of the tree-dwellers, but their coloration is an excellent match with leaves and is capable of limited change. *U. alluaudi*, *U. guentheri* and *U. malahelo* are rare and are not usually available. Some species are known to react to threat by gaping, protruding the red tongue, squawking and raising the tail. The tail is autotomous at the base only – the whole tail is lost.

The arboreal species need large quarters to allow them to leap from branch to branch. Proportionately smaller housing is acceptable for smaller species. Although adhesive feet enable them to cling to the vivarium walls, they seem to prefer bark to glass.

Sexing leaf-tails is based on the swellings under the males' tail base. Preferable groupings are one male to one or two females. Leaf-tails are egg-layers and usually produce 2 eggs per clutch. Some of the species are said to produce 4 per clutch, but this has not been observed in captivity. Eggs may be deposited on or just under the leaf litter and should be removed for incubation. Because *Uroplatus* were not available until rela-

tively recently, little research has been done on breeding. Breeding of *U. fimbriatus* and *U. sikorae* is still rare at present. Photoperiod, temperature and Winter cooling need to be examined for these species. *U. ebenaui*, *U. phantasticus* and *U. henkeli* are showing promise as vivarium subjects. *U. ebenaui* and *U. phantasticus* have produced 3 clutches of 2 eggs in a single season and may be capable of producing more.

FLYING GECKO

Ptychozoon lionotum. These nocturnal geckos from southeast Asian rainforests make interesting vivarium subjects and are fairly easy to keep. The common name stems from their ability to glide (not fly) using flaps of skin on each side of the body, which fold underneath when not in use. Conspicuous webbed feet and a series of flaps along the tail also assist gliding and disguise the gecko's outline when it perches on branches. Even on the ground, Flying Geckos move fast.

▶ *A Flying Gecko* (Ptychozoon lionotum) *needs plenty of room to glide gracefully from branch to branch. Note the extended flaps on either side of the body.*

The feet are extremely adhesive and also possess claws that can be turned upwards when not being used for movement. Flying Geckos grow to 6.5in (16cm) long and are brown and grey with darker markings, making them almost invisible on bark surfaces. They "croak" and bite when picked up – the bite is startling but not dangerous. The tail is thrown readily.

Gliding can only properly occur in a very large vivarium. A pair or trio of Flying Geckos may be housed together. Plants may be used for decoration, but provide cork bark and branches for climbing. These should be easily removable: elaborate furnishings make it difficult to find eggs. *Ptychozoon* need a small water dish, and they normally feed at night unless very hungry.

Males have a row of prominent pre-anal pores and a skin flap either side of the cloaca. Breeding occurs year-round if conditions are right. Eggs are hard-shelled and adhesive and may be stuck to bark – leave them on the laying surface and remove, as for Fan-foots. The same site is often used repeatedly. Raise the young in a small vivarium with conditions similar to that of the adults.

Other species requiring the same treatment as the Flying Gecko: *P. kuhlii* – a slightly larger species with tubercules on the dorsum.

WONDER GECKO

Teratoscincus scincus. These attractive geckos, found from central and southwest Asia to the Arabian peninsula, usually grow to around 7in (18cm). Unlike other members of the genus, this species is noted for its delicate fish-like scales which scrape off easily if handled roughly. The tail also is easily lost. Both will regenerate with suitable diet and conditions. Other notable features of the Wonder Gecko are a large head with round eyes, which give it the alternative common name Frog-eyed Gecko; and comb-like scales on the eyelids and toes – an adaptation to life in sandy areas. A pale ground coloration with darker flecks and stripes produces a pleasing effect which appeals to many keepers. Captive breeding is fairly common, but most of the specimens for sale are still wild-caught imports.

The Wonder Gecko has special needs that make it an unsuitable choice for inexperienced keepers. Although it is a desert dweller and needs a dry atmosphere, it also needs to burrow down to moisture to protect the sensitive skin through which gas exchange (respiration) takes place. For this, both a damp and a dry substrate are required. Providing these can be difficult in a small vivarium. The vivarium may be divided to

● *Are Wonder Geckos aggressive?*

Yes. Males should not be housed together. Gravid females are best removed from the vivarium; they can be aggressive towards males, who tend not to retaliate. In this situation the females have been known to cause serious damage to males.

● *Is it true that Wonder Geckos bark?*

Males will "square up" to the keeper, waving the tail and producing a chirping noise with their scales. They can also "vocalize" and will bite the unwary. This is probably an example of male territorial behaviour. Females tend to be more amenable to the keeper.

● *How long do Wonder Geckos take to mature?*

In the wild, short summers and long hibernating periods (including the first year) mean that Wonder Geckos take 4 years to reach sexual maturity. In captivity, with shorter hibernation (not in the first year), they can mature in 12–18 months.

Vivarium Conditions
Wonder Gecko

Vivarium size Min 30x12x15in (75x30x38cm) for a pair or trio.

Substrate 6in (15cm) deep sand (dampish in half of vivarium), under moss or cork bark.

Habitat Half moderately damp, half dry. Cork bark for hiding places. Pipes or tubes buried in sand for burrowing. Supply a small water dish.

Temperature 32°C (90°F) at cool end, 40°C (104°F) at hot spot; 20°C (68°F) at night. Heat cables may be used in dry end of the vivarium. Photoperiod: 12 hours.

Winter cooling 8–10°C (46–50°F) for 8–10 weeks

Feeding Dusted insects; cuttlefish bone

Incubation Up to 4 annual clutches of 2 eggs buried or laid on the surface. Remove with a spoon – they are hard-shelled but fragile. Incubate on dry sand for 46–60 days at 31°C (88°F).

provide a moderately damp half and a dry half or a plastic box of slightly damp sand with easy access installed at one end. Heat cables may be used in the dry part of the vivarium to heat this end (see Heating and Lighting, pages 18–19). Extra light may not be necessary in a well-lit room unless it is also being used as a heat source. Wonder Geckos need full hibernating conditions rather than a simple Winter cooling; see the discussion of hibernation in the major section on Breeding (pages 36–37).

Male Wonder Geckos can be sexed by the hemipenile swelling under the tail. There are no femoral pores or other indicators of sex. Their courtship behaviour is similar to other geckos,

but the males tend to bite the females more gently so as not to damage the fragile skin. Eggs may be buried but are sometimes laid on the surface of the substrate. Raising the incubation temperature seems to result in the birth of more males, but this link has not yet been proved. Individual rearing of the young is preferable, at a lower maximum temperature than for adults.

Other species requiring similar treatment are *T. keyserlingii* and *T. microlepis*.

◄ *The Wonder Gecko* (Teratoscincus scincus) *has an interesting contrast of scales: large on the snout, fine on the rest of the head, and large and platelike on the body. The skin is delicate and must be handled gently.*

Day Geckos

FAMILY: GEKKONIDAE
GENUS: PHELSUMA

DAY GECKOS ARE FOUND ON MADAGASCAR and other islands in the Indian Ocean, in habitats ranging from moist forests to plantations. There are more than 50 species and subspecies, but some of these are exceedingly rare. Since 1996, only 4 species may be exported legally from Madagascar: the Giant Day Gecko (subspecies *Phelsuma madagascariensis grandis* and *P. m. kochi);* the Gold-dust Day Gecko (*P. laticauda);* the Peacock Day Gecko (*P. quadriocellata);* and the Lined Day Gecko (*P. lineata).* In addition, European import bans have applied to some geckos since the 1980s. Affected species, such as Standing's Day Gecko (*P. standingi),* are in captive-breeding programmes.

Unlike the nocturnal geckos, day geckos are brightly coloured. Within a few species, males and females may have very different coloration. Mature males have well-developed femoral pores and two hemipenile swellings under the tail base. Females have a swelling on each side of the neck. These are endolymphatic glands for storing calcium, and their absence indicates that additional

▶ *The Giant Day Gecko* (Phelsuma madagascariensis grandis) *is brilliant green with scarlet markings. This specimen has regrown part of its tail after shedding it.*

Q&A

● *Are outside enclosures suitable for day geckos?*

... Yes, if conditions are correct. The enclosure must be totally escape-proof. Extremes of heat and cold must be avoided, and the enclosure needs adequate shade and humidity. Ants may be attracted to food containing fruit or honey.

● *Can young geckos be reared communally?*

Squabbling and injury can occur. Progress is easier to monitor with singly-reared young.

● *How do I remove babies from the hatching box?*

Babies are extremely fast-moving. Place the hatching box in a small aquarium, and cover the aquarium with

a sweater tied at the neck with string. Insert your arms down the sleeves of the sweater, remove the lid of the hatching box, enclose one baby in the palm of your hand, and pull your arm back through the sleeve.

● *My day gecko is having trouble sloughing. What might be wrong?*

Too little humidity in the vivarium causes dry skin and inhibits sloughing. Use a spray, or place the gecko in a damp cloth bag or in a box filled with damp moss.

● *My young gecko's tail flops over. Is this normal?*

A floppy tail is due to weakening of the tail base caused by inadequate diet, mainly calcium and vitamin deficiency. Follow instructions for supplements.

Vivarium Conditions

Vivarium size   30x18x30in (75x45x75cm) for larger species; 24in (60cm) length for smaller types.

Substrate   Chopped up pieces of moss, sterile soil, sand or orchid bark compost.

Habitat   Cork bark, bamboo poles or branches, (vertical and horizontal). Broad-leaved plants (*Sansevieria, Scindapsus aureus, Monstera deliciosa*) for climbing, hiding and to maintain humidity.

Temperature 26–28°C (78–82°F) at cool end, 30°C (86°F) at hot spot; 20–23°C (68–73°F) at night. Photoperiod: 14 hours. Provide full-spectrum (UVB) light and basking lamp. Hot rocks are unsuitable.

Humidity   50–85% according to species. *P. m. grandis* has thrived at the lower figure. Spray daily.

Winter cooling   Max 25°C (77°F) during day, 15°C (60°F) at night for 8 weeks. Photoperiod: 10 hours.

Feeding   Dusted insects, Lory nectar foods, sweet fruits and fruit-based baby foods (especially peach and mango); small pieces of cuttlefish bone, important for young and for breeding females. Geckos will lick a hardened mixture of clear honey, soft brown sugar, calcium powder and a pinch of vitamins. Provide a small water dish.

Incubation   2–3 annual clutches of 1–2 eggs. Incubate for 54–70 days at 28°C (82°F), 22°C (72°F) at night, and 75% air humidity; or 45–55 days at a constant 26–28°C (78–82°F). The first egg may hatch up to 7 days before the second one.

calcium is needed to bring the female into breeding condition. All *Phelsuma* species have "adhesive" feet and can walk on vertical surfaces.

Phelsumas tend to be aggressive, and crowding enhances this. Even females can be aggressive to each other and sometimes attack males. It is best to keep pairs or trios, but incompatible partners must be separated. Under the right conditions, many *Phelsumas* become tame enough to take food from forceps or fingers, though small specimens seldom accept handling. Day geckos are swift-moving and will dash for freedom.

Breeding in Captivity

Day geckos usually mate in Spring, after the Winter cooling period is finished and normal vivarium conditions have been restored. Several clutches of eggs are laid in secluded spots inside the vivarium. They should be removed to a separate incubation container. If any of the eggs are adhering to each other, they must not be prised apart – remove them together, very carefully. Make tiny holes for ventilation in the lid of

the container, and line the bottom with small vermiculite moistened in warm water and then squeezed out (see Breeding, pages 38–39). Eggs should be raised off the substrate for incubation. Some species will stick their eggs on the vivarium walls or vegetation. If they cannot be removed easily, these eggs must be incubated in place by taping a small, clear, ventilated plastic container over them. Put a ball of paper towels inside the container and keep slightly moist by dripping water through the holes in the top. Temperature may affect the sex of hatchlings, but this is not yet completely understood. Provide hatchlings with vivarium conditions as for adults and offer them smaller items of the same kinds of food.

▶ *The Peacock Day Gecko* (Phelsuma quadriocellata) *gets its common name from the characteristic turquoise and black "thumbprints" on each side of its body, just behind the front legs.*

Green Iguana

FAMILY: IGUANIDAE
SPECIES: IGUANA IGUANA

MORE THAN A MILLION OF THESE IGUANAS from Mexico to central South America were imported into the US in 1994–95, and 23,500 into the UK. This popularity is despite several drawbacks. The first is size: iguanas in the wild can exceed 79in (2m) – half of which is tail – and commonly grow to 72in (180cm) in captivity. Housing poses a problem long before then, and many iguanas are donated to zoos, sold on or abandoned. Another factor is temperament. Anyone determined to keep iguanas should buy babies, which ought to become tame with proper care. Baby iguanas are both attractive and relatively cheap. Older specimens are expensive and often intractable. Iguanas have sharp claws and powerful tails that can lash. Keepers are bound to be scratched sometimes; treat all lacerations. A third drawback is that in the US iguanas have been linked to outbreaks of salmonella, often where they have been allowed to roam the house. Hygiene must be strictly observed, especially if children are present in the house.

Green Iguanas are solitary animals and should not be housed together; males may even attack a female cagemate. Growth is rapid: a baby iguana that begins in a 30x15x18in (73x38x45cm) vivarium will outgrow it in a matter of weeks.

Nutrition is crucial; see Food and Feeding, pages 29–30, for a discussion of herbivorous diets. The diet should be calcium-rich and high in fibre, and as varied as possible. Chop the food small and mix thoroughly to prevent picking and choosing. Commercial foods are widely available. Do not give the iguanas pizza, burgers, ice cream, etc. Juveniles (up to 2 years) need a diet of 15% vegetable protein and 85% plant material, of which 70% should be vegetables. Metabolic bone disease (MBD; see Health and Disease, page 45) is responsible for most health problems in Green Iguanas. They will thrive outdoors with exposure to natural sunlight, which helps metabolize calcium and may provide some psychological benefits, though this is difficult to prove.

Large Crested Males

Mature males are larger than females, especially their head, crest, jowls, subtympanic scale and thicker tail base. Their femoral pores are larger and more numerous, sometimes with a hardened waxy secretion protruding like a comb. Males may develop a slightly orange colouring, whereas mature females are usually blue-grey. Relatively few keepers attempt to breed Green Iguanas, but it is possible, given adequate space. They are able to breed from 2 years of age before reaching full size. Breeding can be encouraged by reducing the photoperiod from 14 to 10 hours; maintaining the normal day temperature and reducing the night temperature to 20°C (68°F); and halving the quantity (not variety) of food. Maintain for weeks and gradually restore normal conditions

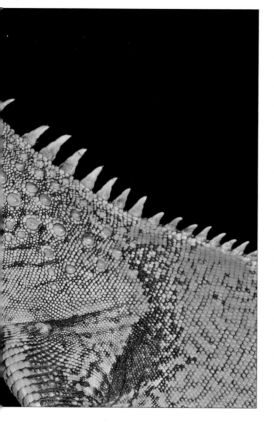

➤ *Green Iguanas* (Iguana iguana) *are spectacularly endowed with crest, scales and jowls. The large circular scale below the ear is the subtympanic scale. Juveniles such as this one are difficult to sex accurately.*

● *Are Green Iguanas really dangerous to keep?*

... The more careless the keeper, the more dangerous the iguana. Many become "silly tame", but they can be unpredictable. Attacks on owners, especially women, are not unheard-of. Do NOT leave Green Iguanas alone with children and domestic pets. For handling large specimens, two people should always be present. If someone is attacked, throw a jacket, blanket or rug over the iguana to subdue it.

● *Is it necessary to take faecal specimens for analysis when buying captive-farmed Green Iguanas?*

Yes. Captive farming is no guarantee that an animal will not be carrying harmful organisms. Analysis should detect these.

● *Should multivitamin and calcium supplements be provided for Green Iguanas living outdoors?*

Yes, but sparingly. Iguanas receiving natural sunlight should not be given additional vitamin D3, but will need calcium 3 times per week.

● *How often should Green Iguanas be fed?*

Babies every day, adults every other day. Stale, uneaten food should be removed. Put the food dish on a flat stone to avoid the substrate being ingested.

● *Are Green Iguanas partially insectivorous?*

Not in the wild, but some captive juveniles will take insects. No more than 3–5 mealworms or crickets per day should be given to young Green Iguanas.

Vivarium Conditions

Vivarium size   A room or part of a room for an adult pair, or outdoor enclosure in suitable climate.

Substrate   Loam or moss for humidity, or newspaper or carpet-type material for ease of removal and cleaning.

Habitat   Firmly fixed branches for climbing and basking; hiding places for young. Plastic plants – Green Iguanas will eat or damage live ones. Make sure that clean water is always available.

Temperature   29.5–32°C (85–90°F) at cool end, 38°C (100°F) at hot spot; 25°C (77°F) at night. Photoperiod: 14 hours. Provide full-spectrum (UVB) light and a basking lamp.

Humidity   60–75%

Winter cooling   Normal daytime temperatures, with a reduction at night to 20°C (68°F) for 6 weeks. Photoperiod: 10 hours.

Feeding Herbivorous. 5% protein, 80% vegetables, 15% fruit and flowers. Sprouted pulses, alfalfa, fresh peas and beans; Romaine, bak-choi (Chinese cabbage), kale, endive, clover, turnip leaves, parsley, collard greens, watercress, mustard cress, zucchini (courgettes), squash, snow peas (mangetout), broccoli, sweet peppers, grated carrot; grape and hibiscus leaves, nasturtium and dandelion; edible flowers; apples, soaked raisins, soft pears, oranges, kiwi and raspberries. No bananas or animal protein.

Incubation   1–2 annual clutches of 10–60 eggs. Incubate for 80–100 days at 30–32°C (86–90°F).

Arboreal Iguanids

IGUANIDS (FAMILY IGUANIDAE) ARE FOUND only in the New World and on the islands of Madagascar, Tonga and Fiji. Many iguanid species have adapted to an arboreal existence. The species below all possess cryptic coloration, which is useful in their way of life. The small Green Anole can change colour in seconds. The two larger species – the Helmeted Iguana and the Plumed Basilisk – have a semi-prehistoric look mainly created by the crest, head adornments and gular (throat) flaps.

HELMETED IGUANA

Corytophanes cristatus. These medium-size tree-dwelling rainforest iguanids, growing to a maximum length of 14in (35cm), are found across Central America and northern South America. Their common name is derived from the crest on the nape in both sexes. This and the gular pouch are extended to make the head appear larger in threat displays by males. Both the crest and gular pouch have a serrated edge of pointed triangular scales. The body is laterally compressed to facilitate movement through the trees, which is also assisted by long, slender limbs. Colouring is variable, mainly brown with darker bands or spots, but sometimes reddish-brown. It varies sometimes depending on ambient temperature and the level of light. Although Helmeted Iguanas are fairly common in the trade, few keepers seem to make serious attempts to breed them.

Male Helmeted Iguanas may be distinguished by their larger crests. They are quarrelsome and should be kept apart. A pair or trio with only one male is a suitable grouping. Because of fairly constant conditions, breeding in the wild can occur any time during the year. Gravid females must be watched for digging or decreased girth. Eggs should be removed for incubation in 1:1 moist vermiculite (see Breeding, pages 38–39, and the chart opposite). The temperature can vary slightly, about 1°C (2°F). Hatchlings can be reared communally under similar conditions to the

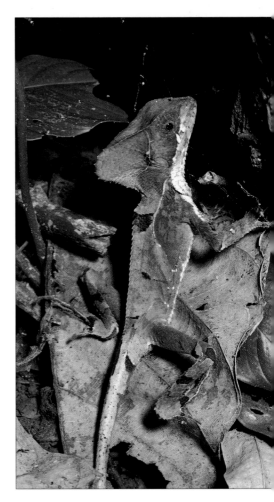

▲ *A Helmeted Iguana* (Corytophanes cristatus) *camouflaged against leaves, where it waits for its insect prey. Colouring can change with light and temperature.*

adults, but as maturity approaches they should be housed apart. Other species that require similar treatment are Bloodsuckers (*Calotes cristellatus*) and casque-headed iguanas (*Laemanctus* species), which need a higher temperature – up to 35°C (95°F) at the hot spot; also, the lowland species of pricklenapes (*Acanthosaura*) and hump-headed dragons (*Gonocephalus*).

GREEN ANOLE

Anolis carolinensis. Also known as the Common Anole, this iguanid is relatively easy to keep and is a good choice for beginners. Primarily green, with a pale belly, these 8in (20cm) lizards are capable of rapid but limited colour changes based on mood or temperature. Green Anoles are native to the US, and another widely-used common name for them is the American Chameleon. However, they are not true chameleons, which are not found on either of the American continents. They are exported in large numbers and are very familiar in pet stores.

Green Anoles are mostly arboreal but they frequently dwell near human habitation. Their adhesive toes enable them to walk on vertical glass surfaces. The males are slightly larger than the females, with a larger head, a pink throat flap or dewlap that extends when displaying, and 2 enlarged post-anal scales. Males are extremely territorial and should not be housed together

▲ *A Green Anole* (Anolis carolinensis) *is an agile, darting creature and can fall from great heights without injuring itself. A spacious vivarium with a number of branches will ensure plenty of exercise for this species.*

Vivarium Conditions
Helmeted Iguana, Green Anole and Plumed Basilisk

VIVARIUM SIZE   All sizes are a minimum requirement for a pair or trio. Due to humidity, the vivarium should be rot-proof.

Helmeted Iguana	36x18x30in (90x45x75cm)
Green Anole	24x15x30in (60x38x75cm)
Plumed Basilisk	60x48x48in (150x120x120cm)

SUBSTRATE Moisture-retentive (potting soil, leaf litter), covered with moss, which can be changed when soiled.

HABITAT Branches for climbing and basking. Living plants will help to maintain humidity levels. A daily spray is essential. For basilisks, plants should be robust or out of the way. Basilisks also require a pool, which can be heated with an aquarium heater or a heater mat placed underneath.

TEMPERATURE Full-spectrum (UVB) light and basking lamp are needed.

Green Anole 22°C (72°F) at cool end, 28°C (82°F) at hot spot; 18–20°C (64–68°F) at night. Photoperiod: 12–14 hours.

Others 25°C (77°F) at cool end, 30°C (86°F) at hot spot; 22–23°C (72–74°F) at night. Photoperiod: 12–14 hours.

HUMIDITY Adequate ventilation of vivarium is needed to avoid stagnant conditions.

Green Anole	65–70%
Others	85–90%

WINTER COOLING

Green Anole 15–18°C (59–65°F) for 8 weeks. Normal daylight is sufficient unless there are live plants; then additional light will be needed, but it must not raise the temperature.

Others	No Winter cooling

FEEDING A wide variety of dusted insects. Some basilisks will take sweet fruit. Give cuttlefish bone to females for calcium supplements.

INCUBATION All three species are egg-layers. Females will bury their eggs in substrate and cover them, so detection can be difficult. Incubate in moist vermiculite.

Helmeted Iguana 2–3 annual clutches of 1–10 eggs. Incubate for 85 days at 30°C (86°F).

Green Anole Up to 6 annual clutches of 2 eggs. Incubate for 40 days at 26.5°C (80°F).

Plumed Basilisk Up to 3 annual clutches of 10–12 eggs. Incubate for 70–74 days at 26.5°C (80°F).

unless they can be put in an exceptionally large enclosure. A large vivarium also provides more scope for furnishing and room for exercise.

The Green Anole breeding season extends over 4 or 5 months, with a short gestation period – only around 3 weeks. Rearing the young individually is recommended, but if reared communally, you should separate them at 7–8 weeks of age. Young Green Anoles need humid conditions and a fairly constant temperature of around 25°C (77°F). Other species requiring similar conditions are the Brown Anole (*A. sagrei*), and the Knight Anole (*A. equestris*), which needs a larger, taller vivarium with 27°C (81°F) at the cool end and 30°C (86°F) at the hot spot, dropping to 20°C (68°F) at night. The Knight Anole needs extra drinking water.

PLUMED BASILISK

Basiliscus plumifrons. Spectacular crests on the heads and backs of the males make this Central American species very popular as vivarium subjects. Large and active, Plumed Basilisks live in close proximity to water and will swim readily. Males can grow to over 24in (60cm) in length, females slightly less. Most imports are wild-caught adults, which do not tame readily. Young captive-bred specimens, which are occasionally available in the trade, tend to be more amenable. They have long whippy tails, long claws and strong hindlimbs suited to arboreal activity. The basic colouring of both sexes is green, sometimes with a blue tinge and light spots along the sides.

Plumed Basilisks require a pool for swimming (they are excellent swimmers), drinking and maintaining humidity. The water should be kept at 25°C (77–78°F). The vivarium heater may be sufficient to keep the pool at the required temperature, but if an aquarium heater is used, it will need to be protected (see Heating and Lighting, pages 18–19). Plants will contribute to humidity, but live ones are subject to damage; use plastic ones to provide decor. A water dish is unnecessary. Because basilisks often defecate in the pool, the water must be changed frequently.

The males' crests make sexing simple. Mating is usually prefaced by vigorous nodding by the male, who then seizes the female's neck, often tearing the skin. The wound heals quickly but

antibiotic ointment may be needed. Several matings may occur, and gestation takes approximately 30–32 days. Breeding can be at any time of the year. Plumed Basilisks are egg-layers and will bury the eggs in a corner of the vivarium. The eggs should be removed and placed in moist vermiculite (1:1 vermiculite to water; see Breeding, pages 38–39) in a clear plastic box which has a few small ventilation holes drilled. Babies may be raised in a 24x12x18in (60x30x45cm) vivarium with a slightly moist substrate, under full-spectrum (UVB) lighting and a basking lamp. A few thin branches, cork bark shelters and a

▲ *A magnificent male Plumed Basilisk* (Basiliscus plumifrons) *in its native Costa Rican rainforest habitat. Captive-bred specimens tend to be paler than wild-caught ones, and the males may have reduced plumes.*

water bowl complete the nursery. A maximum temperature of 26.5°C (80°F) should be maintained, dropping to 22°C (72°F) overnight.

Other species requiring similar treatment to the Plumed Basilisk are the Banded Basilisk (*B. vittatus*) and the Brown Basilisk (*B. basiliscus*), which requires the slightly higher temperature of 30°C (86°F) to incubate the eggs.

● *My Helmeted Iguana has difficulty sloughing. Why could this be?*

... The most likely cause of this is insufficient humidity in the vivarium. (This is true for most lizards that slough.) Increased spraying of the vivarium should help. Check the animal's feet to ensure that skin does not remain on the toes, as unshed skin can lead to loss of digits.

● *Do Helmeted Iguanas need a bathing pool?*

No. Unlike basilisks, they are not bathers or swimmers.

● *Do Green Anoles feed during their cool period?*

Food can be offered but may be refused. Uneaten insects should not be left in the vivarium. Water must be provided for the cool period. A light spray will be needed daily, as they will not drink from a bowl.

● *Is it possible to keep Green Anoles and Brown Anoles together?*

Because of their dissimilar colouring but similar size, they may coexist in a large vivarium with more than one basking spot, but aggression may still occur. Ideally, a single species should be kept by itself.

● *How long do Plumed Basilisks take to hatch?*

It can take hours or more. The hatchling basilisks should not be disturbed – they will dash out of the egg with yolk attached. Leave them until the yolk has been absorbed and they are moving freely around the hatching box.

● *Do baby Plumed Basilisks resemble adults?*

Juveniles up to 3 months have a brownish dorsal surface with darker crossbands especially on the tail. The crests are not evident.

● *How large should a pool be for Plumed Basilisks?*

At least as long as the lizard and 5in (12.5cm) deep, but the larger the better. Vivarium specimens may not use a pool of these minimum dimensions.

● *Can Plumed Basilisks run on water?*

The toes have enlarged flaps along each side which help them to run on water in an upright position. This bipedal gait is not seen in the vivarium – it is only achievable over substantial distances, when they are fleeing from danger in an open space.

● *My Plumed Basilisk keeps scraping its snout against the vivarium glass. Can this be stopped?*

A deep baffleboard along the bottom at the front will prevent this. Scraped snouts can become infected.

Desert Iguanids FAMILY: IGUANIDAE (PART)

ARID AND SEMI-ARID IGUANID SPECIES ARE found from Canada to South America. Although diverse in size and feeding habits, they have similar habitats. The key to keeping them successfully is to provide hot, dry conditions with high-percentage, full-spectrum (UVB) fluorescent light.

COLLARED LIZARDS

Crotaphytus collaris. These especially attractive, colourful lizards are native to the southern-central to southwestern US and to the Mexican state of Sonora. Most in the trade are wild-caught. Males grow to 13–14in (33–36cm) long. Colour and pattern vary slightly. Most have a green dorsum with a series of darker crossbands covered with light spots. The throat is yellow-orange and the collar has 2 black markings. Females have a grey-brown dorsum with a paler vent, dark crossbands and large white spots.

Collared males have a row of post-anal scales and prominent femoral pores; in females these pores are faint and the scales are absent. Mating takes place about 2 weeks after the cool period. Gravid females develop orange markings along the sides of the body and on the neck. If a site is not available, they may deposit their eggs near the waterbowl. Young Collared Lizards should be maintained in a vivarium similar to that of the adults. Other species requiring similar treatment are the Eastern Collared Lizard (*C. collaris collaris*, also known as "Mountain Boomers"), the Black Collared Lizard (*C. bicinctores*) and the Leopard Lizard (*Gambelia wislizenii*).

▶ *A male Collared Lizard* (Crotaphytus collaris) *from the southwestern US. Collared Lizards are more colourful than their close relation, the subspecies Eastern Collared Lizard* (C. collaris collaris).

● Why do baby Collared Lizards have markings similar to females?

... The markings probably evolved to prevent aggression by adult males.

● My Collared Lizard seems hungry all the time. Is this normal?

Collared Lizards are very active, and they consume a lot of food. Feed daily, as many insects as it will eat. If any are left, supply less the following day. If the lizard is eating well but losing weight, faecal analysis for parasite infection is advisable.

● What size insect is appropriate for feeding young Collared Lizards?

Even the young have large heads and wide-gaping jaws which can take surprisingly large prey for their size. Trial and error is the only way to find out.

● If Collared Lizards' eggs are laid in a dry spot, is it worth trying to incubate them?

Desiccated eggs start to collapse quite quickly, but it is worth putting them in moist vermiculite to see if they rehydrate. However, success is not guaranteed.

Vivarium Conditions
Collared Lizards and Blue Spiny Lizards

Vivarium size Min 36x24x24in (90x60x60cm) for a pair or trio.

Substrate Dry, dust-free sand, 3–4in (8–10cm) deep; Collared Lizards will dig and burrow.

Habitat Rocks cemented together to form caves and terraces for climbing. Stumps, driftwood and vineroot. Use drought-loving plants, left in pots, or artificial/dried plants. Ventilate well. Light spray on rocks in morning. Provide a small water dish.

Temperature 29°C (84°F) at cool end, 38°C (100°F) at hot spot; 19–20°C (66–68°F) at night. Photoperiod: 14 hours. Provide a high-percentage full-spectrum (UVB) light and basking lamp.

Winter cooling 10–12°C (50–54°F) for 8 weeks. Photoperiod: normal daylight or 6 hours of artificial light. NOTE: Ensure female Blue Spiny Lizards are not gravid. Litters have been produced as late as December by captive females.

Feeding Dusted insects; pieces of cuttlefish bone.

BLUE SPINY LIZARD

Sceloporus cyanogenys. This lizard is the largest of its genus of approximately 100 iguanid species that are distributed from southwestern Canada into Panama, and reaches a full length of 14in (36cm). Its native habitat is dry, rocky ground from southern Texas into Mexico. Blue Spiny Lizards are strongly built, with keeled and spiny scales that give a rough, prickly appearance. The body is cylindrical with a slight dorso-ventral flattening. Once warmed up, these lizards are extremely agile and fast-moving. Certain species within the genus were formerly called "swifts", while others are known as "fence lizards".

Male Blue Spiny Lizards are easily sexed by their colouring, their prominent femoral pores and a thickened tailbase. They have an almost metallic-blue body and tail on a brown background, with a distinctive dark collar bordered each side with white. The throat is blue, and a long blue patch with a black inner border occurs on each side of the belly. Females are plainer, mostly grey to brown. Males are highly territorial and should not be kept together. When threatened by a rival male, they extend the blue gular pouch and display their blue belly patch. The courtship ritual of Blue Spiny Lizards includes head-bobbing and butting by the male.

◆ *A male Blue Spiny Lizard* (Sceloporus cyanogenys). *This distinctive species makes a good vivarium subject. Wild-caught specimens will bite hard and twist their spiny scales against the handler's fingers to gain release.*

Breeding Conditions

COLLARED LIZARDS	Egg-layer
Clutch size	1–2 clutches per season of 6–8 eggs.
Incubation	56–62 days at 30°C (86°F) in moist vermiculite.
BLUE SPINY LIZARD	Livebearer
Gestation	3–4 months
Litter size	6–18 young
CHUCKWALLA	Egg-layer
Clutch size	2 annual clutches of 8–12 eggs
Gestation	66–75 days at 29.5–31°C (85–88°F) in moist vermiculite.
DESERT HORNED LIZARD	Egg-layer
Clutch size	1 annual clutch of 6–28 eggs
Incubation	60–65 days at 31°C (88°F) in moist vermiculite.
DESERT IGUANA	Egg-layer
Clutch size	1–2 annual clutches of 3–8 eggs
Incubation	67–75 days at 29.5°C (85°F) in moist vermiculite.

● *Should young spiny lizards be cooled over their first winter?*

... This is not necessary. It is better to keep them active and feeding.

● *How large are Blue Spiny neonates?*

The size varies from 6.4–7cm (2.5–2.75in). In a large clutch the young are likely to be smaller than average.

● *Are hot rocks useful for heating Chuckwallas?*

Like most diurnal lizards, Chuckwallas prefer heat radiated from above, as from a basking lamp. Hot rocks are not suitable except to maintain nighttime temperatures.

● *Do baby Chuckwallas need water before they start to feed?*

They may lap moisture from fruit. Try dripping just a few drops of sweet fruit juice or water onto the lips.

● *Are low temperatures detrimental to Chuckwallas?*

Except for the cool period prior to breeding, Chuckwallas need to be maintained at high temperatures. Low temperatures hamper food metabolism and other physiological functions.

Some *Sceloporus* species are egg-layers, but this species is a livebearer. Prior to parturition, the young may be seen moving in the mother's belly. They emerge in membranes from which they break free, and immediately become active. Young Blue Spiny Lizards should be raised in a dry vivarium with full-spectrum (UVB) light at a maximum temperature of 31°C (88°F). From the time they are about 3 months old, the young will need to be separated, especially the males, to prevent inter-male aggression and premature mating. However, under normal circumstances, mating in Blue Spiny Lizards usually does not occur before they are 12 months old.

Similar treatment is needed for the other spiny lizard species: the Desert Spiny Lizard (*S. magister*), the Crevice Spiny Lizard (*S. poinsetti*), and Yarrows Spiny Lizard (*S. jarrovi*), which are all egg-layers; and the Mesquite Spiny Lizard (*S. grammicus*), the Emerald or Malachite Swift Lizard (*S. malachiticus*), the Sagebrush Lizard (*S. graciosus*), the Western Fence Lizard (*S. occidentalis*), and the Eastern Fence Lizard (*S. undulatus*), which are all livebearers.

▲ *Two Chuckwallas* (Sauromalus obesus) *basking on the rocks. Chuckwallas are a sun-loving species and require high temperatures, up to 43°C (110°F).*

CHUCKWALLA
Sauromalus obesus. As the name suggests, these are plump-bodied lizards. Adult males grow to about 17in (43cm) in length. The body is dorsoventrally flattened with wrinkled skin along the sides, and the colouring is brown, usually with a lighter yellow tail. Occasionally the posterior half of the body has red spots. Chuckwallas' natural habitat is in arid, rocky areas extending from the southwestern United States into Mexico. They need a perfectly dry atmosphere, which means a well-ventilated vivarium and no spraying or live plants. Although diurnal, in Summer they tend to spend the hotter part of the day in hiding, and feed mainly in the evening. They can move quickly if attacked, dashing into crevices and flattening their bodies to prevent anything removing them. Hiding places must be well constructed to prevent them being dislodged. Under suitable conditions, Chuckwallas can live for up

Vivarium Conditions
Chuckwalla, Desert Horned Lizard and Desert Iguana

VIVARIUM SIZE

Chuckwalla Min 48x18x18in (122x45x45cm) for a pair of adults.

Others Min 30x15x15in (75x38x38cm) for a pair or trio.

SUBSTRATE Dry dust-free sand: 4in (10cm) deep for Desert Horned Lizard; 2in (5cm) deep for others.

HABITAT Very arid. 75% of all sides or all of top made of ventilation panels. Cork bark or half-round earthenware pipes for hides (Chuckwallas). Rocks and stumps for climbing and basking.

TEMPERATURE 30°C (86°F) at cool end, 43°C (110°F) at hot spot; 21–24°C (70–75°F) at night. Photoperiod: 14 hours. Provide a basking lamp and high-percentage full-spectrum (UVB) light.

WINTER COOLING

Desert Horned Lizard 12–14°C (55–58°F) for 8 weeks. Photoperiod: normal daylight or 6 hours of artificial light.

Others 25°C (77°F) for 8 weeks. Photoperiod: 6–8 hours.

FEEDING Place food in shallow bowl, preferably on a flat stone, to prevent the substrate adhering to it.

Chuckwalla Varied herbivorous diet with vitamin and calcium supplements (see Foods and Feeding, pages 29–30). Dandelions and other edible blooms are particular favourites.

Desert Horned Lizard Dusted insects; occasional waxmoth larvae and adults, small locusts.

Desert Iguana As for Chuckwalla; dusted insects.

to 25 years. American hobbyists should always check the local and state laws before attempting to take this species from the wild.

Mature males have prominent femoral pores, a larger build, shorter, thicker tail and a broader head, often with heavy jowls. They are highly territorial: they should not be kept together in the confined space of a vivarium. Mating occurs around April; some females may produce eggs only every other year. Gestation lasts about 50 days. Supply a box of damp substrate for oviposition, as near to deposition time as possible to prevent humidity. Hatchlings may not eat at first, subsisting on absorbed yolk, but offer food anyway; they should eat sooner or later. Young can be raised communally. Any that are not thriving should be removed and reared separately.

DESERT HORNED LIZARD

Phrynosoma platyrhinos. Also called Horned Toad Lizards, this is one of the most widespread North American species, ranging from southeast Oregon into eastern California, western Arizona and Mexico. Its native habitat is arid, sandy or rocky scrubland. In spite of their squat, spiny appearance, Desert Horned Lizards have quite a placid temperament. They never grow very large – males may only reach 5in (13cm) in length. The colouring consists of wavy dark blotches on a

▲ *Desert Horned Lizards* (Phrynosoma platyrhinos) *have an unusual appearance due to their horns. They are very small but require specialist care.*

grey background. Slight changes of colour can occur, depending on temperature and the colour of the substrate. Members of this genus have been common in the pet trade for years, but they tend not to survive in captivity. This is mainly due to their specialized diet of ants (although other insects are taken). The collection, sale and keeping of certain *Phrynosoma* species is now banned in some parts of the US – check local regulations before buying. *P. platyrhinos*, however, is frequently imported into Europe. Even where they are legal, Desert Horned Lizards are not a good choice for inexperienced keepers.

Males have a thicker tailbase with 2 swellings apparent underneath. Breeding reports for this species are rare, and the young are difficult to raise, possibly requiring slightly more moist conditions than adults. Desert Horned Lizards are egg-layers, though some *Phrynosoma* species are livebearers. Mating occurs in April or May, egg-laying in June or July. Failure to hatch may be due to insufficient Winter cooling or an incorrect ratio of vermiculite to water during incubation.

DESERT IGUANA

Dipsosaurus dorsalis. Large numbers of these iguanas are available in the pet trade, but they have a reputation for being difficult to keep. Most Desert Iguanas are wild-caught and many specimens will have been kept in poor conditions between the time of their capture and sale (see Starting Out, pages 6–8). They often appear lethargic and emaciated, with sunken bellies, as a result of insufficient temperatures and unsuitable foods. Desert Iguanas are comparatively small, with a total length varying from 10–15in (25–38cm). Their background colour is a light grey–brown with darker, broken crossbands of spots, giving a reticulated effect. This colouring tends to lighten with rising body temperature when the animals bask. A faint dorsal crest of keeled scales runs along the spine. Desert Iguanas are native to the southwestern US and Mexico, where their habitat is arid creosote bush

◆ *Desert Iguanas* (Dipsosaurus dorsalis) *are subtly coloured but physically impressive, with a long, thick tail. It is more fragile than it looks, and is easily shed.*

desert, subtropical scrub and primarily sandy areas. Recent research suggests that Desert Iguanas can see ultraviolet light. This ability may help in detecting suitable food plants, especially flowers, and in seeing femoral pore secretions on rocks (useful in mating). This may have implications for other lizard species.

Captive breeding of Desert Iguanas is rare. Males have swellings under the tail base. In the breeding season – April to May in the wild – both sexes develop a pink suffusion along the belly. Prepare a deposition site as for Chuckwallas. Raise the young communally at 27°C (81°F) at the cool end and 40°C (104°F) at the hot spot.

● *Can Desert Horned Lizards be kept with other species?*

... Yes. They are compatible with Lesser Earless Lizards (*Holbrookia maculata*) and Side-blotched Lizards (*Uta stansburiana*), which are both small species. If kept with anything larger, they may be preyed upon.

● *Can Desert Horned Lizards squirt blood from their eyes?*

This means of deterring attackers has been confirmed in the wild, but it never seems to occur in captivity. Under threat these lizards will also feign death by remaining absolutely still and rigid.

● *Why do Desert Iguanas eat their own droppings?*

Their herbivorous diet is not completely processed by the first episode of digestion, and eating the droppings allows the full nutritional benefit to be obtained. This also conserves food in a desert environment.

Wall Lizards and other Lacertids

FAMILY: LACERTIDAE

THERE ARE AROUND 180 LACERTID SPECIES native to Europe, Asia and Africa. They are particularly representative of European reptiles; many are protected. Some are moderate to large lizards, such as the Eyed Lizard and other green lizards of the genus *Lacerta*, but most are small, including the wall lizards (genus *Podarcis*) and the other members of *Lacerta*. All are highly active, regardless of size, and require plenty of space for exercising their climbing skills. Some species are livebearers (viviparous), though the ones in this section are all egg-layers (oviparous).

EYED LIZARD

Lacerta lepida. Reaching an average length of 24in (60cm), this impressive southern European lizard is the largest European species. Its habitat varies from rocky and sandy areas to open scrubland, cultivated land or embankments, at altitudes ranging from sea level to around 3750ft (1100m) in the Pyrenees and the Alps. Mainly terrestrial, the Eyed Lizard is a skilled climber and is known to rob birds' nests. Captive specimens have lived as long as 20 years, which may be a record for lacertid species.

The dorsal surface is blue to green or grey, usually covered in clusters of black spots. Prominent blue spots (ocelli or "eyes") along the sides of many specimens inspired the common name. Colouring varies with region. Captive breeding of this species is widespread. Mature specimens are easily sexed: males are larger and brighter with large heads, prominent femoral pores and hemipenile swellings, while females are smaller and plainer. Males are incompatible. It is best to separate the sexes for hibernation, reintroducing them in Spring for mating. The young are grey-green, with a number of black-bordered light ocelli, and may have a reddish tail. If any aggression occurs between siblings, they must be reared individually. Full sexual maturity is reached at 3 years. Other species requiring similar treatment are the other European "green lizards": the Balkan Green Lizard (*L. trilineata*), the European Green Lizard (*L. viridis*), Schreiber's Green Lizard (*L. schreiberi*), and the Caucasian Green Lizard (*L. strigata*).

BALKAN LIZARD

Podarcis taurica. This southeastern European species is one of the hardiest of the lacertid family, and is readily available in the pet trade. Its maximum adult length is about 6.5in (16cm). Like other small lacertids, the Balkan Lizard is swift and agile with a long, thin tail which is easily

Eyed Lizards (Lacerta lepida) *are the largest of the European lacertid species. Their size and attractive colouring make them popular.*

● *Why do males lacertids not fight when housed together in dealers' premises?*

Males cannot establish a territory in the overcrowded conditions that typically prevail at a dealer's, so the hierarchy is less defined and there is less aggression. However, overcrowding itself is stressful, and scuffles will inevitably occur.

● *Can Eyed Lizards be handled?*

Yes, carefully. Adults have an especially powerful bite and can cause injury if not used to handling. Baby specimens are amenable if handled regularly.

● *Is it possible to keep Eyed Lizards in the same vivarium with other species?*

No. They prey on smaller lizards and may even eat their own young.

● *Is it best to avoid buying Balkan Lizards with broken tails?*

A broken tail should not make a big difference to the overall health of this species; all lacertids have excellent regenerative capability. However, the new tail is never quite as long as the old.

▲ *Balkan Lizards* (Podarcis taurica) *are diurnal and spend long periods basking in the sun with their bodies flattened to increase the surface area.*

● *Why do female Balkan Lizards "wave" their forelegs? Is this territorial aggression?*

No, territorial behaviour in females is rare. This behaviour is common in female lacertids when a male displays. What it signifies is their submission and willingness to mate with him.

Vivarium Conditions
Eyed, Balkan and Fringe-toed Lizards

VIVARIUM SIZE

Eyed Lizard   Min 48x24x24in (130x60x60cm) for a pair of adults.

Others   Min 30x12x18in (75x30x45 cm) for a pair or trio of 1 male to 1 or 2 females.

SUBSTRATE

Eyed Lizard   Dry and sandy, 2in (5cm) deep

Balkan Lizard   Sand 2in (5cm) deep, divided into damp and dry sections (see Housing, pages 14–17).

Fringe-toed Lizards   Loose, dry and sandy, 4in (10cm) deep, with subterranean moisture one end.

HABITAT   Semi-arid. Rocks, logs, branches and stumps for climbing, basking and hiding. Use firmly bedded plants placed out of the way; artificial plants are better for fringe-toes. Ventilate well. Spray daily and supply a small water dish.

TEMPERATURE   Full-spectrum (UVB) light

Eyed Lizard   25.5°C (78°F) at cool end, 38°C (100°F) at hot spot; 17°C (62°F) at night. Photoperiod: 14 hours. Provide a basking lamp.

Balkan Lizard   26°C (78°F) at cool end, 31°C (88°F) at hot spot; 12–13°C (54–55°F) at night. Photoperiod: 14 hours.

Fringe-toed Lizards 25°C (77°F) at cool end, 35°C (95°F) at hot spot; 15–20°C (60–68°F) at night. Photoperiod: 14 hours. Provide a basking lamp.

WINTER COOLING   All in natural daylight

Eyed Lizard   8–10°C (46–50°F) for 8 weeks

Balkan Lizard   5–10°C (41–50°F) for 8–12 weeks

Fringe-toed Lizards   13°C (55°F) for 4–8 weeks

FEEDING   Dusted insects and invertebrates; sweet fruits. Small pieces of cuttlefish bone.

INCUBATION   All in moist vermiculite

Eyed Lizard   1–2 annual clutches of up to 23 eggs in total. Incubate for 70–90 days at 25–28°C (77–82°F).

Balkan Lizard   2 annual clutches of 4–6 eggs. Incubate for 35–45 days at 27–29°C (80–84°F).

Fringe-toed Lizards   2 annual clutches of 4 eggs. Incubate for 45–50 days at 27–29°C (80–84°F).

lost. Although some regional variations occur, the basic colouring of Balkan Lizards is brown. Light stripes and dark markings are usually present. Varying amounts of green are also shown, mainly on the anterior half of the dorsum.

This species requires a relatively dry environment, but dividing the substrate into a dry area and a slightly damp area is advisable (see Housing, pages 14–15). Live plants may be included as long as ventilation is adequate. Wet conditions must be avoided. Balkan lizards thrive outdoors as long as they are protected from frost.

Male Balkan Lizards have prominent femoral pores, a thicker tail base, larger heads and usually more green in their colouring. Females are plainer, often with fewer dark markings. Males will fight and should be kept apart. The young can be raised communally in a small vivarium with full-spectrum (UVB) light, slightly lower temperatures than adults and plenty of hiding places. Any hatchlings that do not thrive should be removed and raised separately.

FRINGE-TOED LIZARDS

Acanthodactylus species. These lizards acquired their common name from fringelike spiny scales on the toes which assist them in moving on loose sand in their native habitat. Most of the 12 to 18 species of the genus are found in semi-arid regions from northern Africa to northwest India; one of them, *Acanthodactylus erythrurus*, occurs in southern Spain. Specimens in the trade are most likely to be *A. boskianus* from northern Africa. Although their vivarium conditions must be on the dry side, fringe-toes require an area with some moisture, creating a cool place in which they can burrow if desired. To achieve this, bury a box of damp sand at the cool end of the vivarium, or fix a divider to create two separate environments (see Housing, pages 14–15).

Fringe-toes are small lizards, varying in length from 6 to 8in (15 to 20cm). When running over distances, they raise their tails in a curve. Males have larger heads, a swollen tail base and prominent femoral pores; females may show reddish colouring on the underside of the tail. Males are incompatible and should be kept with females in pairs or trios. Courtship follows the usual lacertid pattern; the male seizes the female's neck

● *How do I know if eggs have been laid?*

... Gravid females are not always obvious. Watch for prolonged scratching of the substrate and fresh mounds.

● *Will fringe-toed lizards wreck cage furnishings?*

Like many small lacertids, fringe-toes indulge in scratching the substrate, but little if any damage is done to a furnished vivarium.

● *Why are fringe-toed babies coloured differently from the adults?*

The most likely reason is that the babies' red tails, which are waved slowly when in the open, distract predators from the more vulnerable head. The coloration may also inhibit aggression by adults.

● *Which plants are suitable for long-tailed lizards?*

The suitability of plants depends on their tolerance to vivarium conditions. Spider plants (*Chlorophytum* spp), Weeping fig (*Ficus benjamina*) and Citrus species are possibilities. (See Furnishing, pages 22–24).

● *Do long-tailed lizards practise autotomy?*

Like most lacertids, long-tails will throw their tails if they are handled roughly. Be gentle.

Vivarium Conditions
Long-tailed Lizards

Vivarium size   Min 24x12x15in (60x30x38cm) for a pair. Extra height is better for climbing.

Substrate   Moisture-retentive. Keep slightly damp, but not wet. The vivarium should be almost dried out by morning. Supply a small water dish and spray daily.

Habitat Rocks and cork bark on back of vivarium for climbing. Live plants and clusters of twigs.

Temperature   26°C (78°F) at cool end, 30°C (86°F) at hot spot; minimum 20°C (68°F) at night. Photoperiod: 12–14 hours. Full-spectrum (UVB) light and a basking lamp are needed.

Winter cooling   16°C (62°F) for 4–6 weeks. Photoperiod: 6 hours.

Feeding   Dusted insects

Incubation   3 annual clutches of up to 3 eggs each. Incubate for 50–62 days at 24–25°C (75–77°F), with an overnight drop to 21°C (70°F), in moist vermiculite.

region and manoeuvres her into a suitable position for inserting one of his hemipenes. Female fringe-toes indicate their readiness to mate by "waving" their forelimb at the male. The young should be raised in a simply-furnished sandy vivarium at a maximum temperature of 27°C (80°F) with basking lamp and full-spectrum tube and sufficient hiding places. As with the adults, an area of slightly damp substrate is recommended for cooling purposes. Young *Acanthodactylus* have a black body with light stripes; the tail and thighs are bright red. Other species requiring similar treatment are the northern African lacertids belonging to *Psammodromus*,

Latastia and *Adolphus* (formerly known as *Algyroides*). They are still exported, often under the common name Egyptian sand or wall lizards.

LONG-TAILED LIZARDS

Takydromus species. These lacertids from Asia, found from Japan to Indonesia, have appeared for years on dealers' lists as "skinks". There are possibly 12 species of *Takydromus* but taxonomy of the genus is confused. They measure about 14–15in (36cm) long. As the common name suggests, the tails are extremely long – about 2–5 times the body length, according to species. The body is slender, with keeled scales that produce longitudinal ridges along the dorsum. The lateral scales are also keeled and femoral pores number only 5 or less. Most *Takydromus* are brown to olive-green with lighter stripes along the back. Some are terrestrial while others are arboreal. Moist forests and rocky areas are their favoured habitats; the ones with the longest tails often live in grasslands. Most imported specimens belong to *T. sexlineatus*, the southernmost species, but exact identification is often difficult.

Long-tailed lizards are interesting to observe: extremely agile climbers and swift moving, they appear almost to "swim" over plants and branches and will clamber up cork bark. Sufficient height in the vivarium is important. *Takydromus* also require more humid conditions than their semi-arid *Lacerta* and *Podarcis* relations; the vivarium should be slightly damp without being actually wet.

Mature males can be identified by distinct hemipenile swellings at the tail base. They are better kept apart. Raise the neonates communally in a simply furnished, slightly moist vivarium with lighting similar to adults.

◀ *Long-tailed lizards* (Takydromus *species*) *are particularly good climbers. The tail may help to distribute their body weight when moving over grass.*

Skinks FAMILY: SCINCIDAE

THE SKINK FAMILY HAS MORE THAN 800 species. Mainly found in the tropics and in warm temperate regions, their full adult length is from 4in (10cm) to 30in (75cm). Typical skinks have rounded bodies and smooth, polished scales.

BLUE- AND PINK-TONGUED SKINKS

Tiliqua species. The common name is shared by 9 or 10 species and subspecies found in parts of Australia, New Guinea, the Moluccas and parts of Indonesia. Australia has banned exports, but captive-bred young are widely available, and *T. gigas* may be imported from other areas. Blue-tongues hiss when threatened, and may display the tongue in the pink mouth, but they do not normally bite. *T. s. scincoides* and *T. s. intermedia* tame easily; *T. gigas* tend to be feisty.

▲ *Blue-tongued skinks* (Tiliqua *species*) *get their common name from their startling defensive display. However, this behaviour is rarely seen in captivity.*

Blue-tongues have heavy bodies, with a relatively short tail and limbs. Colouring is mostly brown, blue or grey, with darker markings and patches of dark orange. Blue-tongues are omnivorous and fond of snails. Adults can become fat – do not overfeed, and provide large crickets and locusts to chase. Blue-tongues should live to 10 years and possibly over 20. Their total length is 18–22in (45–55cm) for *T. s. scincoides* and *T. s. intermedia*. *T. gigas* is shorter and stouter.

Males have a longer body (foreleg to hindleg) and a slightly thicker tail base. Males in breeding condition may have a barely perceptible swelling

Vivarium Conditions
Blue-tongued, Pink-tongued, Monkey-tailed and Five-lined Skinks

VIVARIUM SIZE

Blue-tongued and Five-lined Skinks   Min 36x18x 18in (92x45x45cm) for one specimen.

Pink-tongued Skink   Min 24x24x36in (60x60x 90cm) for a pair or trio; larger for a colony.

Monkey-tailed Skink   Min 48x24x48in (122x60x 122cm) for one specimen.

SUBSTRATE

Blue-tongued Skinks   Rounded calcareous gravel to help prevent overgrown claws; or newspaper.

Pink-tongued and Five-lined Skinks   Moisture-retentive loam or leaf litter covered with moss.

Monkey-tailed Skink   Newspaper or other absorbent, easily replaced material.

HABITAT   Provide a small water bowl.

Blue-tongued Skinks   Wooden box or half-round earthenware pipe for hides. Logs and plastic plants.

Pink-tongued and Five-lined Skinks   Branches, live plants, cork bark shelters on the substrate.

Monkey-tailed Skink   Sturdy branches with hides and shelters at several levels. On the ground, hollow cork bark logs are ideal. Plastic plants.

TEMPERATURE   Full-spectrum (UVB) light and basking lamps needed. Blue-tongues need a low-wattage heater mat. Gravid Pink-tongued females need UVB light placed vertically near branches.

Monkey-tailed Skink   26°C (79°F) at cool end, 32°C (90°F) at hot spot; 24°C (75°F) at night. Photoperiod: 12 hours.

Five-lined Skink   22°C (72°F) at cool end, 31°C (88°F) at hot spot; 18°C (65°F) at night. Photoperiod: 12 hours.

Others   25.5°C (78°F) at cool end, 32°C (90°F) at hot spot; 15–21°C (60–70°F) at night. Photoperiod: 13–14 hours.

HUMIDITY   Light daily spray

Blue-tongued Skinks	30–40%
Pink-tongued Skink	65%
Monkey-tailed Skink	75%
Five-lined Skink	55–60%

WINTER COOLING

Blue-tongued Skinks   *T. gigas*: 21°C (70°F) at cool end, 27°C (80°F) at hot spot; 12°C (55°F) at night for 8–12 weeks (Oct–Jan). Photoperiod: 8 hours. *T. s. scincoides*/*T. s. intermedia*: hibernate at 8–10°C (46–50°F) for 8–12 weeks (Nov–Feb) in darkness.

Pink-tongued Skink   15°C (60°F) at cool end, 22°C (72°F) at hot spot; 10°C (50°F) at night for 8 weeks. Photoperiod: 8 hours.

Monkey-tailed Skink   24.5°C (76°F) at cool end, 29°C (84°F) at hot spot; 20°C (68°F) at night for 5 weeks. Photoperiod: 10–11 hours.

Five-lined Skink   12°C (55°F) for 8 weeks. Photoperiod: 6 hours; or hibernate in darkness.

FEEDING

Blue-tongued Skinks   Omnivorous. High-fibre diet recommended: 25% protein, 75% vegetables and fruit. Rat and mice pinkies, raw meat, cat or dog food and boiled egg in moderation. Dust food with supplements.

Pink-tongued Skink   Specialist molluscivore – mainly snails. Some specimens can be weaned onto low-fat cat or dog food and convenience foods for carnivorous lizards.

Monkey-tailed Skink   Herbivorous (see Foods and Feeding, pages 29–30; Green Iguanas, pages 82–83).

Five-lined Skink   Dusted insects and invertebrates; fruits and vegetables. Pinkies can be given once every 2 weeks. Carnivorous lizard foods may also be tried. Small pieces of cuttlefish bone.

at each side of the tail base. Ignore the size of the head and the heavy jowls; they may indicate a mature female or an overfed male. Babies can be sexed at birth using body length as an indicator.

After hibernation or the Winter cool period, the female should be placed into the male's vivarium. Evening seems to be preferred for mating. Males will attempt to seize the female's neck and scratch her body. A receptive female will raise her tail and allow mating. Repeat for as long as the female will tolerate it. An unreceptive female pulls away and may attack the male – remove and try 2 days later. Any bites heal quickly.

Blue-tongued skinks are livebearers. The gestation period varies according to conditions. Gravid females bask under the hot spot and the UVB tube, and feed as normal until a week before parturition. Some 24–48 hours before this, the female splays or raises her hind legs off the floor. The young are born in membranes and break free. Females tend to eat any undeveloped ova (mis-shapen yellow lumps) that emerge. Remove the young blue-tongues to a separate vivarium. Babies are independent and may feed the first day. Any that seem intimidated should be reared separately. Feed daily for the first month, then every 2 days for 5 months. The diet should be 50% protein and 50% vegetables and fruit.

A close relation is the smaller Pink-tongued Skink (*T. gerrardii*), which is found from New South Wales to the Cape Peninsula. It may be kept in colonies of one male to several females.

MONKEY-TAILED SKINK

Corucia zebrata. Also known as the Zebra Skink and the Prehensile-tailed Skink, this species is native to the Solomon Islands and Papua New Guinea. It is large and arboreal, with powerful claws and well-developed limbs, and grows to 30in (75cm) in length – half of which is tail. Most specimens available in the trade are wild-caught; success with captive breeding has been limited. Monkey-tailed Skinks are mainly light olive to grey-green in colour, with dark speckles on the back and sides that resemble stripes. The ventral surface is paler or yellow-green. Regional colour variations are common. Monkey-tails can be kept together in a colony in a room fitted

● *Can I keep several blue-tongues together?*

... Some people keep more than one adult specimen together, but fighting can cause severe injuries and limit breeding success. Housing each specimen separately is strongly recommended for this reason.

● *How frequently do blue-tongues breed?*

When mature, they may breed every year for 2 or 3 years, after which breeding tends to be biennial. This is also true for Monkey-tailed Skinks.

● *How tame are Monkey-tailed Skinks?*

This varies with individuals. Some are placid; others appear tame but can experience brief periods of aggressiveness; and a few specimens remain very aggressive in spite of handling. Many young *Corucias* are initially hostile to the keeper, but frequent handling overcomes this. Even a tame specimen may have an "off day" – the bite is powerful!

● *Can Five-lined Skinks' eggs be incubated artificially?*

No. They are better left with the mother; artificial incubation does not seem to be successful for this species. The same is true for Berber Skinks.

➤ *A Monkey-tailed Skink* (Corucia zebrata) *uses its long prehensile tail to cling to a perch. Monkey-tailed Skinks are quite large for an arboreal species and require sturdy branches to support their weight.*

with numerous branches and shelters. House-plants used as furnishings may be eaten – check toxicity before using. Good ventilation to avoid stagnant conditions is necessary. If humidity is too low, shedding may not be completed. Check the feet, as unshed skin can lead to loss of digits.

Sexing Monkey-tails can be difficult. Some males (not all) may have larger heads and slight hemipenile swelling. Probing is awkward and not always effective. Some keepers prefer hemipenile eversion under anaesthesia. You will need to consult a vet or a highly experienced keeper.

Heavy misting at the end of the cool period often initiates breeding behaviour. If adults have been maintained separately, the female should be placed into the male's quarters. Mating can be somewhat violent, with bites from the male leaving scars on the female which take several sloughs before fading. Young Corucias do not feed until after their first slough (usually 8–11 days after birth). Mothers guard their young for up to a month after birth. When the young are independent they can be moved to their own vivarium with conditions as for adults.

FIVE-LINED SKINK

Eumeces fasciatus. This species from the eastern US derives its common name from the lined pattern in the young. The lines fade with growth, as does the blue tail. Its colouring tends to be a uniform shade of brown, with a central row of enlarged scales under the tail. Maximum adult length is about 8in (20cm).

Five-lines are relatively easy to keep. They may be kept in outdoor vivaria if the climate is suitable. This species is commonly sold in pet stores but some keepers may want to collect their own. It is essential to check local or state laws before taking home any wild herptile (see Starting Out, pages 4–5). A field guide will help to identify *Eumeces*: they are not the only lined skinks, and it is possible to confuse them.

Males develop a red colouring on the lower jaw in spring. Females brood their eggs and may produce two clutches in a season. Males should be kept away from each other and from young. Other species requiring similar treatment are the Southeastern Five-lined Skink (*E. inexpectatus*) and the Broad-headed Skink (*E. laticeps*).

Breeding Conditions	
BLUE-TONGUED SKINKS	Livebearers
Gestation	3–6.5 months
Litter size	4–12 young
PINK-TONGUED SKINK	Livebearer
Gestation	2–4.5 months
Litter size	12–25 young
MONKEY-TAILED SKINK	Livebearer
Gestation	6–7 months
Litter size	1–2 young
FIVE-LINED SKINK	Egg-layer
Clutch size	2 annual clutches of 6–9 eggs
Incubation	60–90 days with mother
BERBER SKINK	Egg-layer
Clutch size	2–3 annual clutches of 1–2 eggs
Incubation	60–90 days with mother
BARREL SKINKS	Livebearers
Gestation	About 3 months
Litter size	2 annual litters; 2–20 young

⬆ *The blue tails of juvenile Five-lined Skinks* (Eumeces fasciatus) *seem to stop them being attacked by adult males in the wild. They lose this colouring at about 12 months, when they are mature.*

The *Berber Skink* (Eumeces schneideri) *is widely available, but captive breeding is still a challenge. Maternal incubation is seldom successful in a vivarium.*

BERBER SKINK

Eumeces schneideri. Native to northern Africa and central Asia, this skink is part of the large genus *Eumeces*, which also contains most of the North American skinks. Berbers have adapted to life in hot, arid, sandy areas. They are fairly typical skinks, with heavy bodies, highly polished scales and relatively small limbs. Berber Skinks are quite attractive, with varying colours – they are usually grey-brown with bright orange spots or patches. A comb-like flap of scales protects the ear openings. Apart from coloration, there is no difference between *E. schneideri* and another northwest African form, sometimes referred to as *E. algeriensis* or *E. s. algeriensis*. Taxonomists cannot agree if they are the same species. Both are generally called Berber Skinks.

Males are larger and more brightly coloured than females, which may lack the orange coloration altogether. Males are aggressive; it is best to keep pairs or trios, with one male to one or more females. Separating the sexes for the cool period may help to stimulate mating when the female is reintroduced to the male's quarters. Some 5–7 weeks after mating, the female lays her eggs in a damp area of substrate, often under a

● *What should I do with Berber eggs if the female abandons them?*

... Try incubating them in a mixture of water and vermiculite (1:1 ratio; see Breeding, pages 38–39) at around 29°C (84°F). This will not necessarily be successful.

● *How long do Berber Skinks live?*

Properly cared for, they can reach 20 years or more.

● *Can living plants ever be used with barrel skinks?*

Plastic plants are ideal but non-spiny arid plants can be used – you must avoid too much moisture. Leave plants in their pots and protect against burrowing activities.

piece of cork bark. *Eumeces* females normally guard the eggs and moisten them by urinating. Removing the gravid female to a separate vivarium will prevent interference by the male. While brooding eggs, females do not actively hunt but may take passing insects or possibly food from forceps. As with the Five-lined Skink, it is best to leave the eggs with the mother. One theory is that the mother's urine contains something important for the development of the embryo.

Young Berber Skinks need warm, dry housing at around 30°C (86°F). They can be quarrelsome; separate if necessary. Other species requiring similar treatment are desert Sandfish Skinks (*S. scincus*), which do not brood their eggs.

Vivarium Conditions
Berber and Barrel Skinks

VIVARIUM SIZE

Berber Skink	30x12x15in (75x30x38cm)
Barrel Skinks	24x12x12in (60x30x30cm)

SUBSTRATE   Non-dusty sand, 3in (8cm) deep, divided into a dry and a moderately damp area. Sphagnum moss can be placed over the surface of the damp area.

HABITAT   Firmly bedded rocks and stumps for basking. Cork bark shelters for hides. Plastic plants. Light spray daily. Small water dish.

TEMPERATURE   Provide a full-spectrum (UVB) light and a basking lamp for all species.

Berber Skink   28–30°C (82–86°F) at cool end, 38°C (100°F) at hot spot; 18–20°C (64–68°F) at night. Photoperiod: 12–14 hours.

Barrel Skinks   25–30°C (77–82°F) at cool end, 35°C (95°F) at hot spot; 18–21°C (64–70°F) at night. Photoperiod: 12–14 hours.

WINTER COOLING

Berber Skink 15°C (60°F) during day, 10°C (50°F) at night for 8–10 weeks. Photoperiod: 6 hours.

Barrel Skinks 10–15°C (50–60°F) for 7–8 weeks. Photoperiod: 6 hours.

FEEDING

Berber Skink   Dusted insects and invertebrates; fruits and vegetables. Pinkies can be given once every 2 weeks. Carnivorous lizard foods may also be tried. Provide small pieces of cuttlefish bone.

Barrel Skinks   Dusted insects. Small mealworms.

➤ *The Ocellated Skink* (Chalcides ocellatus) *is one of the desert skinks collectively known as barrel skinks. New specimens tend to be skittish but later settle down.*

BARREL SKINKS

Chalcides species. The various members of this genus, so named for their elongated, cylindrical bodies, are found across southern Europe and northern Africa to Arabia and Pakistan. They have small, exceptionally smooth scales that allow them to move quickly through loose soil and sand. As with certain other skinks, the limbs vary in size in proportion to the body, often being smaller than normal. Barrel skinks mainly inhabit dry, sandy areas, in many cases with grass or other plant cover, but some species may occasionally be found in slightly moist meadows. New acquisitions for the vivarium tend to dive for cover in the sand when approached, but they usually settle down over time and become more visible. The best known species are the Spanish Barrel Skink (*C. bedriagai*); the Eyed or Ocellated Skink (*C. ocellatus*); the Three-toed Skink (*C. chalcides*); and the Sand Skink (*C. sepsoides*). Lengths vary from 6–10in (15–25.5cm) according to species. Autotomy is easily caused in all species by sudden grabs or rough handling.

There is little visible difference between the sexes, except that females have a plumper body. Males of *C. ocellatus* and *C. bedriagai* may have slightly larger heads. Females of *C. sepsoides* and *C. chalcides* tend to be slightly longer than males. Behaviour is the most reliable guide to sexing. Apart from *C. sepsoides* and *C. chalcides*, pairs or trios (with only one male) are recommended; males are incompatible.

Breeding can occur at various times of the year, and often more than one litter is produced. All barrel skinks are livebearers. Neonates should be removed and reared in their own vivarium, as cannibalism is not uncommon. Gravid females should be isolated to reduce this possibility, but they may well be the culprits. Provide similar conditions for babies as for adults, and appropriately small food. The water bowl must be proportionately small to prevent the young falling in and drowning. The young are sexually mature at around 12 months, although this depends on temperature and nutrition.

Other species requiring similar treatment are lance skinks (*Acontias* species) – legless burrowers with shiny, cylindrical bodies, short tails and a specially adapted snout for burrowing.

Common Tegu

FAMILY: TEIIDAE
SPECIES: TUPINAMBIS TEGUIXIN.

ALSO KNOWN AS THE BLACK AND WHITE Tegu, this large South American lizard is a popular pet. Because of their eventual large size – a total length of 48in (122cm) – Common Tegus need considerable space; they should not be kept in conditions that deny them plenty of exercise. This puts them beyond the scope of many potential keepers. Although they are ground-dwellers and dig burrows in the wild, Common Tegus are also excellent climbers and swimmers. Because captive breeding is a rare event, the majority of available specimens are wild-caught imports. Anyone intending to keep one is advised to buy young specimens, as larger ones can be very formidable creatures and do not tame readily. The tail, which accounts for half of their total length, is often used as a whip in defence. Strong jaws and powerful claws, the latter capable of breaking into termite mounds, constitute the rest of

◆ *A Common Tegu* (Tupinambis teguixin) *is an impressive specimen. It is omnivorous and fond of birds' eggs and snails in the wild. In captive males, this liking for eggs extends to those deposited by their own mates.*

their armoury. The long snakelike tongue can be withdrawn into a sheath in the lower jaw. Their colouring is an attractive mixture of black with irregular bands and spots in yellow to white. Although usually thought of as tropical lizards, they have a wide distribution in both tropical and temperate regions; in part of their range they actually hibernate, which poses a problem for the keeper if the exact origin is unknown.

Common Tegus' surroundings should be set up to maximize space. Plants would soon be wrecked – they are unnecessary. In the wild, Tegus readily take to the water, but providing a pool in a confined space is difficult and creates too much humidity. The ideal accommodation for them is in a large outdoor enclosure.

Many keepers make the mistake of supplying a limited diet of raw meat, chicks, thawed rodents or hens eggs. Raw beef is high in phosphorus and low in calcium, which can lead to metabolic bone disease (MBD; see Health and Disease, pages 44–45). Too many rodents or chicks without other foods can produce inability to slough, while a diet of mostly eggs causes biotin deficiency. Wild specimens are fond of eggs but these will be embryonated (fertilized) eggs, which contain biotin, whereas commercial hens' eggs do not. Other foods that Tegus are not fond of, such as vegetables, may be coated with beaten raw egg to tempt the lizards to eat them, but coating should not be done too often.

Sexual maturity is achieved at about 3 years. Mating in captivity usually occurs during May in the northern hemisphere. Males will mate several times with any available females. As with many other lizards, the male bites the female on the neck to subdue her. Breeding requires spacious quarters, a deep substrate, at least 12in (30cm), for digging; and hibernation for temperate species. Given these prerequisites, it is not surprising that captive breeding is uncommon. Gravid females usually show a desire to move away from the male, which means another vivarium of similar size is required. This is just as well, because males will eat their mates' eggs if given the opportunity. Hatching is accomplished very quickly, often in only a matter of seconds, unlike some lizards which may take several hours or even longer. Hatchlings measure around 9.5in (24cm). They tend to have a green colouring which soon disappears. They should be removed from the adults' vivarium immediately after birth and reared separately in similar conditions.

● *How does biotin deficiency show in Common Tegus?*

... Usually as muscle tremors, but these could be confused with the "shivering" caused by a calcium/phosphorus imbalance. Diagnosis is based on an analysis of diet. The first step in curing biotin deficiency is to stop feeding the Tegu unfertilized eggs. Since biotin is part of the vitamin B-complex, a course of these vitamins might be recommended. However, you should seek veterinary advice.

● *How often should Common Tegus be fed?*

Young specimens should be fed daily, adults 3 times a week. Adults may become obese on an unbalanced diet, especially if they lack space to exercise.

● *My Common Tegu is very tame. Can I let it out in the house for exercise?*

Many keepers allow large "tame" lizards to roam at liberty, but this can cause hygiene problems. Caution is needed where there are children and domestic pets – even docile lizards can be unpredictable.

● *What causes my baby Tegu to shake its tail?*

This behaviour is normally only seen in the first 2 or 3 months. The reason is not clear – it may be a defensive mechanism while they are small and vulnerable.

● *Are Common Tegus sociable?*

Females are generally compatible, but males will fight, especially during the breeding season. They are better kept separately, with one or more females, if the enclosure is big enough to house them all.

Vivarium Conditions

Vivarium size	Min 72x48x48in (180x120x120cm) for a single specimen.
Substrate	Newspaper or bark
Habitat	Sturdy branches or stumps for basking. Spray daily but do not allow humidity to build up. Supply a water bowl.
Temperature	28°C (82°F) at cool end, 36.5°C (98°F) at hot spot; 20–21°C (68–70°F) at night. Photoperiod: 12–14 hours. Full-spectrum (UVB) light and basking lamp are needed.
Winter cooling	4–8°C (37–45°F) for 12 weeks, gradually reduced over 4 weeks, and gradually increased again over 4 weeks at the end.
Feeding	30% thawed rodents or chicks, 10–20% large insects and the remainder fruit (avoid bananas), alfalfa pellets, mushrooms or vegetables coated with beaten raw egg. Canned commercial food for lizards may be given as part of the diet, but do not rely on it exclusively.
Incubation	1 annual clutch of 1–50 eggs. Incubate for 60–65 days at 26.5–29°C (80–85°F) in moist vermiculite.

Boas   FAMILY: BOIDAE

AS LARGE, NON-POISONOUS SNAKES, BOAS are in great demand. They kill their prey by suffocation, yet they have gentle dispositions otherwise. Ample space is the first requirement for a healthy boa; exercise prevents obesity and aids thermoregulation. Any heater in the vivarium must be covered. If a snake needs warmth, it will coil round any accessible lamp.

Male boas have longer, thicker tails and larger anal spurs; if in doubt, use probing (see Breeding, pages 34–35). Mating pairs should be full size and healthy. For all but Emerald and Sand Boas, introduce the male into the female's quarters at the end of the cool period; for these 2 species, introduce the males during the cool period. Some breeders like to use 2 or more males, but this can lead to injuries. Leave the male until he loses interest; multiple matings are more productive.

Boas are livebearers. Gravid females stop feeding and seek warmth; try raising the vivarium temperature by 2–3°C (4–6°F). If hides are used,

supply 2. Use slightly moist substrate for the one at the warm end. House neonates singly in ventilated shoe or sweater boxes, placed partly on a heater mat with a thermostat and kept in a spare vivarium to contain escapees. Feed twice a week for the first 18–24 months, then feed weekly.

LARGE BOAS

This group of snakes includes the Common Boa (*Boa constrictor constrictor*), found from northern Mexico through Central and South America, which most people think of as being the definitive species. The Common Boa and its 11 subspecies (some disputed) are closely related to 3 other species from different genera: the Brazilian Rainbow Boa (*Epicrates cenchria cenchria*); the

◆ *Unlike most snakes, Brazilian Rainbow Boas* (Epicrates cenchria cenchria) *retain their striking juvenile colours and patterns into adulthood. The young may be feisty, but adult boas are noted for placidity.*

Vivarium Conditions
Common, Brazilian Rainbow, Emerald Tree and Solomon Islands Boas

VIVARIUM SIZE   For a single specimen

Common Boa	72x36x36in (180x90x90cm)
Brazilian Rainbow Boa	72x24x24in (180x60x60cm)
Emerald Tree Boa	36x24x36in (90x60x90cm)
Solomon Islands Boa	36x24x24in (90x60x60cm)

SUBSTRATE

Emerald Tree Boa	Moisture-retentive material such as leaf litter or moss. Spray daily.
Others	Newspaper for easy cleaning

HABITAT

Emerald Tree Boa   Firmly fixed branches, some horizontal, 1 positioned 12in (30cm) below the spot bulb. Plastic plants. Flat stone and a small water bowl. 60–80% humidity.

Others   Branches optional. Plastic plants fixed to walls. 1 hide at cool end, 1 near hot spot. Large, wide-based water bowl. 20–30% humidity.

TEMPERATURE

Common Boa   28°C (82°F) at cool end, 35°C (95°F) at hot spot; 26.5°C (80°F) at night. Photoperiod: 16 hours.

Brazilian Rainbow Boa   26.5°C (80°F) at cool end, 31°C (88°F) at hot spot; 23°C (74°F) at night. Photoperiod: 16 hours.

Emerald Tree Boa   26°C (79°F) at cool end, 31°C (88°F) at hot spot; 23°C (74°F) at night. Photoperiod: 14 hours.

Solomon Islands Boa   25.5°C (78°F) at cool end, 32°C (90°F) at hot spot; 23°C (74°F) at night. Photoperiod: 14 hours.

WINTER COOLING

Common Boa   26.5°C (80°F) at cool end, 30°C (86°F) at hot spot; 20–22°C (68–72°F) at night for 8–12 weeks. Photoperiod: 10 hours.

Brazilian Rainbow Boa   24°C (75°F) at cool end, 25.5°C (78°F) at hot spot; 18–22°C (64–72°F) at night for 6 weeks. Photoperiod: 10 hours.

Emerald Tree Boa   Normal day temperatures for 8 weeks. Reduce to 19–20°C (66–68°F) at night. Photoperiod: 10 hours.

Solomon Islands Boa   Normal day temperatures for 6 weeks. Reduce to 19–20°C (66–68°F) at night. Photoperiod: 10 hours.

FEEDING   Rodents, quail chicks, day-old hen chicks every 1–2 weeks. Place food on a flat stone or use long forceps – do not feed by hand.

● *Do boas ever bite?*

Never assume that any snake will not bite, especially at feeding time. A bite may be a warning bite, which is quickly released, or a feeding bite, when the snake hangs on until it realizes that the keeper is not food – use forceps. Remain still to avoid injury on the sharp inward-curving teeth. If the snake does not let go soon, you may need help. Two adults should be present.

● *Is constriction a risk to the keeper?*

Boas are usually docile, and the few cases of owners being constricted have been with pythons. Do not provoke the snake, do not handle it alone, and do not let it coil around you; that will minimize the small risk.

● *How can I get my young boa to feed?*

Try scenting thawed pink mice with day-old chick. Providing thin twigs for climbing may encourage Solomon Island Boas. Very tiny specimens may need to be fed on small pieces such as tails.

Emerald Tree Boa (*Corallus canina*); and the Solomon Islands Boa (*Candoia carinata*). All are popular, and captive-bred young are frequently available. Young boas may rear and strike, but adults are known for being tame – "boa" comes from the Portuguese word for "good".

Common Boas range in length from 72–98in (180–250cm); some specimens may be longer. Colouring is variable, mainly light brown or grey with dark saddles. Some develop a pink ventral surface and pink markings along the sides. The saddles are closer together near the tail, where the background colour is red, orange and cream. The large Brazilian Rainbow Boa is particularly attractive. Growing to about 72in (180cm), its background colour is brown and orange with black rings along the dorsal midline. Along the

▶ OVERLEAF *Common Boas* (Boa constrictor *species and subspecies) with red tails are highly prized. Red tails are often seen in specimens from Peru and Surinam.*

Breeding Conditions

GESTATION	Varies with species, temperature ranges and individual females.
Sand Boas and Rosy Boas	4.5–5.5 months
Others	7–8.5 months
LITTER SIZE	
Common Boa	10–50
Rainbow Boa	7–15
Emerald Tree Boa	10–25
Solomon Islands Boa	9–60
Sand Boas	5–20
Rosy Boas	3–5
TEMPERATURE	From neonate to 4–6 months
Common Boa	27–31°C (81–88°F)
Rainbow Boa	29°C (84°F)
Emerald Tree Boa	28°C (82°F)
Solomon Islands Boa	28–29°C (82–84°F)
Sand Boas	27–29°C (81–84°F)
Rosy Boas	27–29°C (81–84°F)

Emerald Tree Boas (Corallus canina) *are arboreal. They seem to benefit from the privacy of leaves, and the young are born in the trees and can climb from birth.*

sides are smaller black rings with light to bright-orange centres. The Emerald Tree Boa (up to 60in/150cm) is bright green with white markings down the centre and a cream or yellow ventral surface. The Solomon Islands Boa, with several colour forms, grows only up to 48in (120cm).

Boas become mature at 2 to 3 years depending on how well they are fed. Like all snakes, some individuals can be difficult to feed. Common Boas, Emerald Tree and Rainbow Boas usually feed on thawed pink mice after their first slough, 3–14 days after birth. Solomon Island Boas produce large litters of very small young, the most difficult of all to feed. They go absolutely rigid when disturbed, so pinky-pumping and force-feeding frequently cause death by trauma.

Other species requiring similar treatment are the Amazon Tree Boa (*Corallus enhydris enhydris*), which can be kept as for the Emerald Tree Boa. It is not suitable for beginners.

DESERT BOAS

(*Eryx* and *Lichanura* species). These desert boas are smaller than their tropical cousins – from 18in (45cm) to 3ft (100cm) – and are easier to house. Sand boas (*Eryx* species) are found from southern Europe to central Africa, Asia and the Middle East; Rosy Boas (*Lichanura trivirgata*) are native to the southwestern US and north-western Mexico. Sand boas have drab colours, usually in varied patterns of light and darker brown. Rosy Boas range from brown and white to orange and silver, with stripes. The taxonomy of both genera needs revising. *L. trivirgata* has possibly 4 subspecies; *Eryx* has 10–11 species with possibly 12 or more subspecies. *Lichanura* is protected and should not be collected from the wild. *Eryx* species are still imported but captive-bred specimens are often available.

Both genera of desert boas are livebearers and can be sexed like other boas. *Eryx* males should be introduced to females at the onset of the Winter cooling period, though mating may not occur until normal temperatures are restored. *Lichanura* males should be introduced after the cool period ends. Raise the young individually as for other boas in small, clear plastic boxes with good ventilation. Provide a shallow water dish inside but avoid increasing the humidity.

The Kenyan Sand Boa (Eryx colubrinus loveridgei) *is the most attractive of the sand boa species. Sand boas are crepuscular but may bask during the day. They also spend long periods buried with just the head showing.*

Vivarium Conditions
Sand Boas and Rosy Boas

VIVARIUM SIZE Min 24x24x15in (60x60x38cm) for a single specimen.

SUBSTRATE Dry, dust-free sand 2–5in (7–12cm) deep.

HABITAT Dry conditions are essential. 2 or 3 cork bark shelters partly buried in substrate; rocks for basking. Branches optional. Small water dish.

TEMPERATURE 26.5°C (80°F) at cool end, 32°C (90°F) at hot spot; 20–22°C (68–72°F) at night. Photoperiod: 14 hours.

WINTER COOLING

Sand Boas Varies with species. *E. c. loveridgei*: 6 weeks at 24–26.5°C (75–79°F) during day, 18°C (65°F) at night, photoperiod 8–10 hours. *E. miliaris, E. tartaricus*: hibernate in darkness at 5–10°C (41–50°F) for 12–16 weeks.

Rosy Boas Hibernate in darkness at 10–13°C (50–55°F) for 8–12 weeks.

FEEDING Small rodents, offered in the evening. Scent with lizard eggs or lizard skin if necessary.

● *How can I control lighting for hatchling boas in boxes?*

... Individual cages can be illuminated, but where sweater boxes or drawer systems are used, the ambient (room) lighting will have to follow a photoperiod. Clear boxes let in the light.

● *Why does my female boa lie almost upside down?*

Gravid female boas sometimes do this – it is thought that they are warming the developing young under the basking lamp.

● *How do I know if my boa is going to give birth?*

The swelling caused by the mass of young will gradually move towards the posterior part of the body and the cloaca may appear slightly swollen.

● *Does food have to be offered with forceps?*

Forceps are only used to simulate movement if necessary. Many snakes readily accept thawed items placed on a stone in their vivarium.

● *Will a water bowl increase humidity too much?*

A small bowl should be used. Put it far away from the heat source and guard against any spillage.

Pythons

FAMILY: BOIDAE
SUB-FAMILY: PYTHONIDAE

IN RECENT YEARS PYTHONS HAVE PROVOKED controversy among hobbyists, attracting some negative publicity. This is mostly because the larger and more dangerous species are easier to keep and breed in captivity, while the more suitable small and medium-sized species, which are just as beautiful, have proved more challenging. However, information about how to keep the smaller species in captivity is improving all the time. Given the correct conditions, they are even more rewarding than their large relatives. Some experienced hobbyists are rising to the challenge of breeding them in captivity.

Three smaller pythons from Australia and Oceania are particularly good vivarium subjects: the Green Tree Python (*Morelia viridis*, formerly *Chondropython viridis*); the black and yellow Jungle Carpet Python (*Morelia spilota cheynei*); and the brown-and-iridescent-purple Children's Python (*Antaresia childreni*, formerly *Liasis childreni*). This last species is particularly prized for the way its skin shimmers as it moves. The Green Tree Python is the largest of the three, growing to a length of 72–80in (180–200cm); the Children's Python, reaching a maximum of 40–47in (102–118cm) long, is the smallest.

The Royal Python (*Python regius*) from western and central Africa, sometimes called the Ball Python, is also becoming popular. It grows to 60in (150cm) long, has an attractive yellow skin patterned with dark-brown or black, and a very docile nature. Large numbers of wild-caught and

Vivarium Conditions
Jungle Carpet, Children's, Royal and Green Tree Pythons

VIVARIUM SIZE   For a single specimen

Children's Python	36x24x24in (90x60x60cm)
Royal Python	35x15x18in (90x38x45cm)
Others	36x24x36in (90x60x90cm)

SUBSTRATE Newspaper and carpet-type material for easy removal and cleaning.

HABITAT

Children's Python   2 hides: 1 at cool end, 1 near hot spot. Flat stone and water bowl.

Others   Horizontal and sloping branches for climbing and perches for basking. Plastic plants and 2 hides: 1 at ground level, the other at a higher level. Water bowl. Spray lightly during breeding season.

TEMPERATURE

Jungle Carpet Python 28°C (82°F) at cool end, 32°C (90°F) at hot spot; 21°C (70°F) at night. Photoperiod: 15 hours.

Children's Python   27°C (81°F) at cool end, 30°C (86°F) at hot spot; 24°C (75°F) at night. Photoperiod: 15 hours.

Royal Python   29.5°C (85°F) at cool end, 35°C (95°F) at hot spot; 24–26.5°C (75–80°F) at night. Photoperiod: 14 hours.

Green Tree Python   27°C (81°F) at cool end, 32°C (90°F) at hot spot; 25°C (77°F) at night. Photoperiod: 15 hours.

HUMIDITY

Jungle Carpet and Green Tree Pythons	55%–65%
Children's Python	35%–45%
Royal Python	60%

WINTER COOLING

Children's Python   20°C (68°F) at cool end, 23°C (73°F) at hot spot; 16°C (62°F) at night for 8–12 weeks. Photoperiod: 9–10 hours.

Royal Python   26.5°C (80°F) at cool end, 29.5°C (85°F) at hot spot; 21–24°C (70–75°F) at night for 8–12 weeks. Photoperiod: 10 hours.

Others   21°C (70°F) at cool end, 24°C (75°F) at hot spot; 18–19°C (64–66°F) at night for 8–10 weeks. Photoperiod: 10 hours.

FEEDING   Rodents, quail chicks, day-old chicks. Feed using forceps.

🡄 *The Jungle Carpet Python* (Morelia spilota cheynei) *is usually fully grown within 3 years, but many females do not breed successfully until 4 or 5 years old.*

captive-farmed specimens have been imported into the US and Europe during the 1990s, primarily from Ghana and Togo. One other variety of small python particularly valued by hobbyists is the more rare Calabar Python (*Calabaria reinhardti*), which has never been bred in captivity. Vivarium conditions are the same as for the Royal Python, except that Calabars need a loose loamy substrate for burrowing.

Most pythons are relatively easy to sex. Males have larger spurs than the females, although the spurs of Children's Pythons are quite small in both males and females. If in doubt, try probing the specimen (see Breeding, pages 34–35).

Feeding Problems

Some species, particularly Royal and Calabar Pythons, are known for being difficult to feed. Imported babies may feed well once they have settled down in the right conditions, but imported adults may not, for a variety of reasons; they may be suffering from the stress of capture and transport, and wild-caught adults tend not to feed from September to February (the breeding season). Gravid females will not feed either.

If you have ruled out all these factors, as well as parasites or bacterial infection, and you are sure you are offering the right kind of food, the snake may need assisted feeding or force-feeding (see Foods and Feeding, pages 32–33). Use mice, fuzzy (unweaned) rats or young gerbils (Calabar Pythons seem to prefer rat pups 3–4 days old). Another possible cause is that the snake may be constipated. Pythons awaiting export are kept in conditions that lead to dehydration. Faeces accumulate and become hardened within the snake, which can affect its ability to feed. If you suspect this is the case, provide a large container of tepid water where the snake can soak. If this does not work, seek advice from a veterinarian.

Breeding Pythons

Place the male in the female's quarters soon after the cool period begins. At the start of the breeding season, female pythons produce follicles in response to environmental stimuli. As these follicles mature in the ovaries, the female becomes swollen as if already gravid. During this period the pythons mate, but fertilization is typically delayed by a few weeks or even months. At this point the keeper may see a mid-body swelling, as if the female has eaten a substantial meal. This "lumping", indicating ovulation, lasts for 8–24 hours. Once the ova have entered the oviduct where they are fertilized, very few females will mate. If a female reaches this stage without mating, any eggs she produces are infertile. Females slough once between ovulation and laying eggs.

◆ *Royal Pythons* (Python regius) *are primarily ground-dwellers and need ground-level hides. They will sometimes climb on sturdy sloping branches.*

Breeding Conditions	
CLUTCH SIZE	1 annual clutch
Jungle Carpet Python	9–28 eggs
Children's Python	7–20 eggs
Royal Python	1–11 eggs
Green Tree Python	6–30 eggs
INCUBATION	In moist vermiculite (0.8:1)
Jungle Carpet Python	52–60 days at 31–32°C (88–90°F)
Children's Python	53–56 days at 28–29°C (82–84°F)
Royal Python	53–60 days at 32°C (90°F)
Green Tree Python	45–52 days at 30–32°C (86–90°F)
TEMPERATURE	From hatchling to 6 months
Jungle Carpet Python	29°C (84°F)
Children's Python	28°C (82°F)
Royal Python	30°C (86°F)
Green Tree Python	28°C (82°F)

In the wild, females coil round the eggs to incubate them. This does not seem to work in captivity – it is difficult to manipulate environmental factors to produce the right conditions. Also, the female may not feed or drink while incubating, and can lose condition, rendering her unsuitable for breeding the following year. For all these reasons, artificial incubation works best.

After the pre-egg-laying slough, place a large plastic container lined with damp sphagnum moss in the female's vivarium. She will lay her eggs on the moss, and you can remove the whole container. Lift the moss and eggs out together and put them in a container of moist vermiculite, burying the eggs so that only the tops are showing. Python eggs need high air humidity during incubation, but if the vermiculite is wet rather than damp, the eggs will absorb too much moisture and may fail to hatch. Weigh the container and eggs at the outset. About 10–14 days before hatching, weigh them again. If the eggs are 10–40% heavier, hatching should be successful.

Young pythons may take hours or even days to emerge completely from their eggs. Be patient. After they have broken free, house them individually. Green Tree Pythons may produce both juvenile colour phases from the same clutch. Hatchling Jungle Carpet Pythons and Green Tree Pythons need perches and should be housed in their own small vivaria. Hatchling Children's Pythons can be housed in shoe boxes with a paper towel substrate, a hide and water bowl.

Q & A ...

● *Is it true that the hatchlings of Green Tree Pythons, Jungle Carpet Pythons and Children's Pythons tend to be aggressive?*

These young snakes are apt to rear up and strike. This is a defence mechanism and can be used to help them feed by wiggling a pink mouse in front of them. After a few weeks they become amenable to handling. No snake should ever be handled before or after feeding.

● *Can Children's Pythons be kept in a more natural set-up? Newspaper or carpet is not very attractive.*

Some keepers use dust-free sand, furnished with rocks and stumps, but this setup is more difficult to maintain. Spot-cleaning (using a sieve to separate faeces from sand) means the substrate remains clean for longer periods, but it will have to be replaced regularly.

● *My hatchling Children's Pythons refuse to accept mice, though many dealers recommend this as an ideal food for young. What else should I try?*

Some specimens readily accept pink mice; others need for the mice to be washed and dried first to remove their natural smell. For the most reluctant feeders, try scenting the mice with lizard skin or lizard egg.

● *Why are most Royal Python hatchlings available as imported specimens? Are they wild-caught?*

Large numbers of these snakes are imported, both as wild-caught and as captive-farmed specimens, and prices are relatively low. This has meant that until recently there was little commercial incentive to breed them in captivity in Europe and the US. True captive-bred specimens are sometimes available now. Your local herpetological society will be able to help.

◀ ▲ *Green Tree Pythons* (Morelia viridis) *change colour dramatically from hatching to adulthood. Hatchlings (left) may be a beautiful yellow or bright brick-red with white markings. As they grow, they gradually develop the adult colouring (above).*

Harmless Snakes FAMILY: COLUBRIDAE

OF AN ESTIMATED 2400 SPECIES OF SNAKE grouped in 13 or 14 families, the family Colubridae is by far the largest, containing more than 1500 species. Colubrids are highly diverse: terrestrial, arboreal, fossorial (adapted to burrowing) and aquatic forms exist. Most are harmless, but a few species are very poisonous.

With nearly all snakes, it is advisable to keep specimens separately. Individual cages can be heated by light bulbs controlled by a thermostat. Housing snakes in a rack system with heater mats and room lighting also works well.

The Colubrid family contains both egg-layers and livebearers. Breeding from immature snakes results in small clutches of undersized hatchlings; mating pairs should be mature and as close to their full size as possible to ensure healthy offspring. After Winter cooling, gradually restore the temperature and photoperiod to normal, and then offer food. Males usually accept 1 or 2 feeds before sloughing, then refuse food until mating is over. Females will accept a number of feeds before sloughing, after which they become receptive to male advances. Introduce the male to the female; if no mating occurs, remove the male and try again in 1 or 2 days.

KING SNAKES AND MILK SNAKES

Lampropeltis species. Native to the region from southern Canada all the way to South America as far as Colombia and Ecuador, these snakes are popular and are widely available through captive breeding. They are of medium length (24–66in/ 60–165cm), placid, easy to keep and attractive.

King snakes will eat other snakes, including venomous species. They must be housed separately. To mate, the male secures the female with a grip on her neck. Once mating is finished, they

---

Vivarium Conditions
King, Milk, Corn, American Rat, Pine, Gopher and Bull Snakes

VIVARIUM SIZE	**WINTER COOLING**
Snakes up to 30in (76cm) long require 24x24x18in (60x60x45cm).	**King, Milk, Corn and American Rat Snakes** Hibernate in darkness for 10–12 weeks at 9–10°C (48–50°F), or 12–15°C (54–60°F) for species from Central and South America.
Snakes 30–60in (76–152cm) long require 36x24x 18in (90x60x45cm).	
Snakes 60–102in (76–259cm) long require 72x24x 24in (180x60x60cm).	**Pine, Gopher and Bull Snakes** Hibernate in darkness for 8–12 weeks at 10°C (50°F).
SUBSTRATE Newspaper, dust-free shavings, or washable carpet-type material.	**FEEDING**
	King, Milk, Corn and American Rat Snakes Rodents of appropriate size. Some prefer mice or rat pups.
HABITAT Dry and well ventilated. 2 hide boxes, flat stone for food and rubbing against, sturdy water bowl. Branches can be fitted.	**Pine, Gopher and Bull Snakes** Rodents; quail chicks or day-old hen chicks.
TEMPERATURE	**INCUBATION** All species are egg-layers. Incubate in moist vermiculite.
King, Milk, Corn and American Rat Snakes 24°C (76°F) at cool end, 30°C (86°F) at hot spot; 19–23°C (66–74°F) at night. Photoperiod: 14 hours.	**King, Milk, Corn and American Rat Snakes** 1 annual clutch of 1–30 eggs depending on species. Incubate for 55–72 days at 25.5–29°C (78–84°F).
Pine, Gopher and Bull Snakes 26.5°C (80°F) at cool end, 30°C (86°F) at hot spot; 18–21°C (65–70°F) at night. Photoperiod: 12–14 hours.	**Pine, Gopher and Bull Snakes** 1 annual clutch of 3–20 eggs. Incubate for 75 days at 24–25.5°C (75–78°F).

The harmless Scarlet King Snake (Lampropeltis triangulum elapsoides) *looks very similar to the highly poisonous Coral Snake, but the red snout and yellow rings (divided from red bands by black rings) identify it.*

need to be separated; hungry females may try to grab and swallow a male. They continue feeding for 4–5 weeks before sloughing and laying eggs. Provide a plastic container with damp vermiculite topped with damp moss. The eggs are deposited 6–15 days after sloughing, and are laid in a clump, which should be kept together.

Remove the hatchlings without disturbing the unhatched eggs. They may be kept in shoe boxes or plastic sandwich boxes with ventilation holes. Provide a paper towel substrate, a small water bowl and hide. The boxes can be placed on a heater tape (snake strip or heater mat) to provide a maximum of 27–28°C (80–82°F). Young will not feed until after the first slough, usually at 6–10 days old. Thawed pink mice are accepted by most hatchlings. As they grow, transfer them to larger units and increase the size of the food.

● *How will I know when Colubrid eggs are close to hatching?*

... The eggs look as if the shell has stretched, then they begin to sweat, after which slits appear. There may be 7–9 days between the first and last eggs hatching.

● *What is meant by "double-clutching"?*

This is a very irresponsible practice by which some keepers manipulate conditions so that their snakes produce 2 clutches of eggs per breeding season. It can deplete the female's reserves and may result in smaller, weaker young.

● *My month-old hatchling king snake has not eaten. Should I start force-feeding it?*

Some new hatchlings may not eat for several weeks and slough a second (or even a third) time before feeding. Hatchlings retain a certain amount of nutrition from the egg yolk. So long as they are producing faeces, they are still using stored food. Be patient, and offer a pink mouse once a week. For Grey-banded and Mountain King Snakes, scenting pink mice with lizard skin or lizard egg may be effective.

◀ *A range of Corn Snakes* (Elaphe guttata) *showing various colour mutations. Some breeders have also developed pattern mutations such as stripes and zigzags.*

CORN AND AMERICAN RAT SNAKES

Elaphe species. These snakes are excellent for beginners: hardy, easy to feed and generally easy to breed. Ranging in length from 39in (100cm) to 102in (260cm), they are widespread across North America, Europe and Asia. As a group they tend to be crepuscular or nocturnal. Rat snakes are so called because they eat rats (as well as mice). Corn snakes and rat snakes are mainly terrestrial, but they are both accomplished climbers. Although individual temperament varies, captive-bred specimens are usually calmer than wild-caught ones. Breeding behaviour is very similar to *Lampropeltis* species.

Corn snakes show some considerable variation in colour. Certain natural forms are available under the names Okeetee and Miami Phase. More exotic mutations have been produced by selective breeding, but many keepers and breeders still prefer the normal form. Hatchling rat snakes have a bold pattern of dark spots or blotches, but usually these disappear with age.

PINE, GOPHER AND BULL SNAKES

Pituophis species. These robust snakes from the US and Mexico range in size from the Gopher Snake (*P. catenifer*) at some 66in (168cm) long to the Northern Pine Snake (*P. melanoleucus melanoleucus*) and the Bull Snake (*P. sayi*), both 100in (254cm) long. The taxonomy is in dispute; a number of subspecies exist, and some experts count the Bull Snake and Gopher Snake as subspecies of *P. melanoleucus*. All *Pituophis* species are popular in spite of their reputation for aggression: they hiss, strike and vibrate their tails. Captive-bred animals may not be as feisty, but handling equipment should be used, since bites can be serious. Their colouring is variable but the usual form is dark patches on a lighter background. Striped forms exist naturally, and patternless forms have been bred selectively.

Once copulation has begun, a male may bite the female's neck if she attempts to move away. Remove the male after mating and reintroduce him on a daily basis until several matings have occurred. Gravid females should be disturbed as little as possible – they tend to be slightly more "snappy" during this period. Supply a suitable box filled with 3in (8cm) of damp vermiculite for

➤ *The Florida Pine Snake* (Pituophis melanoleucus mugitus) *loves to burrow. Unlike many other snakes, it tends to be diurnal except in hot weather.*

● *My rat snake sometimes vibrates its tail in a threatening way. Should I be concerned?*

In captivity this behaviour is merely a defensive ploy. In the wild, however, rat snakes will often follow tail vibrating with rearing up, hissing and lunging forward.

● *Some breeders advertise Red Rat Snakes. Are these a new colour mutation?*

They are a subspecies of corn snake, *Elaphe gutatta rosacea*, also known as the Rosy Rat Snake, which has less black pigmentation than the corn snake.

● *What is a suitable hibernation medium for Pine, Gopher, and Bull Snakes?*

Several inches of sterilized potting soil may be used. Wood shavings (not cedar) or moss is also suitable. Generally speaking, the hibernation medium for most snakes must be dry, otherwise skin problems occur.

● *My young Pine, Gopher, and Bull Snakes tend to be aggressive when handled. Will they become more docile as they get older?*

Baby snakes often hiss and strike out through fear, but this stops when they become more used to being handled. Their bite is harmless when they are young.

oviposition. Females normally remain with their eggs for several days and may resist attempts to remove them for incubation. Rear the hatchlings separately in small ventilated containers using a paper towel substrate. Most hatchlings accept pink mice at first, until they are large enough to graduate to a more varied diet.

WESTERN HOGNOSED SNAKE

Heterodon nasicus. This crepuscular or nocturnal burrowing snake, native to the western US, is very popular with keepers. Attractive but not "flashy", it grows to 24–26in (60–65cm) long. The common name is derived from the hard, upturned scale on the upper lip which aids burrowing and digging out toads, its main prey. As with many burrowing snakes, the body is stout. The dorsum is brown, grey or yellow-grey with dark blotches and spots.

The Western Hognosed Snake breeds successfully in captivity. After Winter cooling, when the snakes have begun feeding, introduce the male to the female – preferably in the early evening when they have just emerged. It is usually advisable to remove hides and the water bowl before mating. If no mating occurs, the male should be

● *Why do Hognosed Snakes pretend to be dead?*

... This is a common response to danger, as a ploy to be left alone. They may writhe and thrash about, then "die" with an open mouth and protruding tongue.

● *Is the Hognosed Snake venomous at all?*

It is said that they produce a mild venom at the rear of the mouth, but there are no reports of keepers being harmed. Occasionally they hiss and strike but seldom bite. They could only inflict damage by "swallowing" a finger to make contact with the rear fangs.

● *How often should Red-sided Garters be fed?*

Babies every day, juveniles every other day, adults twice a week. They should be allowed to eat their fill. Gravid females can be fed as much as they will take.

● *My Red-sided Garter Snake appears to be having convulsions – it rears up, falls, gapes and moves very erratically. What could be wrong?*

These are the symptoms of thiaminase poisoning; expert veterinary treatment is needed.

➤ *The Western Hognosed Snake* (Heterodon nasicus) *makes a better vivarium subject than other hognosed snakes since it can adapt from its natural diet of toads.*

removed and reintroduced the next day. Several successful matings will increase the number of fertile eggs. Provide a box of damp sand covered with moss for oviposition.

Rear the hatchlings separately in small ventilated containers. Pink mice make suitable food, but if the young prove to be difficult feeders, the mice should be scented with frogs, toads, lizards, lizard eggs or chicks. Young do not need to be cooled for their first Winter.

RED-SIDED GARTER SNAKE

Thamnophis sirtalis parietalis. These medium-sized North American snakes have been popular in the hobby for many years. They grow to 20–30in (51–76cm) long and have a ground colour of olive, brown or black with two light lateral stripes and varying amounts of red on the sides.

Captive breeding is relatively easy, but many specimens are still caught in the wild. Initially wild specimens may strike, hiss and discharge an evil-smelling secretion from their anal glands, but they usually settle down with time. Litter size tends to increase with the female's age, peaking in the third year and then reducing. Sperm retention is not uncommon, so birth can be delayed by several months, sometimes extending through hibernation. The young are enclosed in a membrane from which they break free, and the keeper should provide extra humidity to prevent the membranes from drying out before the young emerge. Newborns require conditions similar to the adults. They have their first slough four or five days after birth, and will not feed until this has taken place. It is best to remove newborns and raise them separately.

⬆ *The Red-sided Garter Snake* (Thamnophis sirtalis parietalis) *lives near water in the wild, but damp vivarium conditions will cause skin and respiratory problems.*

Vivarium Conditions
Western Hognosed Snake and Red-sided Garter Snake

VIVARIUM SIZE 25x15x15in (60x38x38cm)	**WINTER COOLING**
SUBSTRATE	**Western Hognosed Snake** 8–12 weeks at 13°C (56°F). Photoperiod: 6 hours.
Western Hognosed Snake Dry, dust-free sand 3in (8cm) deep for burrowing.	**Red-sided Garter Snake** Hibernate in darkness for 12 weeks at 12–15°C (54–60°F) for central and southern species, 10°C (50°F) for northern species.
Red-sided Garter Snake Newspaper, dust-free shavings, or washable carpet-type material.	
HABITAT 2 hide boxes, a flat stone to put food on and for rubbing against, a sturdy water bowl. Branches are optional for the Red-sided Garter Snake; some firmly bedded rocks are needed for the Western Hognosed Snake.	**FEEDING**
	Western Hognosed Snake Rodents of appropriate size. Some prefer mice or rat pups.
	Red-sided Garter Snake Frogs, earthworms and whole fish (including bones). Pink mice scented with fish. Special food is available from dealers.
TEMPERATURE	**INCUBATION**
Western Hognosed Snake 21°C (70°F) at cool end, 28°C (82°F) at hot spot; 18°C (65°F) at night. Photoperiod: 14 hours.	**Western Hognosed Snake** Egg-layer. 1 annual clutch of up to 24 eggs. Incubate for 45–55 days at 28°C (82°F) in moist vermiculite.
Red-sided Garter Snake 20°C (68°F) at cool end, 30°C (86°F) at hot spot; 18°C (65°F) at night. Photoperiod: 12–14 hours.	**Red-sided Garter Snake** Livebearer. Litter of up to 30 young. Gestation: 3–4 months.

Dekay's Snake (Storeria dekayi) *has an impressive threat display that makes it appear as if it will strike, but its worst tactic is discharging its anal scent glands.*

Vivarium Conditions
Dekay's Snake and Rough Green Snake

VIVARIUM SIZE

Dekay's Snake   24x12x12in (60x30x30cm) for up to 6 specimens.

Rough Green Snake   24x18x36in (60x45x90cm) for up to 8 specimens.

SUBSTRATE   2–3in (5–8cm) of loamy soil covered with large bark chips and moss.

HABITAT   Well ventilated. Cork bark hides. Small water dish. Spray daily. Potted plants and climbing branches for Rough Green Snake.

TEMPERATURE   Full-spectrum (UVB) light

Dekay's Snake   24.5°C (76°F) at cool end, 28°C (82°F) at hot spot; 14–15°C (58–60°F) at night. Photoperiod: 12–14 hours.

Rough Green Snake   24.5°C (76°F) at cool end, 30°C (86°F) at hot spot; 14–15°C (58–60°F) at night. Photoperiod: 14 hours.

WINTER COOLING   8–12 weeks at 10–12°C (50–55°F). Photoperiod: normal daylight.

FEEDING

Dekay's Snake   Soft-bodied slugs, earthworms

Rough Green Snake   Dusted crickets

INCUBATION

Dekay's Snake   Livebearer. Litter of up to 30 young. Gestation: 4 months.

Rough Green Snake   Egg-layer. 1–2 annual clutches of 2–7 eggs. Incubate for 40–45 days at 28°C (82°F) in moist vermiculite.

DEKAY'S SNAKE

Storeria dekayi. Sometimes known as the Brown Snake, this species, which grows to an average adult length of 9–14in (23–33cm), is found from southern Canada through the US to Mexico and Honduras. Pollution and the destruction of their native marsh and woodland habitat have depleted populations. Dekay's Snakes are often found near water but are not aquatic. Secretive and mainly crepuscular, they occasionally bask in the daytime. Wild specimens flatten the body, curl the lips and draw back the head into a threatening S-posture. When unused to being handled, they discharge the anal scent glands, but this will stop with time. This insectivorous species is ideal for keepers who do not like the idea of feeding their charges with mammals.

Dekay's Snakes are livebearers. Adult females are usually slightly longer and stouter than the males, and have a shorter tail. Mating occurs in Spring and possibly in Autumn, with the young being born between June and September. Newborns measure some 3.75–4.5in (8–11cm) and are plain brown with a yellow collar. A light spraying at the time of birth will help prevent them from adhering to the substrate, but too much moisture can cause the substrate to compact and suffocate the young.

Babies should be removed to a small vivarium which is slightly more moist but also has a dry area. Finding tiny live foods can be a problem – some US keepers try to solve it by releasing the young snakes into the wild. You must ALWAYS seek expert advice from a local herpetological society before attempting to do this.

ROUGH GREEN SNAKE

Opheodrys aestivus. This harmless North American diurnal snake is sometimes referred to, incorrectly, as the Vine Snake. Its native range extends from New Jersey to the Florida Keys, west as far as Texas and Kansas, and south into Mexico. Rough Green Snakes can move very quickly and they sometimes leap out when the cage is opened. They have a reputation for being difficult to keep in captivity, but with proper care and conditions they will breed regularly.

Males grow to a length of 22–28in (55–70cm); females to 32–34in (80–86cm). Females have a thicker body, and the males have longer tails. The dorsum is an attractive light green, with a white to pale yellow belly. There may be blue dots along the anterior sides.

After Winter cooling, the eggs are laid, usually in April in the northern hemisphere. Another clutch may be produced later in the year. The eggs are buried where there is sufficient dampness, in or under flowerpots, under cork bark or in the substrate. The young measure 6–9in (15–23cm) and slough 5 or 6 days after hatching before starting to feed. Keep them in glass food storage jars with a nylon mesh cover and a layer of sphagnum moss on the floor. A light daily spray will provide drinking water and humidity. After they begin to feed, they can be removed to a small vivarium similar to that of the adults.

● *Can other small snakes be kept with Dekay's Snake?*

... It is not advisable in case the other species are cannibalistic.

● *Can Dekay's Snake be kept in groups?*

You should be able to keep Dekay's Snake in groups of up to 10 (both sexes) without any problems.

● *Is the Rough Green Snake easy to tame?*

If unused to handling it will thrash about and discharge a strong-smelling fluid when picked up. It seldom bites, and its small teeth cannot cause serious damage.

● *Do Rough Green Snakes need a water area?*

In the wild they enter water occasionally, but it is not necessary in captivity. They lap spray water from their habitat, but a small water dish should be provided.

➤ *The Rough Green Snake* (Opheodrys aestivus) *is very swift-moving and agile. It is also sociable and will coexist peacefully with other members of its species.*

Snapping Turtle

FAMILY: CHELYDRIDAE
SPECIES: CHELYDRA SERPENTINA

THESE TOUGH, FEISTY TURTLES ARE FOUND all along the eastern seaboard of North America from southern Canada to the Gulf of Mexico. Despite their very unattractive appearance and aggressive temperament, Snappers are hugely popular. They have large heads with hooked jaws that can gape open even when the head is partially withdrawn. Full withdrawal of the head and the legs is prevented by a small, cross-shaped plastron. The long tail bears a ridge of toothlike scales. Their colouring varies from black to light brown or tan, with grey on the soft parts. Babies have a light spot on each marginal scute of the carapace. Because of salmonella scares blamed on baby turtles, US law forbids the sale of turtles with a shell-length of less than 4in (10cm). But hatchlings of several species, including Snappers, are regularly exported to Britain and Europe.

An adult Snapper can measure 18in (45cm) long. At this size, many turtles have outgrown their quarters and their owners' commitment, and they are often dumped. Only people who are seriously interested should acquire this species. However, Snappers are highly adaptable in the wild and easy to cater for in captivity if there is adequate space. Although mainly aquatic, they also bask on land or rocks. An aquarium should have rocks projecting from the water so that they offer a dry surface, and an outdoor pool should have at least a small land area beside it. The young turtles are particularly fond of basking. All Snappers are very aggressive, particularly at feeding time, and are best kept individually. Always use long forceps for feeding.

Adults may be left outdoors during a cold winter. They will remain at the bottom of the pool, under a layer of ice, if airholes are cut in the top. A deeper pool is less likely to freeze solid, and will provide relief in a hot climate; it may also be partly shaded. Water may look clean even when it is fouled with uneaten food and waste. Dirty water causes diseases, especially eye problems, and must be changed regularly – a big chore for a large tank. Filtration systems can be installed, but turtles do not like turbulent water and partial changes will still be needed. (For information on pools, see Housing, pages 16–17.) If a heater is required, cover it to prevent burns.

Space for Breeding

The captive breeding of Snappers is not practical for most private keepers as it requires a huge amount of space, but it is possible in an outdoor enclosure. Mating usually occurs between April and November in the northern hemisphere, but the peak laying time is in June. Sperm retention often occurs in females, sometimes for up to several years. Eggs and hatchlings may remain in the nest over winter, but after that, hatchlings are better reared individually in small aquaria. They must not be put in the same pool with adults.

Aquarium Conditions	
Aquarium size	Min 72x36x24in (180x90x 60cm) for adults indoors. An outdoor enclosure is best, with a pool, min 60x48in (150x120cm) and 12–18in (30–45cm) deep, and dry land.
Substrate	None, for hygiene
Habitat	Exposed rocks for basking
Temperature	For indoor habitat. Water: 23–25.5°C (74–78°F) during day, 15°C (60°F) at night. Land: 23–25.5°C (74–78°F) at cool end, 29–30°C (84–86°F) at hot spot. Full-spectrum (UVB) light and basking lamp over rocks.
Winter cooling	Max 5°C (41°F) for 8 weeks in water. Photoperiod: normal daylight hours.
Feeding	Varied diet: whole fish, snails, crayfish, earthworms, thawed mice, quail chicks, day-old hen chicks, aquatic insects, shrimps and aquarium plants. Float small pieces of cuttlefish bone to provide extra calcium.
Incubation	1 annual clutch of 25–50 eggs. Incubate for 63–70 days at 30°C (86°F) in moist vermiculite (1:1).

Q&A...

● *How should I handle a Snapper?*

Snappers have a very powerful bite which can cause serious injury. Handle them by the tail and keep them well clear of your body. The head can quickly swing round to bite. They are extremely aggressive when out of water and have been seen to "charge" the owner, attempting to bite his or her feet!

● *Is full-spectrum (UVB) lighting always necessary?*

It would be most beneficial for juvenile turtles kept indoors, although even these often seem to thrive without it as long as their diet is adequate.

● *How often should I change the water?*

If the pool has no filtration system, water should be changed 70–100% weekly. An efficient filtration system will reduce this to around 20–50% per week. A good book on aquarium care should give information on mechanical and biological filtration, and the importance of the nitrogen cycle – the process by which waste is converted to nitrogen.

● *Can aquarium gravel be used a substrate?*

Aquarium gravel is often used, but it will harbour small food particles, and removing it for rinsing is a laborious task unless the tank is very small. Of course, gravel is necessary with an undergravel filtration system.

● *Is it possible to use plants in the aquarium?*

Not really. Many turtles and terrapins, including Snappers, will eat plants or dig them up. Decorative planting is impossible.

● *Can I feed fresh meat to my snapper?*

Lean raw beef is acceptable in small quantities. It is high in phosphorus and low in calcium, and too much of such food can contribute to metabolic bone disease (MBD; see Health and Disease, pages 44–45). If used at all, the beef should have calcium ground in. Animal fats and tinned pet foods should be avoided.

➤ *A Snapping Turtle* (Chelydra serpentina) *needs a varied diet with plenty of calcium. Too much fatty food and not enough swimming space leads to obesity.*

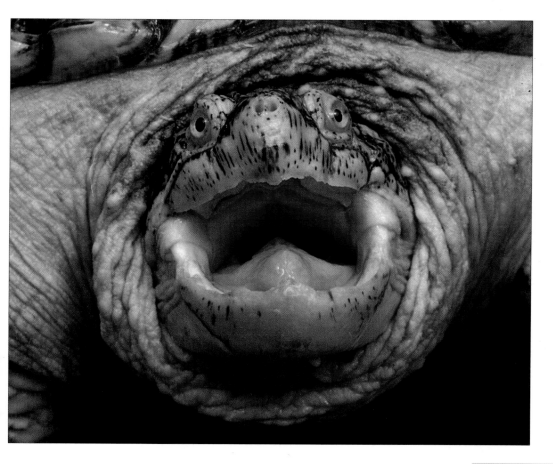

Freshwater Turtles

FAMILY: EMYDIDAE

THIS FAMILY BELONGS TO THE SUBORDER Cryptodira (hidden necks) – its members are able to retract their necks by means of an S-shaped bend in the vertebral column. They are missing 2 intermediate scutes between the carapace and plastron, and in certain species the plastron may be hinged. All species of Emydidae are semi-aquatic and inhabit fresh water. Like other chelonians, they are egg-layers. Although mainly carnivorous, they may also eat varying amounts of plant material, especially the adults.

EUROPEAN POND TURTLE

Emys orbicularis. This species is found throughout Europe, except in the northern and central regions, and is also present in western Asia and northern Africa. Large numbers of hatchlings

▲ *Adult European Pond Turtles* (Emys orbicularis) *are good outdoor subjects. Sunlight helps them dry out so that their soft parts do not develop fungus.*

were formerly exported for the trade, but it is mainly larger specimens that tend to be available now; smaller ones are subject to controls. The oval-shaped carapace is dark with light spots or streaks, and bears a central ridge which disappears with age. The head also has light markings. Adults' shells may reach 12in (30cm) in length.

The European Pond Turtle is a good outdoor subject. It thrives with access to sunlight. If kept indoors, the aquarium must not be covered with glass – it creates a humid atmosphere, and semi-aquatic turtles such as these need to dry out completely. If unable to do so, their soft parts can develop fungus disease (see Health and Disease, pages 44–45). European Pond Turtles may not eat much plant material even as adults.

Mating occurs in Spring to early Summer in the northern hemisphere. Females may store sperm for up to several years. Males can usually be distinguished by their concave plastron and enlarged tailbase. For egg deposition, a suitable area of sandy soil, 12in (30cm) deep, should be provided – this is difficult in all but a very large aquarium. Successful breeding is more likely in a large outdoor enclosure.

Another species requiring similar treatment is the Strip-Necked Turtle (*Mauremys caspica*), formerly classed as two separate species: *Clemmys caspica* and *C. leprosa*.

REEVES' TURTLE

Chinemys reevesi. These small, hardy Asian terrapins have been common in the trade for some years, usually as hatchlings or small specimens. Native to Korea and central and southeastern China, Reeves' have also been introduced into Japan. They are relatively easy to keep. The maximum adult shell length is 8.5in (22cm); housing space does not need to be large. Although they lack bright colouring, they are engaging creatures and can become quite tame. The carapace is dark brown to black; the plastron yellow with dark spots. The neck is striped and the face has a network of light yellow to silver-grey markings. This is an ideal species for outside enclosures. Winter protection will be needed in some areas.

Males possess a thicker tail and have a slightly concave plastron. Reeves' Turtle can be bred in captivity, but spacious quarters are needed; a pool of minimum size 36x36in (90x90cm) is required with a land area for oviposition. Males approach females head-on, butting their head and simultaneously opening and closing the mouth. Unreceptive females will snap at the male to repel him. To prevent bullying, males of disparate sizes should not be kept together. After a successful mating eggs are buried and must be removed for incubation. The young may not feed for several days until they have used up the absorbed yolk. Small aquatic insects and other foods should be supplied. Shallow water (twice the shell depth) and basking facilities are needed.

● *Can I mix turtles and tortoises?*

Generally it is better not to mix species and sizes. Some species are aggressive. Small specimens may be harassed and will lose out at feeding time.

● *Are turtle bowls suitable for babies?*

No, they are too small. Even a plastic tray 18x12x5in (45x30x12cm) used for a hatchling will soon be outgrown, and it is difficult to provide a basking lamp and suspension of full-spectrum (UVB) light over such a container. The best solution is to put babies in their own small aquarium with similar conditions to the adults. Ensure the water is shallow (no more than twice their shell depth) and that the babies do not overheat.

● *Can the pool be planted?*

Large pools can be planted but this reduces space for swimming and feeding. A small planted pool would be difficult to clean and plants would probably be dug up.

● *Can hardy turtles survive Winter outdoors?*

Members of the family Emydidae are not as hardy as the much larger Snapping Turtles. Although European Pond and Reeves Turtles are hardy, they should not be exposed to temperatures below those recommended for hibernation. In cold climates it may be easier to remove them from the pool when they become sluggish in the Autumn, and transfer them to individual hibernation boxes with damp leaves or moss. Put the boxes in a cool place and monitor temperatures. (See Breeding, pages 35–37, for a discussion of hibernation; also see Box Turtles, pages 130–131.)

◥ *Reeves' Turtle* (Chinemys reevesi) *is the only* Chinemys *species widely imported from Asia; the others both lack keels. It is not fond of plant material.*

MISSISSIPPI MAP TURTLE

Graptemys kohni. This species from the south-central United States belongs to a genus with 9 or 10 species, including other map turtles and "sawbacks". Some of these have a limited distribution and their habits in the wild are poorly known. Map turtles have been overexploited in the past; you should investigate their legal status before acquiring any. "Farmed" hatchlings of *G. kohni* are still exported, although the "4-inch Law" applies within the US (see Starting Out, pages 4–5). Babies have a light-brown carapace with circular markings, a dark "toothed" keel and an intricate design on the plastron, but this colouring fades as they mature. The soft parts are striped, and a crescent-shaped mark behind the eyes distinguishes this species. The eyes are white with a dark pupil. Adult Mississippi Map Turtles may reach 10in (25cm) in length but are usually smaller. They are particularly fond of snails and freshwater molluscs, but they tend to become more herbivorous with age.

Hatchlings of this species are prone to fungus if kept too cool and not able to dry out by basking. They may also have difficulty adjusting their buoyancy; water depth should be no more than twice the height of the shell initially. Calcium is particularly important in their diet.

Males are smaller than females and have elongated claws on their forelegs. Breeding of this species by hobbyists is uncommon, and breeding habits in the wild are still poorly known. Outdoor breeding is far more likely to be successful. An area of soft soil will be used to bury the eggs.

Other species requiring similar treatment are the Map Turtle (*G. geographica*) and the False Map Turtle (*G. pseudogeographica*).

SOUTHERN PAINTED TURTLE

Chrysemys picta dorsalis. The members of this genus, found in the central US from southern Illinois to the Gulf of Mexico, have long been popular in the hobby for their bright red colouring. Like other painted turtles, the Southern

Aquarium Conditions
European Pond, Reeves', Mississippi Map and Southern Painted Turtles

AQUARIUM SIZE   Indoors: smaller specimens 30x12x12in (75x30x30cm), large adults min 48x 15x15in (120x38x38cm) with water 8–12in (20–30cm) deep. Outdoors: a large enclosure with access to unfiltered sunlight and a pool min 60x24x10in (150x60x25cm). This is preferable to indoors, especially for adult specimens.

SUBSTRATE   Indoors: none for an indoor aquarium, for hygiene. Outdoors: soil or grass.

HABITAT   A dry basking area such as exposed rocks if indoors. A small sunny land area outdoors.

TEMPERATURE   If kept indoors, all species require a photoperiod of 12–14 hours , a full-spectrum (UVB) light and basking lamp with a hot spot at 29–30°C (84–86°F). The UVB must not be filtered through glass. The following figures are water temperatures for both indoors and outdoors.

European Pond Turtle   25.5–26.5°C (78–89°F) during day; 13–16.5°C (55–62°F) at night.

Reeves' Turtle   22–28°C (71–82°F) during day; 15–20°C (60–68°F) at night

Others   25.5–26.5°C (78–79°F) during day; 20–21°C (68–70°F) at night.

WINTER COOLING   Outdoors if climate permits.

European Pond Turtle   5°C (41°F) for 6–8 weeks under water or in damp leaves or moss.

Reeves' Turtle   7–10°C (45–50°F) for 6–8 weeks. Will hibernate under water or in a box of damp leaves or moss.

Others   Larger specimens: 10–13°C (50–55°F) for 6–8 weeks in water. Smaller specimens: no cooling.

FEEDING   As for Snapping Turtles (page 124) but smaller. *Elodea* or similar plants. Small pieces of cuttlefish bone in the water.

INCUBATION   In moist vermiculite

European Pond Turtle   1 annual clutch of up to 16 eggs. Incubate for 78–80 days at 29–30°C (84–86°F).

Reeves Turtle   1 annual clutch of 2–3 eggs. Incubate for 70–80 days at 25–32°C (77–90°F).

Mississippi Map Turtle   1 annual clutch of up to 12 eggs. Incubate for 70–86 days at 27–30°C (80–86°F).

Southern Painted Turtle   1 annual clutch of 3–15 eggs. Incubate for 68–80 days at 27°C (80°F).

● *Can my baby Map Turtle be placed outside on a sunny day?*

... Sunlight is beneficial but babies could soon overheat in a small, shallow container. Some shade must be available and the period limited according to the temperature.

● *Will Map Turtles eat crickets?*

They can be used, and most aquatic turtles will eat them, but they are not a healthy food because they are low in calcium and high in phosphorus. Also, too many crickets in the aquarium will pollute the water. When they are dropped into the water, they drown; any that remain uneaten they should be removed.

● *When are Southern Painted Turtles mature – how do I know if one is old enough to purchase?*

It is not possible to tell the age of a wild-caught specimen, but a mature male is 3–4in (8–10cm) long, and a female 4–5in (10–12cm). Anything larger than 2in (5cm) is well on its way to maturity and should be reasonably easy to maintain under normal aquarium conditions, even for an inexperienced keeper. With correct treatment, a young adult may live as long as 20 years. Winter hibernation both prolongs the growth period (as growth is suspended for several months) and increases the lifespan.

A female Southern Painted Turtle (Chrysemys picta dorsalis) *can be identified by her short claws. Males use their longer claws to "tickle" females during courtship.*

Painted Turtle is not large; most are under 6in (15cm). They have a broad red to orange stripe along the centre of the dark carapace, and red markings along the marginal scutes. The plastron is light and may have one or two dark spots. Farmed hatchlings are still exported to Europe in substantial numbers, but an inexperienced keeper should begin with specimens that are at least partly grown, as hatchlings need complicated care. Southern Painted Turtles may not need to hibernate in the southern part of their range. In captivity in a warm climate they will remain in the water but may not feed.

Adult males are smaller with elongated claws on the forelegs, a long tail with a thickened base and a slightly concave plastron. As with most turtles, breeding is more likely to occur in an outdoor enclosure, although in some years they may miss breeding altogether.

Other species requiring similar treatment are the groups of turtles known as sliders (*Trachemys* species) and cooters (*Chrysemys* species).

Box Turtles

FAMILY: EMYDIDAE
GENUS: TERRAPENE

THESE SMALL TURTLES FROM THE EASTERN half of the US get their common name from their hinged plastron, which can be completely closed. Most familiar in the pet trade are the subspecies of the Common Box Turtle (*Terrapene carolina*) and those of the Ornate Box Turtle (*T. ornata*). The Spotted Box Turtle (*T. nelsoni*) and the Coahuila Box Turtle (*T. coahuila*) are rare and not seen in the trade. Individuals vary from 4–7in (10–28cm) according to species.

Concern over the collecting and trading of box turtles has meant ever-increasing legislation, so that it is now illegal to collect, sell and possibly even to keep them in some states of the US – you must check with the local environmental agency. However, certain subspecies are still exported.

Box turtles are most suited to an outdoor existence as long as the climate is favourable. The next best choice is a whole or part of a room. In the wild they often inhabit moist regions or areas near standing water, but they will adapt to a terrestrial existence. Outdoors, sunlight must not be filtered through glass or plastic, and shade must be available; hot, dry conditions lead to health problems. Indoors, heat may be provided by a spot lamp with dimmer thermostat. If conditions are unsuitable, the turtles may refuse to eat, though they may also fast even if nothing is wrong. Mushrooms and berries are apparently favoured; small quantities of boiled egg may be accepted. Food should be chopped small and mixed thoroughly. Like all chelonians, box turtles can be prone to vitamin A deficiency. Given the correct conditions, they typically live at least 30 to 40 years; there are claims of family pets that have survived for 100 years.

The basic rules for hibernation should be followed (see Breeding, pages 35–37). Outdoors, the turtles bury themselves; heap dead leaves or moss over the site. Cover the enclosure with old carpets for extra protection against frost. Box turtles can hibernate in this way at around 5°C (41°F); lower temperatures are fatal. If a hibernating box is used, it should be well ventilated and have a deep, loose, moist medium such as leaves, moss or potting soil, squeezed until no more moisture exudes. Check the box regularly for drying or signs of any respiratory trouble.

Vivarium Conditions

VIVARIUM SIZE Min 36x24x15in (90x60x38cm) for 1 specimen. Outdoors if the climate is suitable; 72x72x48in (180x180x 122cm) enclosure.

SUBSTRATE

Indoors 2–4in (5–10cm) deep loose, moisture-retentive material.

Outdoors 8–12in (20–30cm) deep loose soil planted with grass and weeds.

HABITAT

Indoors Shallow tray. Spray daily. 2 or more hides of cork bark, half-round pipes or wooden boxes.

Outdoors Deep walls as box turtles can dig and climb. Divided cover: 1 part mesh, the other clear plastic. Hides and shallow pool with easy access. Rotting logs to attract insects. Spray daily.

TEMPERATURE (indoors) 22–24°C (72–76°F) at cool end, max 28°C°(82°F) at hot spot; 15°C (60°F) at night. Provide full-spectrum (UVB) light.

WINTER COOLING 5°C (41°F) for 8–12 weeks for most; 8–10°C (46–50°F) for 7–8 weeks if from southern part of range.

FEEDING Omnivorous: insects and larvae, thawed pink mice, earthworms, snails and a varied herbivore diet. Canned commercial box turtle foods, canned low-fat dog food. Vitamin supplements once a week, extra calcium twice a week. Place food dish on a broad, flat stone to avoid food being pulled into substrate.

INCUBATION 1 or more annual clutches of 3–5 eggs. Incubate for 70–80 days at 26°C (79°F) in moist vermiculite.

● *What are the symptoms of Vitamin A deficiency?*

... They include closed eyes, clear discharge from the nose – peeling or thickening of the skin. Other factors such as infection may be involved. Consult a veterinarian for advice.

● *I read about turtles brumating. What does it mean?*

Brumation is only partial hibernation (see Breeding, pages 35–37). If normal temperatures are maintained over Winter, box turtles will brumate – they will stop feeding and use up reserves. In this condition they will become weak and may die, so hibernation is essential.

● *What should I do if the hibernating box is dry?*

Spray the box lightly as needed, but overwetting must be avoided; dampness causes respiratory problems.

● *Can several box turtles be housed together?*

Yes, they are fairly sociable. Avoid overcrowding, which leads to poor hygiene and disease. Keep species and subspecies apart to prevent interbreeding.

◀ *Ornate Box Turtles* (Terrapene ornata) *may fast during hot weather. Spray their hiding place daily as needed to provide a retreat from the heat.*

Mating at Any Time of Year

Male box turtles have a concave plastron (except in *T. ornata*) and a longer, thicker tail than the females. Their eyes are often red, whereas those of females yellow-brown. Mating can occur at any time of the year if the sexes are kept together, so keep them separately unless you want to breed them. When hibernation is over and both are feeding well, put the sexes together. The female lays her eggs and buries them in soft soil. Incubating them at slightly higher temperatures (29–30°C/84–86°F) produces mostly females; lower temperatures (22°C/72°F), mainly males. Hatchlings require similar treatment to adults but their diet is mainly carnivorous and insectivorous. They should not be housed with their parents to avoid the transfer of any parasites.

Tortoises FAMILY: TESTUDINIDAE

TORTOISES ARE HUGELY POPULAR REPTILES, and they are not especially difficult to keep, but the majority survive less than 2 years as pets due to their keepers' ignorance of correct treatment. Many of them die during their first Winter in a cold climate. An improper diet can cause shell deformity and an overgrown beak; damp conditions, crowding and poor hygiene promote respiratory problems. Shells crack if dropped – or gnawed by the family dog (this does happen). The shell should be given regular gentle scrubbing with a soft brush and tepid water to prevent bacterial infection. Finally, a number of losses are caused by tortoises digging or climbing out of their vivarium or enclosure and wandering away for ever. Properly constructed quarters prevent this happening (see Housing, pages 16–17).

MEDITERRANEAN TORTOISES

Testudo and *Agrionemys* species. This group of tortoises is found throughout the Mediterranean to the Middle East and Asia Minor. The "Greek" or Spur-thighed (*T. graeca graeca*) Tortoise and Hermann's (*T. hermanni*) tortoise are the most commonly available. Some species are rare or protected; only Horsfield's Tortoise (*Agrionemys horsfieldi*) may still be exported from the wild.

Mediterranean tortoises, especially Horsfield's Tortoise, may not do well in high humidity. They need dry, sunny conditions, preferably outside;

◀ *The Greek Tortoise* (Testudo graeca graeca) *has been put under controls in response to its high mortality rate in northern Europe. Along with Hermann's Tortoise* (T. hermanni), *it is now captive-bred.*

in cooler climates, outdoor and indoor facilities must be combined. A vivarium is not suitable for the large specimens, which can measure up to 14in (35cm). A spotlamp (white light) is better than a heat mat or ceramic heater – tortoises are attracted to visible beams. They bask to raise their body temperature, but as air temperatures approach 29.5°C (85°F) they seek shade.

Males have a longer, thicker tail and may have a concave plastron. They should be kept separately from females except for mating; gravid females can be aggressive, and prefer their own quarters for oviposition. A 12in (30cm) depth of loose sand or soil is needed. Sperm can be stored, and the gestation period may vary from 2–30 months (2 months is more common). Air temperatures at the high end of normal conditions and soil surface temperature 29.5°C (85°F) are

Vivarium Conditions
Mediterranean Tortoises

Vivarium size   Min 72x72x36in (180x180x 90cm) indoors. Adults are better housed in an outdoor enclosure in a suitable climate.

Substrate Indoors: dry, dust-free sand. Outdoors: avoid waterlogged areas and hard surfaces such as patios which can abrade the plastron.

Habitat Indoors: several hides. Outdoors: shade, low shrubs, wooden shelters. A hide box with hay in it for cool nights. Supply a shallow water bowl both indoors and outdoors.

Temperature For indoors: 20–25.5°C (68–78°F) at cool end, 35°C (95°F) at hot spot; 10–15°C (50–60°F) at night. Photoperiod: 14 hours. High-percentage, full-spectrum (UVB) light and a basking lamp are needed.

Winter cooling 5–6°C (41–43°F) for 8–12 weeks. Photoperiod: normal daylight (tortoise is buried).

Feeding   Varied herbivorous diet with leafy vegetables and wild plants; 8–10% calcium by weight – it can be sprinkled on the food as powder and supplied as small pieces of cuttlefish bone. Max 15% fruit. No animal protein. Use vitamins sparingly, especially if kept outdoors. Place food dish on a flat stone.

Incubation   2–3 annual clutches of 6–9 eggs. Incubate 120–160 days at 26–33°C (79–92°F) in moist vermiculite with 70–80% air humidity.

● *How do tortoises prepare for hibernation?*

... In Autumn, the tortoise stops feeding, becomes sluggish and tries to bury itself. Only healthy, well-fed tortoises should be hibernated; sick or malnourished ones will not survive.

● *What kind of quarters does a hibernating Mediterranean Tortoise need?*

If the earth is dry, give them extra frost and rain protection or remove to a large plastic bin (1) buried in the soil and filled with dry peat. Use a broad waterproof cover to keep rain out; leave ventilation space between it and the peat. Alternatively, use a hibernation box (2) in a frost-free outhouse. The box must be at least 24x24x24in (60x60x60cm) with a smaller box (20x20x20in/ 50x50x50cm) inside a layer of wood shavings, styrofoam chips, etc. The inner box should contain dry peat. Stand the box on a large slab of styrofoam and provide ventilation. For both, tape an external thermometer sensor to the tortoise's shell.

● *What should I do at the end of hibernation?*

Provide a shallow, tepid bath and plenty of drinking water to lubricate the mouth and internal organs.

OUTDOORS (1)

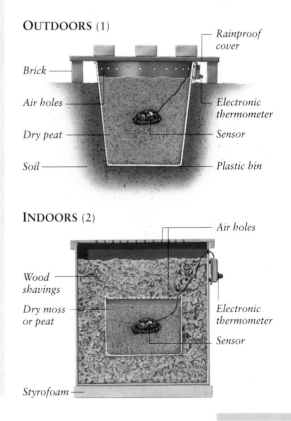

INDOORS (2)

ideal for oviposition. If no suitable site is available, the eggs may be retained and become over-calcified, causing dystocia (egg retention) in the female (see Health and Disease, pages 42–43). Bird incubators (non-turning) may be used for incubation to control the humidity.

Hatchlings should not be disturbed until they have left the egg. An open pen with newspaper substrate, overhead basking lamp and full-spectrum fluorescent light is suitable. Maintain the young at the same temperatures as for adults. They should also be fed the same food, but items need to be finely chopped or grated and mixed well. Supplements are important, especially calcium. A tepid bath twice a week is useful to clean the shell and prevent dehydration.

RED-FOOTED TORTOISE

Chelonoidis carbonaria. These popular South American tortoises (which were previously classified as *Geochelone carbonaria*) are found east and west of the Andes in tropical rainforests. They are highly attractive, with red and yellow scales on the head and legs. Their eventual large size (up to 20in/50cm) means they that will soon outgrow a vivarium. They are not suited to dry conditions, and keepers living in areas of natural high humidity have an advantage if attempting to keep them outdoors. Calcium is particularly important for young and for gravid females.

Male Red-foots have a deep concave plastron and a longer, thicker tail. They tend to be aggressive to each other, often biting heads and legs or attempting to overturn rivals – another reason why spacious quarters are needed. Breeding can occur at almost any time of year if the sexes are kept together, but eggs are usually laid between August and March in the northern hemisphere with appropriate temperatures. Eggs are buried up to 9in (22cm) deep in soil, which is first moistened with urine to soften it. After having mated, the sexes should be kept apart. Any troublesome individuals should also be kept separately.

Place all the young in a clean plastic container and leave them until the yolk sac is absorbed. High humidity, about 90–95%, is essential to prevent premature desiccation of the yolk sac. Soon after the sac has been absorbed, the young

Vivarium Conditions
Red-Footed Tortoise, Leopard Tortoise and Pancake Tortoise

VIVARIUM SIZE For a pair. Larger species are best housed outdoors in suitable climate.		**Leopard Tortoise** 28°C (82°F) at cool end, 35°C (95°F) at hot spot; 18–20°C (65–68°F) at night. Photoperiod: 14 hours.	
Pancake Tortoise 48x30x18in (122x75x45cm)		**Pancake Tortoise** 24°C (75°F) at cool end, 32°C (92°F) at hot spot; 13–15°C (55–60°F) at night. Photoperiod: 14 hours.	
Others Min 96x96x24in (240x240x60cm); ideally, whole or part of a room if indoors.		**HUMIDITY** Red-footed Tortoise only: 85–90%	
SUBSTRATE 2–3in (5–8cm) deep		**WINTER COOLING** Leopard Tortoise only: 7–8 weeks at 25°C (77°F). Photoperiod: 10 hours.	
Red-footed Tortoise Loam or leaf litter		**FEEDING** Varied herbivorous diet (see Foods and Feeding, pages 30–31) with max 20% fruit. Mushrooms, bean sprouts, green beans, broad beans, alfalfa. Vitamins given sparingly if kept outdoors.	
Others Dry, dust-free sand			
HABITAT Keep outside if in a warm climate. Move to heated indoor quarters in cool weather.		**INCUBATION** In moist vermiculite	
Red-footed Tortoise Shade or hides; shallow water dish for drinking and bathing. Spray daily.		**Red-footed Tortoise** 2–3 annual clutches of 3–7 eggs. Incubate for 120–170 days at a constant 28–30°C (82–86°F).	
Others Several hides; small water bowl. Keep conditions dry and ventilate well. No live plants.		**Leopard Tortoise** 2–3 annual clutches of 5–12 eggs. Incubate for 96–180 days at 27–30°C (80-86°F).	
TEMPERATURE For indoors. Provide full-spectrum (UVB) light and basking lamps.		**Pancake Tortoise** 2–3 annual clutches of 1 egg. Incubate for 150–200 days at 29–30°C (84–86°F).	
Red-footed Tortoise 24°C (75°F) at cool end, 32°C (92°F) at hot spot; min 22°C (72°F) at night. Photoperiod: 12–14 hours.			

Red-footed Tortoises (Chelonoidis carbonaria)
require special conditions and are not for the novice.
This specimen is a hatchling – note the egg tooth, which
is for slitting the shell. It drops off soon after hatching.

should be offered food – soft fruit and vegetables, mashed to a smooth consistency with vitamin and calcium supplements. Once they begin feeding, transfer the young to their own vivarium with 90% humidity and reduced the humidity to 85%. A daily tepid bath in shallow water should be given for about half an hour.

Other species requiring similar treatment: Yellow-footed Tortoise (*Chelonoidis denticulata*).

LEOPARD TORTOISE

Geochelone pardalis. Distinctive patterns on the carapace give these tortoises from eastern and southern Africa their common name. Recent European Union controls mean they are not now easily available in Europe, although many are already being maintained in collections. Reaching an adult shell length of 24in (60cm), Leopard Tortoises are not recommended for keepers with

Q & A

● *What depth of substrate is needed for oviposition?*

... At least 12in (30cm) of loose, sandy soil (6–7in/15–18cm for small species). Tortoises usually dig to the length of their hindlegs. If the female reaches bare floor, she may repeatedly excavate new sites and become exhausted.

● *How do I maintain humidity for Red-foot hatchlings?*

Place them in a container in a spare vivarium with a bowl of water on a heater mat. Use a humidity meter (hygrometer).

● *Are Red-foots carnivorous?*

They are known to eat carrion – a thawed rodent or day-old chick should be offered once a month only.

● *Can I keep Red-foots with lizards?*

It is not advisable: given a chance, they will eat lizards. Red-foots have been seen to eat iguanas' tails.

● *Do baby Leopard Tortoises need dry conditions?*

Yes, but they can soon dehydrate. Provide drinking water and 1 or 2 slightly damp hides. They can also be given a shallow, tepid bath twice a week individually.

limited space; hatchlings soon outgrow a small vivarium. The tortoises can be kept outside in warm, dry weather, but cool, wet conditions are not suitable for them. Although they enjoy basking, some shade is needed. In restricted quarters the males should be kept separately and mated females given their own accommodation. Their diet should be high in calcium to build the massive shell. Multivitamin supplements should also be provided (see Foods and Feeding, pages 30–31), but these should be reduced if the tortoises are kept outside in natural sunlight. Most specimens will eat carrion but this should be limited to only 1 thawed rodent, thawed day-old chick or 8oz (18g) can of low-fat dog food per adult per month. Hatchlings should be given no more than a quarter of a pink mouse or a half-teaspoon of canned food per month.

Males have a concave plastron, and a longer, thicker tail. Breeding is not likely to occur in an area smaller than the minimum recommended vivarium size. After breaking out of the egg, the hatchlings will remain still for several days until the yolk is absorbed. They should not be disturbed until they can be seen moving around. When the hatchlings are mobile, place them on damp paper towel in containers with plenty of ventilation until the yolk sac has completely disappeared. The temperature for babies should be 25°C (77°F) at the cool end and 30–32°C (86–90°F) near the hot spot. Overnight they will sit on a low wattage heater mat which can be supplied if the ambient temperature is lower than 21°C (70°F). Full-spectrum (UVB) light is also needed. Food should be finely chopped and well mixed. Calcium is especially important. Multivitamin supplements may be given once a week.

PANCAKE TORTOISE

Malocochersus tornieri. Also known as Tornier's Tortoise, this species from southeastern Africa is the only one in the genus. Its common name comes from the low, flattened body. The carapace length is usually 6–7in (15–18cm) with a height of barely 1.5in (4cm). The thin, flexible plastron permits this tortoise to expand its body and wedge itself in crevices in its dry, rocky native habitat. Because of its lightweight shell, this species can move quickly and is an accomplished climber compared with many other tortoises. Spacious quarters are needed to allow normal activity. Its colouring is variable and tends to fade with age, but many specimens have an attractive "sunburst" pattern of dark and light lines radiating from a light spot. This provides excellent camouflage in the wild.

Pancake Tortoises will breed all year round with constant temperatures, and captive breeding is common. Eggs from clutches produced late in the year may be infertile. A respite from breeding can be achieved by reducing the maximum temperature to 24–26.5°C (75–80°F) and the photoperiod to 10 hours. Separate gravid females from males, and remove eggs from the nesting site for incubation. Raise hatchlings in their own small vivarium with plenty of shelter.

◀ *An adult Pancake Tortoise* (Malocochersus tornieri) *is identified by its flat shell as well as its size – hatchlings have a slightly domed shell and a more circular shape than adults, but change shape as they grow. Even a full-size shell is fairly lightweight, allowing these tortoises to move quickly.*

Common Musk Turtle

FAMILY: KINOSTERNIDAE
SPECIES: STERNOTHERUS ODORATUS

ALSO KNOWN AS THE STINKPOT TURTLE, this 5in (13cm) long species is found along the east coast of North America from Ontario to Florida, and west as far as Wisconsin and central Texas. Two light stripes on the head, barbels on the chin and throat distinguish them from other musk turtles. The plastron has a faint hinge in adults. They can swing the head round as far as the hind limbs and will bite, especially the males. Mainly aquatic, this species may bask but often sits in shallow water with the carapace exposed. Small specimens require less water – they tend to walk on the bottom rather than swim.

Males have a longer tail than females, with a hard blunt spine on the tip, and two areas of rough scales on the inside of each leg. Eggs are buried in loose soil (provide in a tray if indoors) and should be removed for incubation. Raise hatchlings individually in shallow water with conditions and food as for the adults. Other species requiring similar treatment are the mud turtles (*Kinosternon* species). Both they and *Sternotherus* may be subject to legal restrictions in the US – check local laws before acquiring them.

▲ *The Common Musk Turtle* (Sternotherus odoratus) *is easy to keep and is popular despite the foul-smelling fluid exuded from glands under its carapace.*

Aquarium Conditions

Aquarium size	Min 48x15x15in (120x38x 38cm) if indoors, larger outdoors.
Substrate	Outdoors: soil. Indoors: none.
Habitat	Mainly aquatic, with small dry area. Shallow water 5in (13cm) deep with exposed rock.
Temperature	For indoors. Water at 25.5– 29°C (78–84°F) during day; 15–18°C (60–65°F) at night. Photoperiod: 14 hours. Full-spectrum (UVB) light and basking lamp needed.
Winter cooling	7–10°C (45–50°F) for 8–12 weeks in water or a box of damp leaves or moss.
Feeding	Mainly carnivorous: earthworms, crayfish, aquatic insects, shrimps; pellet foods.
Hatching	1 annual clutch of 1–9 eggs. Keep in vermiculite for 60–109 days at 25–29°C (77–84°F).

● *Can I keep several Musk Turtles together?*

... Males are aggressive to each other and will bully any that are smaller. However, in a large outdoor enclosure, small groups (6–8) may coexist. Remember to secure the enclosure to prevent the turtles climbing out.

● *What size should an outdoor pool be?*

The pool should be 30x15x6in (75x40x15cm) for adults, 18x12x2in (45x30x5cm) for hatchlings. Partial water changes or a pond filter are necessary.

● *Will Musk Turtles hibernate outdoors?*

Yes, but if really hard frost occurs in your area, they are better hibernated in a box of slightly damp moss.

● *Can I keep frogs in my turtle pond?*

No. Frogs and their tadpoles (especially the tadpoles) would provide a meal for the turtles.

● *Should I clean the algae from my turtle's shell?*

Yes. A growth of algae is natural, especially on aquatic species, but it can provide a site for infection. Periodic brushing with a toothbrush will remove the algae.

Amphibian Care

Amphibians are extremely sensitive to environmental influences; they are widely regarded as "bio-indicators", which show the health (or otherwise) of this planet. Their requirements are even more exacting than those of reptiles, and most species are still poorly documented. This is particularly true of amphibian health and disease, which is a highly specialist subject. Finding a competent vet may be a real challenge.

Amphibians' tolerance of high temperatures is limited; most are better kept in slightly cool conditions. Their most important requirement is the need for moisture: to allow them to breathe through their skin, it must be kept moist. For this reason, all amphibian species, including the primarily terrestrial ones, need moisture to varying degrees, even though some are adapted to survive periods of drought by burrowing or other strategies. For semi-aquatic and aquatic species, water quality is an additional issue; not only the temperature but also the pH balance (acidity or alkalinity), chlorine, hardness (the presence of dissolved calcium and magnesium salts) and the presence of other minerals or pollutants. You will need to test and possibly treat any water you intend to use in a pool. Larvae are particularly sensitive. Finally, frogs and salamanders can poison themselves if large amounts of their own waste products are allowed to build up in a small body of water such as a bowl. Be sure to change the water frequently.

▶ *Female Marbled Newt* (Triturus marmoratus) *see page 197.*

What is an Amphibian?

AMPHIBIANS ARE A CLASS OF VERTEBRATES descended from primitive forerunners of the reptiles that adapted to life on land. Although their name refers to a life spent partly in water and partly on land, some species are wholly terrestrial, while others are wholly aquatic. All three types exist in all three orders. Even the terrestrial species retain their dependence on moisture.

Amphibians have colonized a range of different habitats. Newts and salamanders are mostly restricted to cool, moist regions, whereas frogs and toads have adapted to all types of habitat, even arid deserts. Unlike reptiles, amphibians have retained the larval stage, starting life as eggs

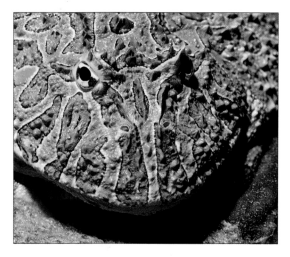

and metamorphosing through stages to the adult form. In a very few cases the eggs develop inside the female and emerge as well-developed larvae or even fully-formed young, as in the Alpine Salamander (*Salamandra atra*).

Permeable Skin

An amphibian's flexible skin is endowed with mucus glands, which produce secretions to keep it moist. This gives many species a slimy coating. The skin is also permeable, allowing the exchange of gases and moisture. Respiration can also occur through the mouth lining. Members of the largest salamander family (Plethodontidae) have evolved without lungs and rely on the latter two methods for their oxygen supply.

The permeable skin has other uses. Certain desert species can absorb moisture from damp sand when buried; others can store water in the bladder. Some frogs and a few salamanders encase themselves in a cocoon to prevent water loss during droughts. They can remain buried for lengthy periods. A few species of arboreal frog cover themselves with a waxy coating to keep moist in hot, dry conditions. The skin and mouth lining can work in reverse in some amphibians,

◀ *A female Horned Frog* (Ceratophrys ornata). *Though the warty skin would suggest a "toad" to most people, there is actually no difference between frogs and toads.*

Amphibian Classification

ORDER	COMMON NAME	FAMILIES	GENERA	SPECIES
Urodela (*or* Caudata)	Salamanders and Newts	9	60	360
Anura (*or* Salientia)	Frogs and Toads	20	303	3495
Gymnophiona (*or* Apoda)	Caecilians*	5	34	163

*Caecilians – wormlike amphibians that are fossorial or aquatic – are not dealt with in this book. They require specialized treatment and very few species tend to be available in the pet trade.

● *What is the difference between frogs and toads?*

... Squat, rough-skinned species are commonly called "toads"; "frogs" are smooth-skinned. Both skin types occur in both groups. In scientific literature, "frogs" is used to describe both.

● *How long do amphibians live in captivity?*

Common Toads (*Bufo bufo*) and Fire Salamanders (*Salamandra salamandra*) reportedly live over 20 years; Asian giant salamanders (*Andrias* species) have survived 52 years. Lifespan in the wild is not known.

● *Is it true that some salamanders are blind?*

Yes. The blind species have adapted to living in dark caves. Others may have small eyes that can only differentiate between light and darkness.

● *Are all amphibians poisonous?*

The toxicity of all species is not known. Some are highly toxic; others may simply taste unpleasant. Humans eat several species after cooking them.

● *Should amphibians be handled?*

Only during removal for cleaning or moving. Your hand is too hot for them; holding for even a short time can kill them. Wet hands or gloves prevent damage to their skin. Always wear disposable gloves and wash your hands afterwards. Avoid mouth and eye contact. Do not allow young children to touch amphibians at all.

◀ *A Strawberry Arrow-poison Frog* (Dendrobates pumilio) *in a bromeliad. The bright colours warn off predators, permitting the frogs to be active in daylight.*

permitting water to escape from the body in order to cool the animal by evaporation.

Chromatophores in the skin (see What is a Reptile?, pages 12–13) enable some frog species to change colour, reflecting heat and preventing dehydration. Noxious substances secreted by glands provide extra protection, but some predators can eat even the most toxic amphibians.

Warning Colours and Body Shape

Colour also provides protection, and some toxic species exhibit bright warning colours. Others, less flamboyant and less toxic, rely on camouflage. Some amphibians mimic the coloration of toxic species. Some species have a cryptic (camouflage) coloration on their dorsal surface and

warning colours on the ventral surface. The colours are exposed to predators by twisting the body, a reaction known as the "unken reflex". Countershading – a light belly with a dark dorsal surface, as seen in many fish – is common, especially among frogs that enter water to breed. This makes the frogs less visible to predators and prey from above or below.

Both frogs and toads lose their tails during metamorphosis. They have a short body with four limbs. Adaptation has produced streamlined frogs with powerful hind legs for jumping or swimming; squat-bodied forms with short legs for burrowing; and slimmer, long-legged forms with "adhesive" toes for climbing trees. Newts and salamanders have four limbs and an elongated body, and retain the tail. Certain aquatic forms, such as olms and amphiumas, have evolved an eel-like body and reduced limbs; sirens, also aquatic, have lost the hindlimbs.

Housing – the Vivarium

Before bringing home an amphibian, make sure that you are well prepared. (See Starting Out, pages 4–9.) Some basic research into your chosen species will assist in selecting and furnishing the vivarium. Is the amphibian arboreal? Is it an active jumper? Does it need a water area; if so, how deep and how wide? What kind of substrate and how deep should it be? Some species may need special facilities such as leaves or branches overhanging the water, or covered terrestrial spawning sites. Plants are required by some species and can be very useful for furnishing the vivarium. Some aquarium plants can be used – a good book on these should give details of which can grow out of water.

Water quality is important. This subject is often dealt with in books on fishkeeping. Water treatments are advertised in the aquarium trade, and manufacturers often supply leaflets. Because amphibians are moisture-dependent, problems can arise due to the quality of the local tap water (see box on this page). As a last resort, rainwater or pondwater can be boiled to kill any harmful organisms, but even rainwater can contain undesirable substances – acid rain will be detrimental to the health of any specimen kept in it.

Mains Water Problems

Chlorination
Chlorine can be dispersed by allowing tap water to stand in a wide container for at least 24 hours.

---

pH Imbalance
Most amphibians prefer water that is neutral to slightly acid. Acidity or alkalinity (pH) is expressed as a number between 0 and 14. Below 7 is acid, 7 is neutral, above it is alkaline. The minimum pH for amphibians is 5.9, the maximum is 7.6. Some species from limestone areas are used to higher alkalinity.

Water Hardness
"Hard" water from dissolved minerals can be harmful, especially to larvae, but water from domestic water softeners can also be unsuitable. Boil some water and allow it to stand for at last 24 hours in a wide container. Then use only the top half of it.

Rot-Proof and Escape-Proof

An amphibian vivarium must be rot-proof to withstand moisture. Although fibreglass and plastic can be used, most keepers choose a standard all-glass aquarium fitted with an escape-proof lid. Top access is the only choice for a fully aquatic setup, but it can present problems (see Housing in the Reptile Care section, pages 14–17). For terrestrial setups or those requiring only shallow water, there are prefabricated glass models with front overlapping doors. Keep in mind that the gap between them will allow the escape of small amphibians and insect prey. Sliding doors are another alternative. Yet another popular choice is a sloping front, where the front glass panel pulls forward for access; this may also be used for

GLASS VIVARIUM

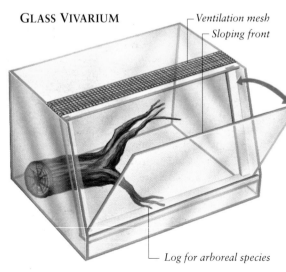

— Ventilation mesh
— Sloping front
— Log for arboreal species

◀ *A front-opening all-glass vivarium is popular for small terrestrial amphibians. Furnishing and servicing is easy. A semi-aquatic habitat could also be provided by adding a shallow preformed pool or tray.*

shallow water. If either of these models is custom-built by you at home, you can choose how high to position the access panel to allow for substrate or water. The panel must be secured so that it cannot be pushed out. Check carefully for any small gaps. Amphibians are expert escapers and can climb up glass to squeeze through tiny gaps.

A glass vivarium must be placed on styrofoam tiles or slabs at least 0.25in (6mm) thick to prevent the base cracking. Once the substrate medium or water has been added, the vivarium must not be moved – it is likely to break.

Crowding and Disease

Overcrowding leads to infectious diseases and must be avoided. Frogs produce substantial amounts of liquid and solid waste that quickly pollute the substrate unless it is changed frequently. With certain small species and the correct vivarium layout, it is possible to maintain a balanced system. Some planted Dendrobatid frog vivaria have functioned perfectly for up to 17 years with minimum maintenance, but never with more than four frogs; an overloaded system cannot cope with waste. Strict quarantining of any new introductions helps to prevent disease.

● *Are there any advantages to mixed collections?*

... In general, no. Many amphibians are cannibalistic and will eat young. Animals from one area may be carriers of diseases to which they are immune but their companions are not. A toxic specimen may poison another one, especially a wild-caught toxic animal with a non-toxic captive-bred one. Finally, some species hybridize if housed together; valuable genetic material can be lost by this.

● *How do I test my tap water?*

Many aquarist stores test water samples. They also sell kits for checking water hardness, pH, ammonia, nitrite, nitrate, etc. Chlorination and hard water can both be treated at home. An aquarist store will also have products that remove certain harmful substances.

● *Do I need another vivarium for breeding?*

Breeding requirements may be different from the everyday ones. For certain species it may be advisable to have a terrestrial set-up for most of the year and then to transfer the occupants to an aquatic set-up for breeding. Alternatively, you may choose a divided tank with a water area. (If fitting dividers, grind the edges smooth before sticking into place with silicone sealer.)

● *What is the best choice of vivarium for a semi-aquatic habitat with a pool?*

Any kind of all-glass vivarium-aquarium can be used as long as the dimensions are adequate. You can fit a divider (as above) or use a plastic tray for the pool area. This can easily be removed for water changes.

● *What kind of filtration system is best; and is it always necessary?*

Water in shallow pools (as found in a semi-aquatic habitat) should be partially changed at least weekly. Aquarium plants use up some nitrogenous waste but are not completely effective. A filtration system is inappropriate for a small shallow pool; all systems need a minimum depth that varies according to the type of system. For deeper pools used with larger or totally aquatic species, an undergravel filter or sponge filter is probably better than external canister filters or internal power filters. The latter create too much turbulence and can suck in eggs, tadpoles and larvae.

◀ *A Fire Salamander* (Salamandra salamandra) *climbs out of its vivarium pool. Like many amphibians, it is a poor swimmer and requires only shallow water. Facilities for leaving the pool must be provided.*

Heating, Lighting and Humidity

MANY AMPHIBIANS NEED NO ADDITIONAL heating – in fact, they may be adversely affected by high temperatures, which can pose problems during hot Summers. In the wild amphibians have more opportunity to hide away from the heat, but in the confines of the vivarium this may not be possible. For keepers living in hotter regions, temperate species may be unsuitable unless cooling units can be installed. If heating is necessary, do not use powerful localized heat sources inside the vivarium; they will dry it out and damage the amphibians' moist skin.

Vivarium temperature is affected by the ambient (room) temperature. Avoid positions near sunny windows or radiators. As previously mentioned, the vivarium must be set up, and the day and night temperatures monitored, well before

you introduce the occupants. For tropical specie the overnight temperature must not be allowe to drop too much; it may even be necessary t insulate the vivarium to prevent this, thoug most can withstand a slight drop. Once it i warmed up, a deep substrate in a well-furnishe vivarium will act as a storage heater, giving ou heat at night, and will help to preserve the tem perature level overnight.

Heater mats should not be placed under vivarium that has a deep substrate; a build-up o heat will damage the mat and crack the glas vivarium base. If two vivaria are side by side, th

◄ *A* Surinam Horned Frog (Ceratophrys cornuta) *buried in damp moss. A layer of sphagnum moss, with its water-holding qualities, helps to maintain humidity.*

HEATING CABLE

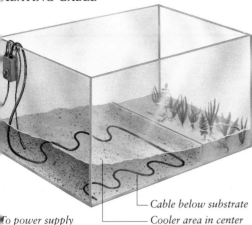

Cable below substrate

To power supply *Cooler area in center*

Although many keepers use subsoil cables, others claim that a heated floor is unnatural for amphibians. It is not advisable to use cables with fossorial species.

...mat can be sandwiched between them, unless it is the type with insulation on one side; this type can be taped to the outside of a single vivarium. Heater mats are moisture-proof but not water-proof; they cannot be used underwater, but they can be used inside the vivarium as long as they are above the water level.

Because of the potential danger from moisture and electricity in close proximity, caution is necessary when providing heat for amphibians. Some electrical fittings are affected by condensation, so you should obtain skilled advice before installation. All heat sources must be controlled by a good-quality thermostat to prevent over-heating. It is better to use 2 or more low-wattage heaters than a single powerful heater.

Ventilation and Humidity

Newts and salamanders, being mainly terrestrial, need less air humidity; they will thrive as long as the substrate is sufficiently moist. Species from rainforest areas, such as the arboreal salamanders *Bolitoglossa*, need moister surroundings and a higher air humidity. Frogs and toads also vary in their requirements. Rainforest species in their natural habitat may exist in 100% relative humidity, which is difficult to create in the vivarium without sealing it. Since some air is necessary, this is hardly feasible. Ventilation and high

● *Are soil-heating cables satisfactory?*

... Yes; these flexible heat cables can be laid out on part of the vivarium base before the substrate is added. Hiding places should be provided in both the heated and the unheated areas of the vivarium. This will provide the occupants with a choice of temperatures.

● *What is the best method of heating a water area in a semi-aquatic set-up?*

An aquarium heater with thermostat may be used as long as it is protected. This will also encourage evaporation to increase air humidity. It may not be sufficient to heat the whole vivarium, in which case extra heating will be necessary. A heater mat underneath the water area, outside the vivarium, is effective if there is no substrate to create a barrier to the incoming heat.

● *How can I stop the front glass of my frog vivarium constantly misting up?*

This is bound to happen where high humidity is needed. You may have to sacrifice some visibility for the sake of the occupants' welfare. A narrow ventilation strip in the top, as near to the front as possible, and perhaps another fitted above substrate level at the base of the front glass, will allow some of the condensation to escape. Some misting is bound to occur after spraying the vivarium.

● *Is it possible to use a misting system to maintain humidity?*

Misting systems can be used, and good results have been reported with tropical frogs, especially in inducing breeding behaviour. Purpose-built systems are available, and the units designed for asthma relief can be adapted if you are reasonably skilful.

Misting timer. This American timing controller, which is used with a misting system, is an example of the sophisticated hi-tech equipment that is now available to the keeper.

humidity levels may seem like a contradiction, but both are necessary. In practice many rainforest frogs do well in less than their natural air humidity levels, so provide some ventilation and spray the vivarium when necessary. Small aquarium air pumps or even computer fans can be used to force air into the vivarium. Air humidity is also affected by the type of substrate and the density of planting. Check humidity levels with a humidity meter (hygrometer).

While continually adding water by daily spraying or misting, you may need to siphon off surplus to prevent flooding. Alternatively, drainage taps could be built into the system. Water areas need regular water changes or, if large enough, a filtration system. Any spray water or replacement water must be at the same temperature as the vivarium to avoid chilling the occupants.

Lighting

Except during the breeding season, relatively few amphibians are diurnal, so they do not require special arrangements for lighting. Many strictly nocturnal species will steadfastly refuse to move until darkness falls. Crepuscular species usually become active around dusk, leaving their hiding places to seek food. Heavy rains will sometimes bring them out in daylight. Diurnal activity in

▶ *Red-eyed Treefrogs* (Agalychnis callidryas) *mating. Most amphibians are nocturnal and need little light, but it will be required if the vivarium is planted. Extra light also makes observation easier for the keeper.*

such species may mean that they are seeking moisture, although a more typical response to overly dry conditions is to huddle further into a corner to try to avoid desiccation. Amphibians sometimes remain out in the daytime if they are sick and too weak to move.

Extra light is often provided primarily for the benefit of the keeper. You must ensure that it does not produce extra heat, which is harmful to amphibians. Use a tungsten-filament spotlamp beaming down through the cover glass to provide heat and light. More than one lamp may be necessary in a large vivarium. The bulb (40 watts) should be at least 4in (10cm) away from the cover glass, which should be 0.2in (6mm) thick. This is wasteful of electricity, but it is safe. A dimmer-type thermostat is recommended, as this will prevent the light going on and off all day. In some cases a "non-light" heat source may be needed overnight.

If the vivarium is planted, then light is a daily requirement for the health of the plants. Choosing shade-tolerant plants and a relatively bright location is often sufficient. (The vivarium must not be positioned near a sunny window, however, as this may make it too hot for amphibians! See Heating, pages 144–45.) Plants in a dim location may need extra lighting.

Photoperiod and Breeding

Photoperiod – the number of hours of light in a 24-hour period – affects amphibian behaviour, especially breeding. If temperate species are kept without additional lighting, their behaviour will be controlled by the natural daylight. If artificial light is provided, use a timer to control the photoperiod, gradually adjusting it to increase the hours of daylight in Spring and decrease them as Winter approaches. For sub-tropical and tropical species, the daylight hours should be more constant throughout the year, but you will still need a timer to provide the correct photoperiod. Frequent variations in photoperiod will disturb and confuse the occupants of the vivarium.

◀ *Illuminated tadpoles* (Rana species). *Although many tadpoles do well with ordinary light, additional overhead lighting will encourage algae and infusoria. Spotlamps are unsuitable as they would heat the water.*

● *Is ultraviolet light (UV) dangerous to amphibians?*

... High doses of UV can be fatal. In studies, over-exposure led to death or deformity in frog tadpoles. There are other implications. The disappearance of some amphibian species, especially those at high altitudes, may be linked to the depletion of the Earth's ozone layer, allowing more UV (especially the dangerous lower wavelengths; see Heating and Lighting in Reptile Care, pages 20–21) to fall onto the earth's surface.

● *Do diurnal frogs need full-spectrum (UVB) fluorescent tubes?*

Several fluorescent tubes are available. Some are designed especially for iguanas or heliothermic lizards. UVB and UVA contents are expressed as percentages of the total light produced. Higher percentages (over 2%) are unsuitable for diurnal frogs, but a 2% tube is harmless. Arrow-poison frogs and mantellas show no ill effects from lower percentages.

● *Do frogs benefit from UVB?*

This is an unresolved debate. Most amphibians in the wild receive sufficient nutrients for all their needs from their diet, but there is evidence – mainly anecdotal – that some UVB is beneficial, especially to young froglets. Cases of rickets and shivering fits have been observed in Dendrobatid froglets, European Green Treefrogs and mantellas, even when dietary supplements were provided; installing full-spectrum light cured the problem.

● *Should the fluorescent tube be inside the vivarium?*

UV wavelengths are filtered out when light passes through glass, therefore the tube should be inside the vivarium if it is to provide any benefit. A ventilation mesh that would allow the light to pass through would also reduce humidity and permit insects to escape. Use an aquarium-type fluorescent kit with moisture-proof caps and the starter unit outside the vivarium. Caution: Always remember to switch the light off before placing your hands in the vivarium.

Furnishing the Vivarium

FOR MANY TERRESTRIAL SPECIES, A SIMPLE set-up consisting of a suitable substrate and several hiding places is sufficient. The rest of the furnishing is a matter of personal choice. Logs, stones or plants can be used as desired. Curved pieces of cork bark make suitable caves, providing privacy and moisture. In the case of larger species such as horned frogs, many keepers forgo a natural habitat in favour of strictly hygienic housing. These species spend the day partially buried, and their surroundings soon become soiled as a result of copious defecation. They are often kept in clinical set-ups on a disposable substrate such as foam rubber or wet paper towel. The animals seem to thrive in these surroundings even though they are unable to burrow. If you prefer, you can use a normal substrate, but this must be replaced frequently. Remember to provide a dish of clean water.

Certain species need a water area for the duration of the breeding season. This may range from an extensive, fully aquatic set-up to a shallow pool or simply a secluded moist spot in which the eggs can be deposited. (For a discussion of water quality see Housing, pages 142–143.)

▲ *An arrow-poison frog* (Dendrobates tinctorius) *in a tropical rainforest vivarium with Sweetheart Vine* (Philodendron scandens) *and a moss substrate.*

● *Can bromeliad plants be used with amphibians?*

... Yes. Bromeliads (not those with spines along the leaves) are well suited to humid vivaria. Spray before planting and rinse the water-filled axils to remove traces of insecticide.

● *Which plants are best for arboreal frogs?*

Three useful climbers are: Devil's Ivy or Pothos (*Scindapsus aureus*); Sweetheart Vine (*Philodendron scandens*); and Creeping Fig (*Ficus pumila*) – also available in a variegated form. These grow well, even in very wet conditions. Others include: Dragon Plant (*Cordyline* and *Dracaena* species); Prayer Plants and Rabbits Foot Plant (*Maranta* species); Peace Lily (*Spathiphyllum*); Persian Shield (*Strobilanthes*); Wax Plant (*Hoya carnosa*); Aluminium Plant (*Pilea*);

Snakeskin Plant (*Fittonia*); and some *Peperomia* species (not hairy-leaved types). Goosefoot or Arrowhead Vine needs a large vivarium. Tropical ferns are suitable but many hardy ferns need cool conditions.

● *Which aquarium plants grow in wet soil?*

The following are suitable: Amazon sword – smaller species (*Echinodorus paniculatus*); Dwarf Anubias (*Anubias nana*); Japanese Rush (*Acorus gramineus*); Pygmy Chain Sword (*Echinodorus tenellus*); some dwarf Cryptocorynes (such as *Cryptocoryne nevillii*); Malayan or Borneo Sword (*Aglaonema simplex*); and Red Hygrophila (*Alternathera rosaefolia*). Note: When choosing aquarium plants, select young specimens; mature plants removed from the water will flop if deprived of their accustomed support.

Suitable Substrates

The substrate should be moisture-retentive regardless of the level of humidity in the vivarium. Materials that develop mould are not suitable (see Furnishing in Reptile Care, pages 22–23). A layer of sphagnum moss can be rinsed when necessary, but you will eventually need to replace it. Moss can be "temperamental"; without adequate light and correct substrate it will die. Another reason for this may be spray water that is too hard or too alkaline. Sometimes it regrows if left – or if fresh clumps are planted on the dead ones. Java moss (*Vesicularia dubyana*) thrives in the splash zone of waterfalls.

Combinations of peaty soil, chopped (milled) sphagnum moss, orchid bark, leaf litter and ground fir bark provide a loose substrate for burrowing. Burrowers from arid regions will need a more sandy mixture. Do not use ordinary builders' sand – it is dusty when dry and compacts almost solid when wet. Use a dust-free sand mixed with ground fir bark or orchid bark. If a moist area is needed, use a plastic container filled with damp medium. Being able to find moisture is crucial for most species. Some keepers use aquarium gravel, but not all types are appropriate. If well-rounded it will not harm the amphibians' skin, and it provides a permeable layer through which faeces can percolate into the soil below. Remember that gravel is not suitable for fossorial amphibians.

Housing small amphibians, especially arboreal species, provides great scope for planting. The basic principles are the same as for a rainforest habitat (see Furnishing in Reptile Care, pages 24–25). Terraces will enhance the vivarium's appearance and provide extra climbing space. Driftwood, branches or cork bark "logs" can be used. Cork on the rear wall will support climbing plants and make an attractive backdrop.

Points to Remember About Plants

- Set up the vivarium and give it time to settle before introducing the occupants.
- Inspect all plants for slugs and other pests.
- If plants become spindly, replace them.
- Leave plants in their pots – this makes replacement easier.
- Certain plants thrive better in higher, well drained areas.
- Some plants are invasive and will choke others if not kept pruned.
- Many common houseplants are suitable for vivarium use.
- Some aquarium plants are bog plants and do well in the lower, wet areas.
- A number of different plants will provide variety of shape, texture and colour.
- Leave a clearing at the front for feeding.

SETTING UP A BALANCED VIVARIUM

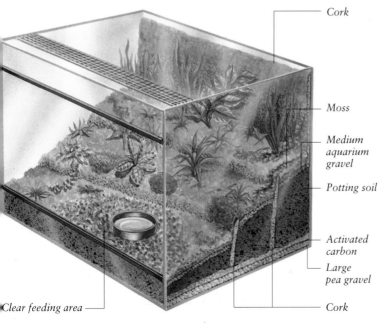

Cork

Moss

Medium aquarium gravel

Potting soil

Activated carbon

Large pea gravel

Cork

Clear feeding area

◀ *A balanced vivarium is a low-maintenance ecosystem for just a few inhabitants. It is suitable for many frogs, especially Dendrobatids. Use live plants; let them grow thick and bushy. Spraying washes faeces into the soil, where they are converted to plant food.*

Foods and Feeding

ALL AMPHIBIANS EAT INSECTS BUT LARGE frogs and toads also eat small rats, mice, day-old chicks and quail chicks, and large salamanders will take pink mice (see Foods and Feeding in Reptile Care, pages 28–29). None of these items needs to be fed live; food can be thawed out and presented in forceps, which are wiggled to simulate the movement of live prey. All of these items are complete foods, so nutritional supplements are unnecessary. (For a discussion of supplements, see Foods and Feeding in Reptile Care, pages 28–29.) Large crickets, locusts and other items provide variety.

For other amphibians, a wide range of live insects can be given. Earthworms (*Lumbricus* species) are an excellent food, and flying insects such as houseflies and bluebottles (blowflies) are eagerly taken by frogs and toads. The larvae (maggots) can be purchased from anglers' suppliers and left to mature, but some keepers avoid them. Maggots themselves are indigestible.

A steady, uncontaminated supply of aquatic creatures can be farmed at home by setting up a small pool in a sunny spot and adding water fleas. Occasional additions of dried yeast, liquid fish fry food, or liquified horse or cow dung will encourage growth. (Overfeeding can cause pollution.) Open water butts can be used for water fleas. They often provide a supply of gnat larvae.

Food for Small Mouths

Frogs with small mouths need small prey such as fruit flies (*Drosophila* species), aphids and small crickets. Aphids (winged and wingless) are nutritious, but you should only use green ones; black and woolly aphids will usually be rejected. Aphid-infested shoots can placed in the vivarium. Gather aphids by sweeping a fine-mesh net through long grass, or by pushing it upwards against leaves. Springtails are useful for tiny froglets. They can be sieved from dead leaves, or cultured in tubs of damp peat and fed on mushrooms, fish flake and bits of fresh vegetables.

● *How do I hatch flies and bluebottles for feeding?*

... Place the larvae in clean sawdust and allow them to pupate, then transfer a number of them to clean, slightly damp sawdust, in a small jar with a hole in the lid. Plug the lid with cotton wool. When the flies hatch, put the jar in the vivarium and remove the plug. Chill the flies before dusting them with vitamin supplements.

● *Where do I obtain infusoria?*

Some aquarist shops supply infusoria cultures. You can start your own cultures by placing bruised lettuce leaves in a jar of water and standing it in sunlight. The infusoria water will turn green. Do not allow the water in the larvae rearing tank to turn green; this reduces the amount of oxygen available to the larvae.

● *Will any amphibians eat slugs?*

Slugs are a popular food for salamanders but they must be from uncontaminated sources. Any with an unpleasant taste will be rejected. The small, soft-bodied white, light grey and light brown forms usually found in gardens are favourites.

● *When I feed crickets to my amphibians, some always fall into the pool and drown. Can I prevent this?*

Both crickets and locusts need a small raft or ramp to stop them drowning in any water that is present.

● *Can uneaten live crickets be left in the vivarium for another time?*

A few will not matter, but in general this is not a good idea. It is better to avoid having large numbers of crickets roaming around the vivarium – they can damage amphibians, especially their eyes, which the crickets will chew. If some leftover live crickets are unavoidable, be sure to leave some food for them. Uneaten dead crickets should be removed from the vivarium in the interest of hygiene.

Adult Black Cricket
(x125%)

Newts in their aquatic stage of development are especially fond of worms, and will eat a variety of small water insects and their larvae, such as water fleas (*Daphnia* and *Cyclops* species), bloodworms (*Chironomous* larvae), gnat larvae (*Culex* species) and tubifex worms. Keep the latter under cool, running water for several hours, to clean out the gut. Some of these aquatic foods may be available from aquarist suppliers. Newts will also eat frog tadpoles, and will butt their way into spawn to eat the eggs. To avoid these problems, do not try to breed both newts and frogs in the same tank.

Because many amphibians are nocturnal, prey such as earthworms disappear into the substrate before they can be eaten. Try offering them in forceps, placing them in front of the animal. Mealworms and waxworms die almost instantaneously if they get wet. Place the former in a small dish; offer the latter with forceps.

➤ *The aquatic species shown here will be taken by newt larvae, the others by metamorphosed frogs and newts. Crickets need to be of an appropriate size, relative to the size of your amphibians.*

Feeding Larval Amphibians

Tadpoles and larval salamanders have very different feeding habits. Larval salamanders are carnivores, whereas tadpoles are mainly herbivorous. They graze the inside of the tank and will eat finely-powdered fish flake food. Many also reach a stage where they can feed on a small piece of raw lean beef suspended by a cotton thread. This should be changed daily to prevent pollution. Tadpoles of some frog species are cannibalistic and will eat their own siblings. These species must be reared separately.

Larval salamanders and newts need a supply of small creatures, starting with a small daily amount of infusoria (the tiny organisms found in "green water"). Later they will eat water fleas, followed by bloodworms, whiteworms (*Enchytrae* species), grindal worms, microworms and small earthworms. To ensure a regular supply of water fleas, set up and stock a tank beforehand. (These fleas also eat infusoria; supply enough for them as well.) The fleas and worms are commonly available from aquarist shops. Whiteworms are very fattening and should be used sparingly in combination with other foods.

FOOD FOR YOUNG AMPHIBIANS

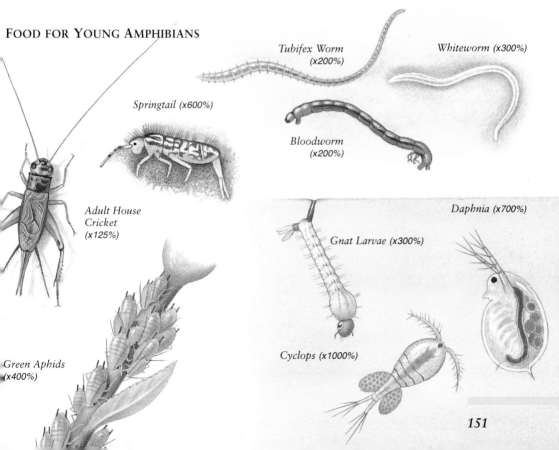

Tubifex Worm (x200%)

Whiteworm (x300%)

Springtail (x600%)

Bloodworm (x200%)

Adult House Cricket (x125%)

Daphnia (x700%)

Gnat Larvae (x300%)

Cyclops (x1000%)

Green Aphids (x400%)

151

Breeding

AMPHIBIANS HAVE DEVELOPED A RANGE OF fascinating breeding strategies. External fertilization is more common in frogs and toads; internal fertilization in newts and salamanders – but there are exceptions. Although most amphibians lay eggs, a few are livebearers. Clutch sizes in frogs and toads can vary from one egg to over 20,000, laid singly, in clumps or in strings, protected by gelatinous coating. Salamanders lay fewer eggs, though aquatic species may produce 400 at once. Some need no water, others need a large deep area. Many species lay their eggs on land in suitably moist spots or near water.

Clues to Sexing

Sexual dichromatism (colour difference) is rare among frogs and toads, so – especially in immature specimens – other characteristics are a more reliable guide. In many species, mature females are larger and plumper than the males. Mature males may have a vocal sac – a fold of skin or a "disc" under the chin. In a few species the sac may have a patch of colour, which becomes visible when expanded. Males of species that breed in water may have webbed fingers or nuptial "pads" (roughened areas of skin) on the fingers, forearms, chest, belly or chin. Male frogs with a pale belly sometimes have two thin tubes which are visible just under the skin. These can be seen by placing the animal in a clear container and holding it up to the light.

Male newts and salamanders are often more intensely coloured, females comparatively drab. Females are usually stouter than males, with rounder bodies. Some males have thicker limbs, and the cloaca may become swollen during the breeding season. Male aquatic newts develop a dorsal crest or a threadlike extension to the tail. In species such as *Cynops*, the male's tail may broaden. Some salamanders develop nuptial pads similar to those of frogs and toads. If none of these characteristics is obvious, males can be identified by the following behaviour: calling (frogs and toads); territorial behaviour, rubbing or head-butting (salamanders); or attempted amplexus or tail-waving (aquatic newts).

Courtship Rituals and Mating

Many amphibians are prolific breeders. Huge numbers congregate in pools in the Spring. Male frogs and toads attract females and challenge other males by calling. They seize the approaching females in a grip called "amplexus", which stimulates egg production in the females. The female may be gripped around the armpits, the waist, or (in some Dendrobatid frogs) the neck. In species that do not use amplexus, eggs are fertilized as the female moves away after spawning. Amplexus by adhesion occurs in some short-legged, plump-bodied species such as *Kaloula*, *Gastrophryne* and *Breviceps*; a secretion produced by cells in the male's abdomen holds the female fast until mating is completed.

◀ *A male Marbled Newt* (Triturus marmoratus) *showing the dorsal crest. The crest disappears after breeding, but may be visible as short dark and light cross-bands along the back which can aid sexing.*

Courtship of Red-spotted Newts (Notopthalmus viridescens). *They perform an elaborate aquatic "dance" to encourage the female to take up the spermatophore (sperm capsule) previously deposited by the male.*

Many salamanders and newts also engage in complex courtship rituals. More primitive salamander species practise external fertilization, but many use internal fertilization – the male produces a sperm capsule (spermatophore) and passes it to the female. Amplexus is also common in salamanders, using the limbs (and in some cases the tail) to hold the female. Scent also plays a part in the courtship ritual; newts that do not use amplexus vibrate their tails to propel scent to the female. Other methods involve rubbing the male's scent onto the female's body.

Parental Care

Amphibians that produce huge clutches of eggs can afford to leave the eggs' survival to chance. Those that lay fewer eggs provide parental care to increase the survival rate. Eggs may be entwined around the male's legs; carried on the back, in the vocal sac or in pouches; or even swallowed by the female and nourished in her stomach. Some frogs transport their larvae to small pools to continue developing; as the eggs hatch, the tadpoles move onto the back of a parent (not always the female) to be carried.

These methods are most common in frogs and toads. Salamanders, if they tend their eggs at all, usually do little more than guard them. Parental care by the male is more common in fish and amphibians than in other vertebrates.

⬛ *For breeding, a rainy season as in the tropics can be simulated by heavy spraying or misting, or you can make a rain chamber. There are several ways to do this; you will need to research the needs of the individual species. An internal pump (as shown) can draw in free-floating spawn, so some form of guard is needed.*

A HOMEMADE RAIN CHAMBER

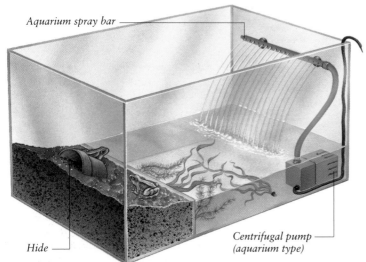

Aquarium spray bar

Hide

Centrifugal pump
(aquarium type)

Making a Rain Chamber

Remove frogs to an empty tank containing a stone or other means of climbing out of the water. The tank should have an overflow system to keep the water at the desired level. Heavy rainfall can be simulated in any of the following ways:

- Place a container of water with a perforated base on a mesh cover so that the water trickles down.

- Use an external aquarium canister filter to draw the water up and pour it onto a perforated plastic cover.

- A similar pump can deliver the water through an aquarium spray bar fixed to the tank wall near the top.

- A misting system might also have the desired effect.

This treatment may have to continue for a week or more before breeding occurs. Note: if using the normal vivarium, the "rain" must be limited to the water section to avoid washing away the land area.

Breeding in the Vivarium

In the wild, males often outnumber females at breeding time, and competition may be a prerequisite for successful breeding. In captivity, a single pair may breed successfully, but if not, breeding can sometimes be triggered by increasing the number of males. In some species, an early-mating couple can act as the catalyst for others. If there are too many males, however, mating may be difficult. Too many females can also inhibit breeding, and some female frogs will eat the eggs of other females.

Tropical species will breed at almost any time of the year if conditions are suitable. Temperate species tend to have a fixed seasonal cycle, and require an annual cool period; for temperate species in captivity, 2 months at 7–8°C (45°F) is usually adequate. (For a general discussion of hibernation, see Breeding in the Reptile Care section, pages 34–37.) A box of slightly damp moss in a frost-free situation provides a suitable environment for terrestrial species. Alternatively, the normal vivarium can be partly filled with a layer of moss. Drain the water area first. Some aquatic species can also undergo this cool period in their usual aquarium.

To prepare for the cool period, withhold food for at least a week before hibernation if the amphibians' appetite has not decreased naturally. After hibernation, increase the temperature gradually – temperate species respond to normal Spring temperature rises and lengthening days. These steps, together with the provision of a suitable water area, usually induce breeding behaviour. Spraying in imitation of Spring rain can also be an effective trigger.

For species that encounter both dry and rainy seasons in the wild, spawning follows the rainy season. In these cases, normal spraying is not always sufficient – you will need to simulate a rainy season. One method of providing simulated rainfall is by using a rain chamber. The chamber will need a suitable spawning site for particular species according to where they lay eggs. These may be deposited in burrows, in foam nests on branches, on leaves overhanging water, on grass stalks above the water, in water-filled bromeliads or under logs. If spawning is continuing, remove the eggs. If it has finished, remove either the adults or the eggs.

Care of Eggs and Young

Many adult amphibians have cannibalistic tendencies and should be separated from eggs and young. Some species also have cannibalistic larvae that must be raised separately. At the end of a prolonged breeding season, adults may also eat hatching larvae. Some aquatic newts, which stick eggs on water plants and fold leaves over them, eat their own eggs. To prevent this, either remove the egg-laden plants or keep the newts well fed. Salamander eggs that are laid on land can be removed, with some of the surrounding substrate, to a small container. Similar treatment is advisable for frog and toad eggs that are laid on land. Some frog and toad eggs need to be placed close to water, so that the tadpoles can reach it easily; place the egg mass on a mound of wet paper towel surrounded by water. The eggs of arrow-poison frogs need particular treatment; some can be removed for artificial rearing, while others must be left to the parents. (See Arrow-poison Frogs, pages 166–169.)

⬆ *Artificial rearing of Dendrobatid tadpoles in individual containers. A duplicate set of containers (with aged water) is needed for a daily change. This system is laborious but prevents cannibalism.*

● *If separating adults and eggs, which should I move?*

... If spawning takes place in the adults' normal housing, the eggs should be removed to a separate tank for hatching; if not, the eggs can remain and the adults should be returned to their usual vivarium. Caution: do not add water before removing the adults – some species may drown.

● *Does sperm retention occur in amphibians?*

It does occur in some salamanders that practise internal fertilization. The sperm is stored and used to fertilize eggs at a later date.

● *How long do hatching and metamorphosis take?*

Both depend on temperature and species. Some desert frog tadpoles metamorphose in several days; their breeding pools are only temporary. In cool regions tadpoles and larvae may overwinter and metamorphose the following year.

● *What happens to larvae at metamorphosis?*

Larval salamanders lose their external gills and lateral sensory line. Some skeletal changes occur. Tail fins are resorbed and permeability of the skin alters. Frogs and toads resorb the tail. The rasping larval teeth are lost and the mouth grows. The long herbivorous intestine shortens to adapt to a carnivorous diet. The limbs develop; hindlegs first, followed by the forelimbs.

● *How do I raise frog tadpoles?*

Set up hatching and rearing tanks well before hatching. These may be quite simple, but ensure plenty of room – for communal rearing, not more than 20–30 tadpoles to a tank with a surface area of 24 x 12in (60 x 30cm). See Housing, pages 142–143, for a discussion of water quality. Change 25% of the water every week; stand replacement water uncovered for 24 hours to dechlorinate it. Algae for grazing will grow in good light. Prevent "green water" – coloured by free-swimming algae – by introducing some *Daphnia* (see Foods and Feeding, page 150–151). These will multiply and can be used to feed newt larvae (or adults). Provide a small raft for metamorphosing froglets to climb on. This will help you net them for moving to a vivarium.

● *Do salamander and newt larvae need different food from frog tadpoles?*

"Tadpoles" are larvae of frogs and toads only. Larvae that metamorphose on land eat insects or worms; there is no grazing or infusoria stage. See Foods and Feeding, pages 150–151, for more information.

Health and Disease

CHOOSING A HEALTHY AMPHIBIAN CAN BE difficult. The trauma of capture and shipping can aggravate or bring on disease, and close confinement can result in ammonia poisoning from the animals' own waste. As a buyer, you may not be able to observe the animals' normal activities; most amphibians are secretive and nocturnal, and spend the day hiding or clinging to the glass. Do not buy stock from dirty, overcrowded tanks, especially if dead specimens are present. Avoid emaciated animals or those with rubbed snouts or other skin blemishes. Some amphibians are naturally slender, but emaciation is evident as prominent bones and a shrunken belly. Most amphibians (with the exception of toads) should have moist, shiny skin. You should also be alert for wrinkled, tight skin and "pinched" muscles on the limbs, which are signs of dehydration.

Precautions and Hygiene

Aquaria that have housed fish or other animals should be thoroughly sterilized and rinsed before they are reused. Substrate materials can be sterilized by heating – except moss, which should be rinsed thoroughly, or preferably frozen for 4–5 weeks. (See Furnishing in Reptile Care, pages 22–25, for treatment of plants.) Bromeliads or other plants that hold water should be flushed out several times with clean water. Aquatic plants should be purchased from an aquarist supplier (not taken from the wild) and should be rinsed well before being put in the tank.

Poor hygiene and overcrowding cause health problems. Dirty conditions can produce a build-up of toxic ammonia and encourage the rapid spread of pathogens and parasites. Replacing soiled furnishings is not enough. The vivarium

COMMON AMPHIBIAN HEALTH PROBLEMS

By law, many conditions must be treated by a professional. A veterinary surgeon will explain what you are legally allowed to do.

Ulcerative Dermatitis

Symptoms: Also called "red leg", it frequently occurs as red haemorrhages on thighs and posterior part of the abdomen, followed by ulcers. (Note: some species have red patches in this area as part of their normal coloration.)

Comments: The most common bacterial infection. Highly contagious, it can appear on any part of the body, leading to septicaemia and death. Topical and oral antibiotics may be needed. Emergency treatment using a chelated copper-based fish remedy (see the manufacturer's instructions) may help.

Bacterial Tuberculosis

Symptoms: In the final stages the skin is covered with lumps, which eventually burst. Swollen eyes may also occur

Comments: Tends to appear in debilitated animals. Attacks internal organs first. No effective treatment known; usually well advanced by the time external symptoms appear.

Velvet Disease (as in tropical fish)

Symptoms: Grey slime, usually on the body of aquatic species.

Comments: Caused by protozoan parasites such as Oodinium and Trichodina. Treatments can be purchased at aquarist shops.

Spindly Leg Syndrome

Symptoms: Seen in newly-metamorphosed froglets (Dendrobatids and other species). Forelimbs are thin and useless, and may be in the wrong position.

Comments: Cause unknown. It seems to occur after intensive breeding. The most likely explanation is an unknown dietary deficiency in the mother. The condition is irreversible.

◀ *A Madagascan Reed Frog (*Heterixalus madagascariensis) *with an ulcerated snout due to bacterial infection. This is often caused by scraping against glass.*

Dietary Deficiencies

Symptoms: A host of problems, from metabolic bone diseases (see Health and Disease in Reptile Care, pages 44–45), reduced infertility and eye trouble, to loss of appetite, general listlessness and reduced growth.

Comments: Deficiencies can be avoided by a varied diet with appropriate vitamin and calcium supplements. It is often difficult to pinpoint exact causes. Over-reliance on deficient foods such as mealworms, raw beef and waxworms causes problems. Large species kept in restricted quarters and overfed on high-protein or high-fat foods are also likely to be obese.

Prolapses

Symptoms: Intestinal prolapses occur mainly in obese females of larger frog species. A mass of pink flesh appears protruding from the cloaca.

Comments: Veterinary treatment is required. Lubricate the affected area with surgical jelly and pack the animal in wet paper towels to prevent desiccation.

Poisoning

Symptoms: Range from hyperactivity to paralysis of hindlimbs. Affected animals (especially frogs) will try to move, only to collapse with hindlimbs outstretched.

Comments: Causes include disinfectants; unsuitable medicines; ammonia build-up (dirty conditions); poor water quality (particularly in larvae); and skin toxins of other species. Other causes are disease and internal damage. Isolate the animal in a clean container under a continuous flow of clean, dechlorinated water at the appropriate temperature until it revives and starts feeding. The best treatment is prevention.

Common Fungal Infections

Symptoms: In aquatic species, a white "furry" growth; in terrestrial species, a brown slime. Followed by ulceration in both cases.

Comments: Amphibian skin is easily infected, especially if previously damaged. Dirty conditions also frequently result in skin infections.

needs cleaning with dilute (3%) bleach, followed by thorough rinsing to prevent any residue leaching into the system. Household disinfectants and proprietary vivarium disinfectants are dangerous to amphibians.

Maladaptation and Quarantine

Sometimes animals do not adjust well to captivity; the size and layout of the vivarium may be unsuitable. Hiding places are essential. A glass tank can be confusing, causing rubbed or damaged snouts, especially in jumpers such as frogs of the genus *Rana*. New introductions should be disturbed as little as possible and the tank walls shaded if necessary until the occupants have settled in. Poor appetite, or weight loss in spite of feeding, is a sign that something is wrong. Check that environmental conditions (temperature, humidity, lighting, water quality, etc.) are correct. If so, investigate other possibilities such as parasites, bullying by cagemates or incompatibility due to skin toxins in different species. Other possible factors include unfamiliar foods or feeding at the wrong time of day.

Captive-bred specimens should be relatively healthy, but a quarantine period of 30 days is advisable. Wild-caught imports need 60 days or longer; some disease organisms have extended life cycles. Unquarantined amphibians must not be put with established specimens, especially if the latter are captive-bred. Quarantine is a burden but it helps prevent expensive losses and the refurbishment of an established vivarium.

Treating Disease

For the novice keeper, accurate diagnosis is the biggest problem. Amphibian diseases have not been well researched, and it may be difficult to find qualified advice. It may be illegal to treat some conditions yourself – consulting a veterinary surgeon is advisable. Different medications may be needed for different organisms – several types may be present in cultures obtained from swabs. For example, a white "cottony" growth in and around the mouth could be fungal or bacterial, or both. Many amphibian keepers use fishkeeping remedies, but this should not be attempted by the inexperienced. Sick amphibians should be moved immediately to a separate

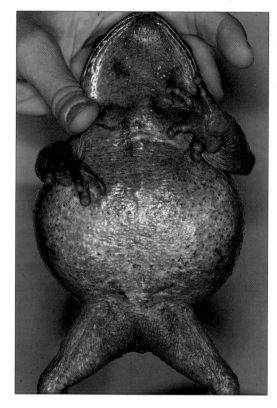

◄ *A Blomberg's Toad* (Bufo blombergi) *showing red-leg disease on its inner legs. The infection can appear on any part of the body, is contagious, and can be fatal.*

container. Having removed a sick animal, it is also advisable to remove its companions to clean quarters to reduce the risk of further infection.

Like reptiles, amphibians are widely subject to parasites (see Health and Disease in Reptile Care, pages 40–42). A common prescription treatment is fenbendazole, though this is not effective against tapeworms. Some tapeworm remedies are dangerous to amphibians – you must seek professional advice. New animals in quarantine should always be treated for worms.

Amphibians carry numerous protozoans in the gut, most of them harmless, but some types can be harmful if the animal is stressed. Secondary bacterial, fungal and viral infections can also occur in these circumstances. Faecal samples are needed for positive identification. The usual treatment is metronidazole, obtained from a veterinarian. Certain protozoans can cause intestinal upsets such as enteritis.

● *How do I give a medicine to an amphibian?*

... Oral dosing of small amphibians using a plastic pipette requires skilled assistance; the jaws of small specimens break easily. For larger specimens, a credit card is useful for opening the mouth. You may add medication to the water of aquatic species, or paint or dab it onto terrestrial ones. Powdered medication may give better adhesion.

● *How do I quarantine amphibians?*

Sick animals must always be quarantined individually to avoid cross-infection, even if their disease appears to be the same. A plastic tank is ideal – it is lightweight and easily cleaned. Furnishing should be minimal: disposable substrate, disposable or easy-to-sterilize hide boxes and plastic (washable) plants for cover. A thick layer of unbleached, wet paper towel is a good substrate; it facilitates the collection of faeces for analysis, which should be done as soon as possible. Avoid drying out the tank. Spray the substrate when necessary and supply a shallow bowl of clean, dechlorinated water into which the animal(s) can climb. Minimizing disturbance and shading the tank help to reduce stress during quarantine.

● *Can I treat fungal infections myself?*

Yes. For emergency treatment for fungal diseases, use a 50% solution of hydrogen peroxide dabbed on the affected areas, or (for aquatic species) a 10-minute bath in a 0.05% solution of malachite green (an aquarium remedy).

● *Is there any treatment for spindly leg?*

No. Once it develops, spindly leg is irreversible, although there are various claims for prevention. These include: vitaminizing food insects at every feed; a full-spectrum (UVB) light suspended over the tadpoles; adding powdered iodine bird block to tadpole food; and high-protein diets for tadpoles. None of these is completely effective when tested, and it is impossible to know whether spindly leg would have appeared without the treatment. Its occurrence can be erratic in consecutive clutches or even within a single clutch.

● *What causes frogs to swell up and die?*

Severe swelling of the abdomen (and limbs) is usually caused by metabolic malfunction such as kidney damage. This may be due to bacterial infection, worms, chemicals, or even an overdose of vitamin D3. Dirty conditions are probably a contributing factor. This problem is difficult to treat and is often fatal.

● *Will my amphibians be harmed if they accidentally eat stones with their food?*

Amphibians occasionally ingest stones or other items that adhere to the tongue or to the prey. These may be passed out harmlessly, but if they become impacted they will require surgical removal – not a practical option for small amphibians. Prevent the problem by using suitable substrates, and avoid placing food directly onto the substrate.

● *Can human antiseptics be used on amphibians?*

No. Many of these are dangerous to amphibians. For treating minor wounds, ask a veterinarian for a non-cytotoxic antiseptic such as a 0.75% chlorhexidine solution or other safe preparation.

● *How do I treat for worms?*

Treatment for roundworms is usually fenbendazole, only obtainable from a veterinary surgeon, who will advise on dosage. Since some tapeworm remedies are dangerous to amphibians, qualified advice is essential. Treatment for worms should be carried out in quarantine accommodation, as this will prevent contamination of the permanent vivarium.

▶ *Spindly leg syndrome in Dendrobatid froglets. The "figure eight" shape of the body often accompanies this condition and becomes evident before the abnormal front limbs appear.*

Amphibian Species

Most amphibians are nocturnal and secretive and sometimes drably coloured – not ideal qualities for vivarium subjects. However, their breeding habits are fascinating, and they have ensured a loyal following among many keepers. Each species has an appeal of its own – some are truly "jewels". Although numerous species are slimy (a word often wrongly used to describe all reptiles and amphibians), this merely serves to protect them against desiccation and in some cases against predators.

Relatively few amphibian species reach a large size. Newts and salamanders rarely grow to more than 8in (20cm) long, frogs and toads 4in (10cm) long – though the latter two have bodies that are more squat than long. In spite of their size, however, some need spacious accommodation because of their jumping ability. *Rana* species and certain others have been omitted for this reason, but there remains considerable choice. With proper care, many of these creatures can live for more than 10 years, and some may live as long as 20 years.

Many amphibians secrete toxins through their skin, and some, such as Dendrobatid species, are extremely poisonous if wild-caught. They should be handled with care, and young children should not be allowed to touch them at all. In general, it is best not to handle amphibians except when absolutely necessary, because they can quickly overheat.

▶ *Blue Arrow-poison Frog* (Dendrobates azureus) *see page 166.*

True Toads

FAMILY: BUFONIDAE

THIS LARGE FAMILY HAS OVER 20 GENERA. Best known in the hobby is the genus *Bufo*, often referred to as "true toads". The 150-odd species of *Bufo* are widespread, from rainforests to semi-deserts and high altitudes. Most are crepuscular to nocturnal, hiding in slightly damp refuges during the day. A few species may be active during the day, basking for limited periods. Although mostly terrestrial, all are good climbers – the vivarium must be escape-proof. Most of these toads have squat bodies with rough, warty skin, although spiny and smooth skins also occur. Toxic secretions can be produced. Many *Bufo* species are known to live for 20 years or more.

OAK TOAD

Bufo quercicus. Found mainly in the southeastern coastal plain, this is the smallest toad in the US, at only 1.25in (3cm) long. Oak Toads are fascinating creatures and many are extremely attractive, but they are less popular than larger species. Nevertheless, they have often been taken from the wild – always check local laws before doing so. Unlike most toads, they are mainly diurnal, but they can be difficult to spot in their native habitat. Oak Toads will thrive in a small vivarium but breeding is more likely to succeed in more spacious quarters, outdoor enclosures or a converted greenhouse. They will not disturb the furnishings, so decorative planting is possible. Individuals make small burrows under the hides and tend to use them regularly. Males have darker throats than females.

In the wild, breeding is sparked off by warm, heavy rain and may occur between April and September in the northern hemisphere. Shallow ponds or ditches are used for spawning. Compared with many bufonids and other species of amphibian, Oak Toads produce a rather modest number of eggs – only 600–700. If you breed them, it would be best to share out the spawn or return some to the wild – but only in the appropriate area and after seeking expert legal advice.

▲ *Oak Toad* (Bufo quercicus) *colouring varies from an almost uniform black to grey with dark blotches and coloured warts. A light dorsal stripe like this is typical.*

▶ *European Green Toads* (Bufo viridis) *breed every Spring in warm, shallow pools. An outdoor enclosure or converted greenhouse is best for this purpose.*

If attempting breeding in a vivarium, a pool will be needed. Following a cool period, spray heavily to simulate rainfall. Remove the spawn to a prepared rearing tank (see Breeding, pages 154–155). Tadpoles should be fed fish flake food and not overcrowded.

EUROPEAN GREEN TOAD

Bufo viridis. This species is found throughout much of central and eastern Europe, into central and southern Asia and north Africa. Its full adult length is up to 4in (10cm). Colouring and patterns vary widely. The most attractive forms have a pale, almost white background with irregular green markings and occasionally red spots. North African forms tend to be brown, the green often being dark or even barely visible. In parts of its range this toad is now protected. Available specimens in the trade are likely to be from northern Africa. Captive-bred toads are occasionally advertised – check their place of origin if possible, as Winter treatment varies accordingly.

● *Does handling toads really cause warts, or is that just superstition?*

... This is pure superstition. Their skin secretions are only produced under extreme stress, and will not cause warts. However, any cuts on the keeper's skin will be irritated by contact, as will the eyes and mouth (all mucous membranes). Toads should be handled gently only when necessary and basic hygiene precautions should be observed.

● *Can true toads be kept outdoors?*

Cane Toads need warm nights and are best kept indoors due to the risk of escape. Oak Toads and European Green Toads can be kept outdoors in a suitable climate. The enclosure should be escape-proof and secured against predators. It should have a small pool, several hides out of direct sunlight, a loose sandy area for burrowing and suitable outdoor plants.

● *How do I hibernate European Green Toads?*

Put the torpid toads in a ventilated box with slightly damp moss or dead leaves and place in a frost-free position. If hibernating in an outdoor facility, remove any water and cover the hibernation site with leaves, straw, styrofoam slabs, etc. for extra protection.

● *What is meant by "breeding stagnancy"?*

According to this theory, some amphibians that use transient pools will not breed twice in the same vivarium. Moving them to new quarters, or replacing the substrate before the breeding season, may work.

● *How many tadpoles can be kept together?*

Overcrowding should be avoided; 30 tadpoles in a tank measuring 24x12x12in (60x30x30cm) should give them sufficient room. This does not apply to Cane Toads (see following page), which are pests as well as prolific breeders and should not be bred.

The European Green Toad does not readily breed in a vivarium; success is more likely in an outdoor enclosure with a pool (min 12x12x3in/ 30x30x8cm) or a converted greenhouse. Males are smaller than females and have loose skin folds on the throat, as well as nuptial pads on the fingers during the breeding season. Breeding is triggered by a gradual increase in temperature, photoperiod and spraying. The huge numbers of eggs in a clutch can cause problems, as infertile eggs rot and pollute the pool. The desired number of eggs should be removed to a prepared rearing tank. Tadpoles metamorphose at about 2–3 months depending on conditions.

● *Is it possible for Cane Toads to live with other herps?*

... No. They are toxic to other species and will eat almost anything that moves, including smaller Cane Toads. Only specimens of similar size should be kept together.

● *How do I keep Cane Toads from breeding, as I don't want to have to deal with 30,000 tadpoles?*

To avoid breeding, keep males and females separate and, as additional insurance, do not provide a pool. Under NO circumstances should you EVER release any cane toads – including tadpoles – into the wild; consult a vet about the most appropriate action to take.

Vivarium Conditions
Oak Toad, European Green Toad and Cane Toad

VIVARIUM SIZE   Rot-proof vivarium needed.

Oak Toad   30x12x12in (75x30x30cm) for 5–6 specimens.

European Green Toad   36x12x15in (90x30x 38cm) for 3–4 specimens.

Cane Toad   Min 48x15x15in (120x38x38cm) for 2–3 specimens.

SUBSTRATE

Oak Toad Loose sandy soil or loam with a moisture-retentive area covering 25% of the vivarium.

European Green Toad   Sandy soil with damper area (sand, chopped sphagnum moss, orchid bark mulch) covering 25% of the vivarium.

Cane Toad Loose sandy soil or loam covered with moss. Cane Toads produce copious waste; substrate must be replaced frequently.

HABITAT

Oak Toad   Several hides in different areas. Logs, rocks and plants as desired. Small water bowl. Occasional light spray to prevent arid conditions.

European Green Toad Hides in both dry and damp areas. Plants must tolerate dry conditions. Small water bowl and light evening spray.

Cane Toad   Several hides, some in a moderately damp area. Large water container for occasional bathing. Light daily spray – wet conditions must be avoided. Sturdy plants optional; leave in pots.

TEMPERATURE

Oak Toad   18–25.5°C (65–78°F) during day; 13– 15°C (55–60°F) at night. Photoperiod: 14 hours.

European Green Toad   21–25.5°C (70–78°F) during day; min 13°C (56°F) at night. Photoperiod: 14 hours.

Cane Toad   25°C (77°F) during day; 20–21°C (68–70°F) at night. Photoperiod: 14 hours.

BREEDING CONDITIONING   Cane Toads have "pest" status in some areas and are rarely bred in captivity. It is best not to breed them. They produce 30,000 eggs, which cannot easily be reared or disposed of.

Oak Toad   Bright light is essential in the vivarium; also, a pool, min 15x12x3in (38x30x8cm). Reduce temperature to 10°C (50°F) for 8–9 weeks, then spray heavily to fill the pool. Photoperiod: normal daylight hours.

European Green Toad   Provide a pool as for Oak Toads. Northern species: 5–7°C (41–45°F) for 10– 12 weeks. Southern species: 10°C (50°F) for 8–9 weeks. Photoperiod: normal daylight hours.

FEEDING

Oak Toad and European Green Toad   Dusted insects, earthworms.

Cane Toad   Thawed rodents and pieces of chick wiggled in forceps, dusted insects.

HATCHING

Oak Toad   1 annual clutch of 600–700 eggs. Remove desired number of eggs to a separate tank. Keep for 15–18 days at 20°C (68°F).

European Green Toad   1 annual clutch of 12,000 eggs. Remove desired number of eggs to a separate tank. Keep for 15–18 days at 18.5°C (65°F).

CANE TOAD

Bufo marinus. Originally found in Central and South America and southern Texas, Cane Toads are probably best known because of their pest status in Australia (and other areas), where they were introduced to control the sugar cane beetle; they have preyed on native species to the extent that scientists are now looking for some means of biological control of the toads. Cane Toads are large – up to 9in (23cm) long – and in spite of their dull brown colouring they are popular as pets. They are commonly available and relatively cheap. But be careful: Cane Toads can produce a powerful toxin from the parotoid glands when attacked. Under extreme provocation this can be sprayed over a distance up to 39in (1m). Children and domestic pets should be kept away from them. Avoid handling unless necessary – normal, gentle handling does not cause toxin release, but always wash your hands thoroughly afterwards. Both eggs and tadpoles also contain toxins and should be handled with care as well.

Like the other true toads, Cane Toads do not require a pool unless breeding, but they will sit in a large water bowl occasionally if their skin

Cane Toads (Bufo marinus) have drab colouring, but are popular due to their size and temperament. They tame easily and will sit waiting to be fed! They also secrete a strong toxin if attacked. Handle with care.

becomes too dry. Extra heating is not normally needed, but their requirement for relatively high night temperatures may mean that they must be kept indoors unless in a warm climate.

Females are much larger than males. During the breeding season, males develop nuptial pads on the forelimbs and produce a "trilling" call. It seems that few, if any, keepers attempt to breed this species – no breeding reports are available. When spawning does occur, a prodigious number of eggs (30,000) is produced; raising this many tadpoles with the problems of filtration and feeding would be a mammoth task. If spawn is produced, raising just a few might be successful. Unwanted specimens must not be dumped in the wild; they can take over whole ecosystems, as in Australia, and prey on other species, including small mammals. For this reason, and the sheer number of eggs involved, it is best for the amateur hobbyist not to breed Cane Toads at all.

Arrow-poison
Frogs FAMILY: DENDROBATIDAE

DENDROBATID FROGS FROM CENTRAL AND South America produce some of the strongest natural toxins known to humans. Three species in particular (*Phyllobates terriblis*, *P. aurotaenia* and *P. bicolor*) were traditionally used by the indigenous peoples of Colombia to poison blow-pipe darts. The secretions produced by one tiny frog are enough to cover 50 arrowheads, and contact with the smallest trace of the toxin is enough to kill a person. Dendrobatids kept in captivity and denied their natural diet of toxic insects eventually lose their potency. Largely for this reason, there are no records of keepers being harmed. Their brilliant "warning" colours make them particularly attractive to the hobbyist.

Very few individual Dendrobatid species have a common name, so most keepers refer to the species name. The most commonly available species in the pet trade are *Dendrobates pumilio*,

◆ *The Strawberry Arrow-poison Frog* (Dendrobates pumilio) *is only about 1in (2.5cm) long. It is difficult to breed in captivity; eggs must be left with the parents.*

D. auratus, *D. azureus*, *D. tinctorius*, *P. bicolor*, *D. reticulatus* and *D. leucomelas*. Collectively they are known as Dendrobatids, dart-poison frogs, arrow-poison frogs and poison frogs.

Several colour forms of certain species occur. Because of the resulting taxonomic uncertainty, some species are placed in complexes. Generally speaking, mature females are slightly larger and plumper than males, and males of some species have broader "plates" on the forelimbs. Calling males can be identified by an extended throat pouch. However, in some cases behaviour is the only sure guide to gender. Unlike many other amphibians, Dendrobatids are diurnal, and their breeding behaviour is fascinating to observe.

● *Are arrow-poison frogs dangerous to touch?*

With time, wild-caught specimens lose their toxicity in captivity, and captive-bred poison frogs do not have any skin toxins. Nevertheless, they should be handled only when necessary. Wear disposable gloves or coax the frogs into a small container.

● *How often should arrow-poison frogs be fed?*

Fruit flies or crickets dusted with vitamin powder can be offered daily, unless large numbers of food insects remain uneaten in the vivarium overnight. Daily spraying with water often knocks down additional insects hiding in the plants.

● *Are Dendrobatids seasonal breeders?*

Most species breed throughout the year. *E. tricolor* and *D. ventrimaculatus* can be particularly intensive breeders and soon "burn out" if allowed to breed without restriction. A slightly cooler, drier period with reduced photoperiod every 4–5 months could be tried to slow them down. Extremely hot weather – too hot to use lighting – may inhibit breeding, but it can also be fatal. (See also "Spindly Leg" Syndrome in Health and Disease, pages 157 and 159.)

Vivarium Conditions

Vivarium size   Min 24x12x15in (60x30x45cm) for a pair or trio of smaller species. More height allows plant growth and provides climbing facilities. Larger species need min 30x18x24in (75x 45x60cm).

Substrate	Moisture-retentive

Habitat   Rainforest. Cork bark logs, driftwood, waterfalls and suitable plants for decoration and cover. (Plants such as bromeliads need drainage at the base. Plant in cork bark logs filled with moss and orchid bark compost.) An unplanted area at the front provides a clearing for feeding.

Humidity   90%. Use a misting system or spray daily with tepid water. Excess water must be syphoned or drained off.

Temperature   23–27°C (75–80°F) during day; 20–21°C (68–70°F) at night.

Feeding   Dusted fruitflies, crickets, green aphids; occasional small waxworms, whiteworms and rice flour beetle larvae. Springtails are useful for froglets of the smaller species. The frogs will adapt to regular feeding in early evening.

🔺 Dendrobates leucomelas, *displaying nature's classic warning colours, yellow and black. There is also an orange and black form of this species.*

Courtship and Mating

Given the correct husbandry, many Dendrobatid species need little stimulus to spawn; mainly they need to be well fed and healthy. Dendrobatids have some of the most complex social behaviour of any amphibian group, and courtship can last from a few hours to several days. A calling male is approached by a receptive female who then paws his back and makes forward butting motions with her chest. In a few species, the male may grasp the female's head with his forelimbs (amplexus). Rival males of other species indulge in ritualized amplexus, attempting to press their opponent to the ground. This usually results in a wrestling match. Similar behaviour is seen in females, with the "pressed" female remaining prone for some time while the winner courts the male. A single pair may breed, or a female may approach 2, 3 or 4 males. Be careful: where several females are kept together, they will often eat each other's eggs.

Most Dendrobatids seek a secluded spawning site, but occasionally the eggs are deposited on leaves of plants, or even on the substrate. Items with a smooth clean surface such as shallow plastic lids or a petri dish base make ideal spawning sites in the vivarium. You will also need to provide some cover – half coconut shells, small plastic tubs, large plastic leaves or flowerpots with an entrance cut out are suitable. A lining of green or black plastic inside the spawning site facilitates the removal of the eggs for hatching.

Breeding Conditions

CLUTCH SIZE 12–15 annual clutches of 1–30 eggs according to species and other factors (the age and size of the female, etc.) are possible, but this is excessive and will exhaust the frogs.

HATCHING

Group 1 Includes *Dendrobates auratus, D. azureus, D. leucomelas, D. tinctorius, D. truncatus, Eppipedobates trivittatus, E. tricolor, Phyllobates vittatus, P. lugubris, P. terriblis, P. bicolor* and *Colostethus* species: Remove to a petri dish or container with tepid water to just touch their base. Do not submerge. Maintain the level and cover container to retain humidity. Hatching takes 9–14 days at 78–80°F (26–28°C) but can drop to 70°F (21°C) at night.

Group 2 Includes *D. histrionicus, D. pumilio* and *D. lehmanni*: Leave eggs where they are laid to be raised by parents.

Group 3 Includes *D. ventrimaculatus, D. reticulatus, D. fantasticus, D. imitator* and *D. quinquevittatus*: As for Group 1 above.

For captive breeding purposes, 3 groups of Dendrobatids can be distinguished:

Group 1 is the largest and includes species whose eggs can be raised artificially. In the wild, hatchling tadpoles are transported to small pools. If left in the vivarium, they may be transported, but froglets tend to be undersized.

Group 2 is the smallest. The eggs are laid on leaves rather than on prepared spawning sites, and hatching tadpoles are carried to water-filled bromeliads and deposited there. Females make regular visits and feed tadpoles on infertile eggs; for this reason, Group 2 species are often called Oophages. Breeding this group poses practical problems: males are highly territorial and need a large vivarium. Artificial rearing is difficult, but may be possible using dried yolk of hens' eggs. It is probably better to leave the eggs and let the parents raise them.

Group 3 breeding behaviour is flexible. Eggs can be removed as for Group 1 or left as in Group 2. Removal is probably advisable. Tadpoles that are raised by the parents tend to be undersized at metamorphosis, although they eventually reach full size. Froglets require very small food.

Care and Feeding of Tadpoles

When they are free of the jelly and swimming, transfer tadpoles to individual plastic containers with 0.75in (1.5cm) of dechlorinated water at 25°C (77°F). Tadpoles are nocturnal feeders; food should be supplied in late evening. The following day, net the tadpoles and transfer them to containers with clean water that has been left to stand for 24 hours. Most accept a 50/50 mixture of finely-ground fish flake food and fish conditioning food. A pinch of powdered cuttlefish bone and multivitamin powder may be added. Stir gently to send food to the bottom, encouraging

◀ *A male and female* Dendrobates azureus. *Their brilliant blue colouring is extremely unusual in frogs, making this a highly sought-after species. Their desirability is typically reflected in the price they command.*

▲ *A female Reticulated Poison-dart Frog* (Dendrobates reticulatus) *carries two newly hatched tadpoles on her back, transporting them to the nearest water source. These tadpoles can survive in the tiniest amounts of water, hardly more than a teaspoon full.*

● *Should infertile eggs be removed or treated with an antifungal agent?*

... No. Infertile eggs, even with fungus, do not normally affect healthy eggs. Moving infertile eggs may damage fertile ones or cause the contents of the infertile eggs to leak onto them. Antifungal agents are thought to cause damage to the nervous system. This damage shows up in young frogs.

● *Is it necessary to raise tadpoles singly?*

Tadpoles of many species are cannibalistic and must be raised singly. In at least two cases, *D. auratus* and *D. truncatus*, sibling tadpoles (from the same clutch) have been raised communally in small aquaria. Adequate food must be provided. Tadpoles from different species should not be mixed.

tadpoles to feed there rather than at the surface, where they would suck in air. Mosquito larvae, bloodworms, *Daphnia* and other live foods may carry parasites; avoid them.

Metamorphosis takes 8–12 weeks according to species and temperature; higher temperatures produce smaller froglets. When all the limbs have developed and the tail is partially resorbed, remove froglets to a small aquarium with a shelving layer of rounded aquarium gravel and 0.75in (1.5cm) of water.

As tadpoles become froglets, the tail disappears. At this point, place the froglets in small clear containers with some ventilation and wet kitchen towel or moss substrate until feeding is observed. Then they can be transferred to a nursery vivarium similar to the adults' but furnished with hiding places and a few plant cuttings for privacy. Small food is needed.

▶ OVERLEAF: *Golden Arrow-poison Frogs* (Phyllobates bicolor) *are the second most toxic Dendrobatid species. Juveniles like these lose their poison on a captive diet.*

Fire-bellied Toads

FAMILY: DISCOGLOSSIDAE
GENUS : BOMBINA

THESE SMALL, HARDY TOADS HAVE BEEN popular in the hobby for years and are fairly easy to keep. Although they are mostly crepuscular, fire-bellied toads are often active during the day, particularly in the breeding season. They feed in shallow water, ducking down to grab aquatic insects. These toads are well-known for their "Unken reflex" when startled (see What is an Amphibian?, pages 140–141), but this response fades in captivity. If they are attacked, the glands along the back give off a poisonous white substance. The degree of toxicity is not known. The tongue is disc-shaped and fixed to the back of the mouth, meaning that the toads cannot feed by flicking it. Instead, they seize food in their jaws and stuff it into the mouth with their forelimbs. If food is placed in a dish, the toads will learn to eat from it – this is useful, as it stops insects from drowning and polluting the water. Fire-bellied toads do well outdoors.

There are 4 species in the genus. The tiny 2in (5cm) long European Fire-bellied Toad (*Bombina bombina*) comes from eastern Europe and parts of Asia. Its background colouring on the dorsal surface is brown with irregular green spots; the ventral surface is orange or red with dark markings. Of a similar size, the Yellow-bellied Toad (*B. variegata*) is found in central and southern Europe. Its dorsal surface is grey, brown or olive with prominent warts, its venter yellow to orange with grey or black markings. The Oriental Fire-bellied Toad (*B. orientalis*) from Korea and northern China seems to be the most frequently seen in captivity and is easy to breed. Slightly larger than the previous species at about 2.5–3in (7–8cm) long, Orientals have a bright green back with black splotches, and the belly is red to orange with black patches. The largest species, at 3.5–3.75in (9–9.5cm) long, is the Giant Fire-bellied Toad (*B. maxima*), found in Vietnam and southern China. Its colouring is similar to that of the Oriental Fire-bellies, but the Giant species has more warts on its back.

● *How do I keep the water clean when rearing tadpoles?*

... If tadpoles are being reared in containers, gently net them and place them in similar containers with dechlorinated water at the same temperature. If the tadpoles are kept in a small aquarium, debris can be syphoned off and partial water changes made. Water added to the aquarium should be 24 hours old and at the same temperature as the aquarium water.

● *Will Bombinas eat their own tadpoles?*

Yes; this is why the eggs are removed.

● *How often should* Bombina *tadpoles be fed?*

Tadpoles and froglets should be fed daily. If any extra food is left in the water, cut back slightly the next day; if all food disappears within a few hours, offer a bit more.

● *Can the colour of fire-bellies be influenced by conditions such as diet or habitat?*

The ventral colouring of captive-bred specimens tends to be paler than that of wild-caught ones. To intensify it, some keepers add special canary colouring food to the fish flake used to feed the tadpoles. The same effect may be achieved using freeze-dried brine shrimp.

➤ *A Yellow-bellied Toad* (Bombina variegata) *shows its warning colours. As with any amphibian, handle as little as possible and wash your hands immediately.*

Calls to Mating

In the breeding season males develop thicker forelimbs, nuptial pads appear, and the back takes on a rougher texture. Females are slightly larger and plumper. As the photoperiod and temperature begin to increase in the Spring, males begin to vocalize their mating calls to attract the notice of females. A receptive female allows a male to mount in amplexus. Spawning takes place 12–24 hours later. Small eggs, about 0.08in (2mm), are laid either singly or in small clumps on the plants. They should be transferred to a prepared rearing tank; several may be needed if there is a large number of eggs. The tadpoles soon begin taking food such as daphnia and tubifex. However, these may be sources of disease, so a high-protein fish flake food is safer. Raw lean beef or beef heart may be given occasionally in the later stages of development, but uneaten meat must be removed after 12 hours.

After 4 weeks the tadpoles have developed all 4 limbs and begin to metamorphose. At this stage they should be placed in a container with shelving gravel. This provides a gradual slope so that the toadlets can crawl out of the water. The baby toads should be kept in an aquarium at similar temperatures to the tadpoles. Wet paper towel or foam rubber are suitable substrates which can easily be replaced when soiled. Toadlets will eat small crickets and fruit flies, but green flies and aphids are particularly nutritious. When the toadlets are 1 month old, the crickets should be dusted first with vitamin and calcium supplements twice a week. Any toadlets that do not seem to be thriving by then should be removed from the aquarium and reared separately.

◄ *Oriental Fire-bellied Toads* (Bombina orientalis) *are more brilliantly coloured if caught wild than if captive-bred. They are mature at 8–9 months if well fed.*

Vivarium Conditions

VIVARIUM SIZE   36x15x15in (90x38x38cm) for 6–8 specimens, divided using a 2in (5cm) glass wall siliconed into place. Water area 15x15in (38x 38cm), 1.5in (3cm) deep.

SUBSTRATE   Loose, sandy soil topped with sphagnum moss for land area.

HABITAT   Land area: several cork bark shelters, plants optional. Spray lightly to keep the substrate slightly damp. Water area: plants such as *Elodea*.

TEMPERATURE   18–25°C (64–77°F) during day; 12–15°C (54–60°F) at night. Photoperiod: normal daylight hours (if kept in a vivarium in a well-lit room), or 14 hours (if using a fluorescent tube to provide light).

WINTER COOLING   Provide plenty of substrate and moss for burrowing.

B. orientalis and *B. maxima*   10°C (50°F) for 8–12 weeks. Photoperiod: normal daylight hours.

B. bombina and *B. variegata*   4–6°C (39–43°F) for 8–12 weeks. Photoperiod: normal daylight hours.

FEEDING   Insectivorous. Dusted crickets, occasional mealworms, hedgerow sweepings.

HATCHING   1–2 annual clutches of up to 100 eggs. Keep in rearing tank with 2in (5cm) day-old water at 21–23°C (70–74°F). Tadpoles emerge at 2–5 days and lie on the tank bottom until the yolk sac has been absorbed. After this, they graze algae; increase the water depth to 4–6in (10–15cm).

Treefrogs FAMILY: HYLIDAE

THIS FAMILY CONTAINS OVER 450 SPECIES (about 37 genera) found in a variety of habitats. They are often referred to as "typical" treefrogs since they are mostly arboreal and possess adhesive discs on the fingers and toes. However, some species are terrestrial and others semi-aquatic. Most are well suited to vivarium life.

EUROPEAN GREEN TREEFROG

Hyla arborea. These frogs are very familiar to European keepers. Their range excludes Britain but extends to the Caspian Sea, and a related form is found in southwest Asia. Although only 2in (5cm) long, they need spacious quarters for their arboreal lifestyle. Mainly nocturnal, they will often spend the day exposed to hot sunlight. Colouring varies; normally leaf-green, the frogs can change to brown or light beige. Males can be heard calling over considerable distances on quiet summer nights. The ideal place to keep this species is a covered outdoor enclosure or converted greenhouse, especially if you attempt to breed them. Overcrowding must be avoided.

Males are slightly smaller than females, with loose skin and yellow coloration on the throat. Spawning usually occurs when day length and day and night temperatures are suitable. Heavy rainfall often stimulates breeding in frogs kept outdoors, even if they are not directly exposed to it. Eggs are usually scattered, singly or in small clumps – they will adhere to the pool sides or to aquatic plants and should be removed for hatching. Gentle aeration or undergravel filtration can be used with the rearing tank, but partial water changes will be needed. Bright light over the tank encourages the growth of algae, which make up the tadpole diet, along with finely powdered fish flake food, fish pellets, blanched parsley and lettuce. Cover the tank with mesh to prevent the metamorphosing froglets from climbing out, and provide small rafts or ramps as soon as forelimbs start to develop. The froglets should be raised in moist, planted vivaria and fed on small dusted insects. Young European Green Treefrogs are more diurnal and seem to benefit from low-percentage full-spectrum (UVB) light.

A calling male American Green Treefrog (Hyla cinerea). This is a readily available species which needs spacious quarters in order to breed.

Other species requiring similar treatment are the European Stripeless Treefrog (*H. meridion-lis*), American Green Treefrog (*H. cinerea*), Barking Treefrog (*H. gratiosa*), Grey Treefrog (*H. versicolor*) and Pacific Treefrog (*H. regilla*).

WHITE'S TREEFROG

Litoria caerulea. These frogs from Australia and New Guinea are also known as Dumpy Treefrogs due to their rotund 4in (10cm) long body and plump limbs. Captive-bred specimens are widely available. The usual colour is a bright, waxy green, but limited colour changes to dark green, brown or almost blue occur. Occasionally a specimen may have white spots. Although White's Treefrogs are crepuscular to nocturnal and should normally be fed in the late evening,

◄ *White's Treefrog* (Litoria caerulea). *During dry seasons this species aestivates. Skin is not sloughed but retained, providing a dry coating to prevent water loss.*

Vivarium Conditions
European Treefrog, White's Treefrog, Red-eyed Treefrog and Marsupial Frog

VIVARIUM SIZE Rot-proof vivarium needed.

European Green Treefrog An outdoor enclosure is best: min 60x18x30in (150x45x60cm) for 3 males and 2 females; water area 24x24in (60x60cm) min 5in (13cm) deep.

White's Treefrog 36x18x30in (90x45x75cm) for 1–2 pairs; water area 1in (2.5cm) deep.

Red-eyed Treefrog and Marsupial Frog 24x24x30in (60x60x75cm) for 6–7 specimens; water area 24x 8x3in (60x20x8cm).

SUBSTRATE Moisture-retentive, topped by a layer of moss.

HABITAT Arboreal set-up including branches, hides, cork bark slabs and plants. White's Treefrog needs particularly sturdy branches.

TEMPERATURE Provide low-percentage, full-spectrum (UVB) light.

European Green Treefrog 18–26.5°C (64°F–80°F) during day; 12–18°C (54–64°F) at night. Photoperiod: 14 hours.

White's Treefrog 22–26.5°C (72°F–80°F) during day; 18°C (64°F) at night. Photoperiod: 14 hours.

Red-eyed Treefrog and Marsupial Frog 22–26.5°C (72°F–80°F) during day; 20–22°C (68–72°F) at night. Photoperiod: 14 hours.

HUMIDITY	Spray daily.
European Green Treefrog	70–75%
White's Treefrog	80%
Red-eyed Treefrog	85%
Marsupial Frog	75–85%

BREEDING CONDITIONING

European Green Treefrog Hibernate for 3 months at 8–10°C (46–50°F). Photoperiod: normal daylight hours.

White's Treefrog Withhold daily misting for 4–6 weeks and reduce temperature to max 23°C (74°F). Water depth 3in (8cm). Photoperiod: 10 hours.

Red-eyed Treefrog Reduce humidity to 65–70% for 8–10 weeks, then mist heavily until normal humidity (85%) is reached. Photoperiod: 11 hours.

Marsupial Frog Slightly drier period (65–70% humidity) for 3–4 weeks. Photoperiod: 10 hours.

FEEDING Dusted insects, including flying insects (bluebottles, moths etc.). White's Treefrog will take young mice; maximum of 1 per fortnight.

HATCHING Keep in separate rearing tank with 3–4in (8–10cm) of water. Change water regularly.

European Green Treefrog 1–2 annual clutches of 150–300 eggs. Keep for 10–20 days at 20–26.5°C (68–80°F).

White's Treefrog 3–4 annual clutches of 150–300 eggs. Keep for 3 days at 24°C (75°F).

Red-eyed Treefrog 2 annual clutches of 20–75 eggs. Keep for 7–10 days at 25.5–26.5°C (78–80°F).

Marsupial Frog 2–3 annual clutches of up to 200 eggs, hatched inside the mother's pouch.

they sometimes also feed during the day, especially after spraying.

Males tend to be slightly smaller than females and have a grey, slightly wrinkled throat patch. An aestivation period (see Breeding, pages 152–153) helps to stimulate breeding. If breeding in a separate tank, the frogs can be transferred to new quarters when they are "awake". At this point you should gradually restore temperatures to normal. A rain chamber may also be useful with this species (see Breeding, pages 154–155). The eggs should be hatched in a spacious rearing tank. Care and feeding of the tadpoles is as for European Green Treefrogs in this section. Metamorphosis usually takes about 32 days. The froglets need conditions similar to the adults'.

RED-EYED TREEFROG

Agalychnis callidryas. Although strictly nocturnal, these attractive frogs from Central American lowland rainforests are extremely popular. The body is light green, the belly white. Along the sides are blue and white vertical bars. Orange feet and red eyes complete the impressive livery. Their maximum length is 2.75in (7cm), and females are larger than males. Their long, slender limbs are equipped with adhesive discs. In the vivarium, the frogs typically spend the day huddled on a leaf or on the glass with their limbs tucked in tightly, making them into a small green "blob" that can be difficult to spot against the foliage.

Like most other tropical species, Red-eyed Treefrogs may breed at any time of the year, but mating may be stimulated by reducing misting to produce slightly drier conditions, followed by heavy misting. Under the right conditions, males begin calling and attempt to seize females. Eggs are deposited over the water on a leaf, stem or branch – or even on the vivarium glass. The egg mass should be misted gently twice daily to prevent it from drying out. Tadpoles drop into the water when they are sufficiently developed. If the

▲ *A Red-eyed Tree Frog* (Agalychnis callidryas) *is flamboyant and unmistakable. The red eyes and flash patches are appealing, but these will not be seen during the night, which is when the frogs are active.*

egg mass is not directly over the water, position a large water bowl underneath it.

Net the tadpoles and remove to a planted aquarium with 6in (15cm) of water at 26.5°C (80°F) – warmer than for other treefrog species. Otherwise, care and feeding are as for other tadpoles but infusoria are needed in early stages; see other species in this section, and the discussion of feeding larval amphibians on pages 150–151.

Other tree frog species requiring similar treatment are *Phyllomedusa* species, *Hyla ebraccata* and *Hyla leucophyllata.*

MARSUPIAL FROG

Gastrotheca riobambae. This species, sometimes also known as the Pouched Treefrog, comes from Central America, mainly Ecuador. It is less arboreal in its habits than the other tree frogs, preferring to climb instead in low vegetation. Its colouring is variable; the dorsum is light brown to green with brown longitudinal bands. Marsupial Frogs are mainly crepuscular to nocturnal and will tolerate colder conditions than recommended; they may be kept outdoors as long as they are protected from frost. They will take advantage of hiding places but often spend the day on branches, bark or glass walls. Light will be needed if living plants are used for decoration. Although not necessary for the frogs themselves, it allows better observation by the keeper.

The unusual breeding method of the Marsupial Frog makes this species an interesting vivarium subject. Adult females may reach around 2.75in (7cm) in length and have a small horseshoe-shaped opening (the pouch) towards the posterior end of the dorsum. In some members of the genus the eggs undergo complete development in the females' pouch, although for this and a few other species development is only partial. Males are slightly smaller than females and have a dark throat sac.

Breeding may occur at any time of the year, but a dry period (created by withholding daily misting) can stimulate breeding behaviour. Spawning of Marsupial Frogs occurs on land. Once in amplexus, the male produces a white liquid that he beats into a foam using his hindlegs. The female arches her rear end upwards; as the eggs emerge, they slide towards the pouch, which is held open by the male's toes. He then uses alternate movements of his hindlimbs to push the eggs into the pouch. The tadpoles develop within the pouch; after 5–6 weeks they are apparent as raised lumps under the skin. To release the tadpoles, the female enters the water and holds open her pouch with one toe. The tadpoles should be netted and placed in rearing tanks with water at around 22–24°C (72–75°F).

▲ *The Marsupial Frog* (Gastrotheca riobambae) *is so named because the female develops a pouch on her back in which to carry developing tadpoles.*

● *Are treefrogs a good choice for beginners?*

... Beginners can manage temperate species such as *H. arborea* and *H. cinerea.* Tropical species need some experience.

Can I mix various species of the family Hylidae?

No. They may hybridize, and White's Treefrog will try to eat smaller frogs.

How do I hibernate European Green Treefrogs?

Outdoors – they will bury into soft soil, or vegetation. Extra protection (dead leaves, old straw, or styrofoam slabs) should be placed over them. Indoors – they can be placed in a small vivarium with plenty of leaves or moss, then removed to a frost-free outhouse. See also Q&A, European Green Toad, page 163.

● *What is a suitable sex ratio for breeding Red-eyes?*

The usual ratio is 2 males to 1 female. The size of the vivarium will determine the total number of inhabitants possible. Remember that overcrowding leads to pollution and disease.

● *What happens if infertile eggs enter the pouch of the Marsupial Frog?*

These and underdeveloped or dead embryos are scraped out by the female's toe when the live tadpoles are being released.

● *Can large numbers of tadpoles be raised together?*

Overcrowding is thought to produce growth inhibitors in tadpoles, so it is better to rear smaller numbers in several containers or tanks. As a rough guide, 20–30 tadpoles need a surface area of 24x12in (60x30cm).

Horned Frogs

FAMILY: LEPTODACTYLIDAE
GENUS: CERATOPHRYS

THESE SOUTH AMERICAN AMPHIBIANS HAVE a reputation for eating almost anything, including their owners' fingers. They grow from 2.5 to 9in (6–22.5cm) in length and have squat, rounded bodies, large heads and wide mouths. Their dorsal colouring is a combination of light to dark green, red and brown. The common name refers to the horn-like projection over each eye, which is more apparent in some species than others – there are about 7 in the genus. The most common are the Argentine Horned Frog (*C. ornata*), the Chacoan Horned Frog (*C. cranwelli*), the Colombian Horned Frog (*C. calcarata*) and the Surinam Horned Frog (*C. cornuta*). All are bred on a commercial scale in the US. Many of the specimens for sale are hybrids, which can make identification difficult.

Horned frogs must be housed singly. They will attempt to eat companions of virtually equal size, as well as anything smaller. If the substrate in the vivarium is suitable, they spend much of their time half-buried in it. However, their huge appetites result in copious amounts of waste, and a clinical set-up may be preferable. In this case,

● *How often should I feed my horned frog?*

... Adult frogs easily become obese; 1 mouse every 7–14 days is adequate. Newly metamorphosed frogs should be fed every 2 days – as they grow, feed them larger portions but less often. With this regime they will be fully grown in 12–18 months. Froglets fed too often will mature too early (from 6 months on), and will put on weight as fat instead of muscle and bone.

● *Can I give goldfish to my horned frog?*

The frogs will certainly eat the fish, but this is not advisable, as goldfish often carry parasites.

● *Is aquarium pea gravel a suitable substrate?*

No. If gravel is ingested it can cause a blockage in the frog's digestive tract and kill the frog.

● *How do I handle my horned frog when cleaning out its vivarium?*

Small specimens can be approached from behind and cupped in both hands, then placed in a clean container with a small amount of aged water. For larger specimens a plastic scoop can be used.

Vivarium Conditions

Vivarium size 18x12x12in (46x30x30cm) for a single specimen.

Substrate Layers of wet paper towel or foam rubber for hygiene; or (in a large vivarium) moisture-retentive substrate such as leaf litter or moss to a depth of 3in (8cm), changed frequently. Some keepers maintain frogs in 0.5in (1cm) of water.

Habitat Cork bark hides, robust plants in pots, water bowl for bathing.

Temperature 25.5–30°C (78–86°F) during day; 22–24°C (72–75°F) at night. Photoperiod: 12–14 hours.

Humidity 80%. Spray vivarium daily.

Feeding Large insects, full-grown mice and even complete day-old chicks. Calcium supplements.

Breeding conditioning Withhold food for 3 weeks, then gradually lower the temperature to 15°C (60°F) and reduce the photoperiod to 8 hours. Provide 4in (10cm) extra substrate for burrowing and let it dry out slightly. After 8 weeks, reverse the process, slowly returning conditions to normal. For the next 4 weeks, feed the frogs every 3–4 days, then move them to a rain chamber. The water in the chamber should be at 28–29°C (82–84°F), with a depth of 1.5in (3.5cm) – horned frogs can easily drown if the water is too deep.

Hatching 1–2 annual clutches of up to 5000 eggs. Keep for 24–36 hours in a prepared container with 9–10in (22.5–25cm) of dechlorinated water at the same temperature as the water in the rain chamber and with an undergravel filtration system.

the frogs will adapt to not burrowing. Normal daylight is usually sufficient for light. In warm conditions additional heat may not be needed.

Male horned frogs are slightly smaller than the females, and are often more brightly coloured with a dark, loose throat (vocal sac). In breeding condition they develop nuptial pads on their forefeet for gripping females. To induce mating, you will need to simulate a rainy season, which is best achieved using a rain chamber (see Breeding, pages 154–155). Watch for cannibalism; not even mating couples are safe. The male calls for a few days before amplexus takes place.

When spawning occurs, the eggs may be left in the chamber, the adults removed and the water depth increased; or the eggs may be removed and put in a separate tank for hatching. Horned frog tadpoles are highly cannibalistic and should be housed individually if possible. If using individual containers, change the water daily; if using a communal rearing tank, undergravel filtration and partial water changes will be needed. The tadpoles eat large quantities of tubifex or blood worms, frozen (thawed) brine shrimp, and strips of beefheart. Given optimum conditions, they can be 3.5in (9cm) long with back legs and faint traces of colour within 4 weeks. When front legs appear, float pieces of cork or styrofoam in the water for the froglets to climb on. They should be reared individually in plastic cups with ventilated lids and wet paper towel for substrate; clean these daily. Tails are absorbed in a few days. Feed the frogs dusted insects, graduating to thawed pink mice and pieces of thawed chick.

▶ *Baby horned frogs* (Ceratophrys *species*) *are just as aggressive as the adults. Once metamorphosed, they must be reared singly.*

◀ *An adult Surinam Horned Frog* (Ceratophrys cornuta). *These fast-growing frogs need calcium supplements.*

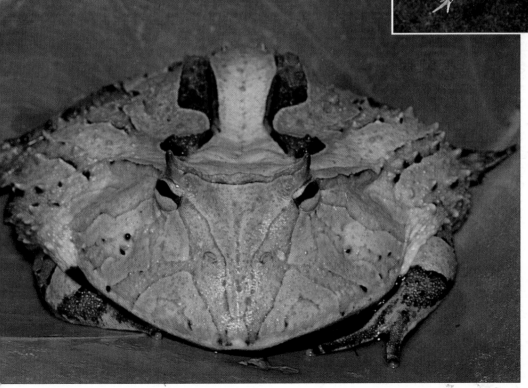

Tomato Frogs and Crevice Creepers FAMILY: MICROHYLIDAE

ALSO KNOWN AS THE NARROW-MOUTHED frogs, the family Microhylidae comprises over 50 genera, found in much of the world except Europe and some parts of North America. Many species lack teeth and feed mainly on termites and ants. Only a few species have been studied.

TOMATO FROGS

Dyscophus species. These plump, slow-moving, terrestrial Madagascan frogs are diurnal but remain buried during the day. Their colouring ranges from bright red-orange in *D. antongili* to a less vivid red-brown in *D. guineti* and *D. insularis*, which are are sometimes called false tomato frogs. *D. antongili* is controlled under CITES, but captive-bred specimens may still be available with the appropriate local licences. The largest *D. antongili* specimens reach 4in (10.5cm); other species are smaller. Although all tomato frogs are fairly easy to keep, breeding them is challenging.

Tomato frogs (here Dyscophus antongili) *produce a white skin secretion under stress that causes swelling on contact. Wear disposable gloves and handle with care.*

Females are larger than males, and those from *D. antongili* and *D. guineti* have stronger webbing on the feet; in the latter species, a dark dorsal pattern is more common in males, whereas females more commonly have a red dorsal reticulations. *D. insularis* males have a black throat sac and may have more dark spots on the venter.

A rain chamber is needed to induce mating (see Breeding, pages 154–155, and Horned Frogs, pages 178–179). Leave the eggs in water in the chamber or remove them to a prepared rearing tank. Tadpoles are filter-feeders and should be fed infusoria and finely ground fish flake food. Gentle filtration or aeration and frequent water changes are essential when keeping hundreds of tadpoles together. As metamorphosis begins,

● *Is breeding conditioning only for breeding; will frogs get sick or die without it?*

No; it is simply the case that without the conditioning, the frogs will not breed. This is not detrimental to their health, as adverse conditions in nature often mean that breeding is not triggered, and the frogs must wait until conditions are right. If you do not wish to breed your frogs, you can omit this regime.

● *Should the vivarium be totally dry when conditioning for breeding?*

For tomato frogs, part of the substrate should remain damp and a small water bowl be provided also. For crevice creepers, allow the terrarium to dry for 6–7 weeks followed by heavy spraying and a slight rise in temperature; if this fails, a rain chamber (see Breeding, pages 154–155) may be necessary. The frogs must have a moist layer under the soil during the dry period. A small funnel inserted in the substrate will carry tepid water down to the lower layer. Add more if needed.

● *How do I provide aeration for tadpoles?*

An airstone (air diffuser) powered by a small air pump should be fitted in the rearing tank. Airstones are widely available from aquarist shops.

● *What are the best conditions for froglets?*

A scaled-down version of the adult set-up – each species may be kept communally. Feed daily.

provide miniature rafts or ramps for the froglets to climb on, or they will drown. A low-percentage, full-spectrum (UVB) light may be beneficial.

CREVICE CREEPERS

Phrynomerus species. These small (2in/5cm long) plump frogs survive extended droughts in their native sub-Saharan habitat by burrowing into soft soil. *P. bifasciatus*, also known as the Rubber Frog, and the Red-backed Crevice Creeper (*P. microps*) are common in the trade. The background colouring is dark brown to black with red-spotted limbs and a red stripe along each side of the dorsum. *P. microps* has a red dorsal surface and males may possess a black throat or darker ventral colouring. Both species produce powerful skin toxins and should not be kept with other frogs. Males are smaller than females.

Mating is stimulated by the rainy season. Captive breeding is rare; a group of 8 or 9 may produce better results than pairs. After spawning, transfer the eggs to a prepared rearing tank, or leave them in the rain chamber and remove the adults. When hatched, the tadpoles will remain suspended vertically in the water. Feed tadpoles as tomato frog tadpoles; light encourages the growth of infusoria. Aeration will be needed if large numbers of tadpoles are kept together.

Vivarium Conditions
Tomato Frogs and Crevice Creepers

VIVARIUM SIZE   30x15x15in (75x38x38cm) for 2 tomato frogs or 4–6 crevice creepers, divided into a land area and a water area 3in (8cm) deep.

SUBSTRATE

Tomato Frogs   Loose, loamy soil 3in (8cm) deep, topped with a layer of moss.

Crevice Creepers   Loose, sandy soil 6in (15cm) deep, mixed with chopped sphagnum moss.

HABITAT   Aquatic plants; low-growing plants on land optional. Cork bark hides on the land substrate. Ramps for climbing out of the water.

TEMPERATURE   24–26°C (75–79°F) during day; 22°C (72°F) at night. Photoperiod: 12–14 hours. Provide a low-percentage full-spectrum (UVB) light, especially if there are low-growing plants.

HUMIDITY   75%. Spray substrate daily.

BREEDING CONDITIONING   Reduce temperature to 22°C (72°F) and stop spraying. After 6 weeks, restore normal daytime temperatures and begin to mist. Remove frogs to a rain chamber or mist vivarium heavily (with drainage to prevent flooding). Leave a few days until spawning occurs. If the male stops calling and no spawning has taken place, remove frogs to the vivarium or stop misting.

FEEDING   Dusted insects

HATCHING

Tomato Frogs   Up to 3 annual clutches of 1000–1500 eggs. Keep for several days at 28°C (82°F) in 4in (10cm) of water in a tank or in the rain chamber. If in the rain chamber, young can be removed to a separate rearing tank.

Crevice Creepers   Up to 3 annual clutches of 400–1500 eggs. Hatching as for tomato frogs.

Spadefoot Toad and Malaysian Horned Frog

FAMILY: PELOBATIDAE

THE MEMBERS OF THIS FROG FAMILY NEED relatively specialized care and conditions, and some degree of experience in the keeper. Owing to their fossorial and secretive habits, Spadefoots are not as popular as many other frogs, but in compensation they are interesting to study.

SPADEFOOT TOAD

Pelobates fuscus. Also known as the European Spadefoot and the Garlic Toad, these mainly nocturnal 3in (8cm) toads are one of 4 species of European spadefoot toad and are found across Europe as far as the Aral Sea. Their colouring is variable; the dorsum may be grey, yellow-patterned or light brown with darker spots, stripes or marbling. This species can be kept outdoors in an enclosure or a converted greenhouse.

◆ *The European Spadefoot Toad* (Pelobates fuscus) *buries itself in holes dug with the hard "spades" on its hindlimbs. Use a substrate that allows excavation.*

Vivarium Conditions
Spadefoot Toad and Malaysian Horned Frog

VIVARIUM SIZE	
Spadefoot Toad 36x15x15in (90x38x38cm) for a pair. A third of the vivarium should be a pool 4in (10cm) deep.	
Malaysian Horned Frog 30x12x15in (75x30x38cm) for a single specimen.	
SUBSTRATE	
Spadefoot Toad Sandy soil 4in (10cm) deep, with a small area moderately damp.	
Malaysian Horned Frog Loam and moss covered with a 2in (5cm) layer of dead leaves.	
HABITAT	
Spadefoot Toad Cork bark hides in both dry and damp areas. A few strands of *Elodea* in pool. Spray occasionally to maintain slightly damp area.	
Malaysian Horned Frog A few cork bark hides on the substrate. Spray twice in the evening.	
TEMPERATURE	
Spadefoot Toad 18–28°C (64–82°F) during day; 12–18°C (54–64°F) at night. Photoperiod: 14 hours.	
Malaysian Horned Frog 24–25.5°C (75–78°F) during day; 24°C (75°F) at night. Photoperiod: 12 hours.	
HUMIDITY	
Spadefoot Toad	Low humidity
Malaysian Horned Frog	80–90%
BREEDING CONDITIONING	
Spadefoot Toad Hibernate in darkness for 8–12 weeks at 7°C (45°F).	
Malaysian Horned Frog In a long aquarium with water area 18x12x3in (45x30x8cm). Reduce water to 1in (2.5cm), temperature to 20°C (68°F) for 2–3 weeks; gradually restore to normal. Add frogs and spray heavily to fill pool. Photoperiod: 10 hours.	
FEEDING	
Spadefoot Toad Dusted insects, earthworms.	
Malaysian Horned Frog Dusted insects, occasional mice or strip of raw, lean beef.	
HATCHING	
Spadefoot Toad 1 annual clutch of up to 800 eggs. Keep for 7 days at 16°C (61°F).	
Malaysian Horned Frog 2 clutches of up to 600 eggs. Keep for 12 days at 23–24°C (73–75°F).	

Females are slightly larger and plumper than males. Breeding males develop a large oval gland on the outside of the upper arms and light granules on the lower arm and hand. Spawning occurs in Spring. Once pairs are in amplexus, remove any surplus males. Eggs are laid in short, thick strands and should be removed to a prepared rearing tank with a similar water depth and temperature to the usual tank. For rearing details, see Breeding, pages 154–155. Tadpoles can be reared communally.

Other species that require similar treatment are: Eastern Spadefoot (*P. syriacus*), Western Spadefoot (*P. cultripes*), Moroccan Spadefoot (*P. varaldii*) and Parsley Frog (*Pelodytes punctatus*) – provide bark or branches for climbing.

MALAYSIAN HORNED FROG

Megophrys nasuta. This nocturnal species from Thailand, Malaysia and the Indo-Australian archipelago is also a spadefoot toad. It is popular among hobbyists and frequently available. Its brown coloration is a perfect match for dead leaves. Malaysian Horned Frogs are quite robust, with females reaching almost 6in (15cm). Males may be only half the size of females.

Both sexes must be fed well before breeding is attempted. A rain chamber may be effective, otherwise the pair should be placed in a separate breeding tank similar to the normal vivarium. Once spawning is over, the adults should be removed. The eggs are usually stuck to the roof of cork bark arches or logs placed just above the water surface, from which the tadpoles slide down to the water on threads. After 7–8 days the tadpoles develop a funnel-shaped mouth which they use to suck up any organisms and particles from the water's surface. Feed them infusoria and very finely-ground fish flake food. As the limbs develop, lower the water level and provide small rafts or ramps. Froglets should be reared separately in small ventilated containers at around 23°C (73°F) with wet paper towel for substrate. Feed on small dusted insects.

Q&A...

● *Why are spadefoots called Garlic Toads?*

When disturbed they produce a garlic-scented secretion. It can irritate, especially if the keeper's hands have cuts.

● *Is filtration needed for the tadpoles?*

As with all tadpoles, the water must be kept clean. Power filters will suck them in. Gentle undergravel filtration and water changes should be used.

● *Can I use foam rubber as a substrate for the land area?*

Some keepers use it with cork bark hides, but it needs frequent cleaning. Also, the frogs cannot burrow into it as they would with soil.

● *What kind of leaves are suitable for the substrate for the Malaysian Horned Frog?*

Oak and beech leaves are long lasting; heating them will kill off any unwanted insects.

● *Are Malaysian Horned Frogs cannibalistic?*

Yes, they are highly cannibalistic. Specimens should be kept separately except when breeding.

◄ *The Malaysian Horned Frog* (Megophrys nasuta) *is unmistakable, with its angular head, sharp snout and "horns". It does well in captivity, although specimens often arrive in poor health due to neglect during transit.*

Clawed Toads

FAMILY: PIPIDAE

THESE AMPHIBIANS ARE CHARACTERIZED by flattened bodies and powerful hindlimbs with claws on the 3 inner toes. Sensory organs, especially near the mouth, aid the search for food; they are more important than eyesight in the murky water that members of Pipidae inhabit.

CLAWED TOAD

Xenopus laevis. This is the largest of the African clawed toads, reaching 4in (10cm). Once used in pregnancy testing, it is a familiar vivarium subject and is common in the trade. The colouring is usually brown, sometimes with irregular darker markings; the belly is light, often with dark spots. Albino forms are frequently available. The Clawed Toad tolerates a wide range of temperatures (although extremes should be avoided in the vivarium). Escaped or released specimens have become established, preying on the eggs, tadpoles, fish eggs and fry of native species. The Clawed Toad is now regarded as a pest, and local laws in the US may prohibit its sale or keeping.

Females are larger than the males and have 3 small projections (labial flaps) around the cloaca. Breeding males develop black nuptial pads on the fingers. The spawning ritual is common to all

● *Are Pipidae safe to handle?*

Their skin is not known to be toxic, but amphibians should not be handled – it is not good for them (see What is an Amphibian?, pages 140–141). Netting is the easiest way to remove them, as they tend to be slippery. They will climb out of an uncovered tank.

● *Can I use pellet foods for clawed toads?*

There is a type of pellet food developed for aquatic frogs and small turtles. For Dwarfs, they should be broken. If the toads refuse them, stop using them.

● *Can clawed toads be kept with other species?*

This is not a good idea. Other creatures would be eaten if they were small enough; or, if they were not eaten by the toads, they might eat the toads' eggs during spawning.

● *Should food items for clawed toads be dusted?*

It is difficult to dust food for aquatic frogs, such as these. Occasional pieces of raw lean beef can have vitamins and calcium well ground in before using.

▶ *An albino Clawed Toad* (Xenopus laevis). *Like all Pipidae, it breeds under water and will eat almost any living thing that will fit into its mouth.*

Aquarium Conditions
Clawed Toad and Dwarf Clawed Toad

AQUARIUM SIZE	Clawed Toad Raise water temperature to 28°C (82–83°F) for 6–7 days. Reduce water level to 4in (10cm) and add water at 10°C (50°F) to full depth.
Clawed Toad 30x12x15in (75x30x38cm) for 1–2 specimens, with water 5–6in (13–15cm) deep.	
Dwarf Clawed Toad 36x12x15in (90x30x 38cm) for 6–10 specimens, with water 10–11in (25–27cm) deep.	Dwarf Clawed Toad Raise water temperature to 26.5°C (80°F) for 6–7 days.
SUBSTRATE Gravel needed if using plants.	FEEDING Earthworms, tubifex, bloodworm, aquatic crustaceans, aquatic insects.
HABITAT Hides including half earthenware pots, rock, bogwood. Raft for Clawed Toads. Aquarium plants for Dwarf Clawed Toads. Dim lighting.	HATCHING In a prepared rearing tank.
	Clawed Toad 2 annual clutches of 500–600 eggs. Keep for 2–3 days at 21–26°C (70–78°F).
TEMPERATURE (Water) 20–25.5°C (68–78°F).	Dwarf Clawed Toad 2 annual clutches of 700–1000 eggs. Keep at 26.5°C (80°F), gradually
BREEDING CONDITIONING 2–3 weeks at 20°C (68°F) for both, followed by:	reduced over 3 or 4 days to 25°C (77°F).

Pipidae (with variations in *Pipa* species). Once in amplexus the pair swim in a vertical circle; as they reach the surface, belly upwards, the female releases eggs for fertilization by the male. The "acrobatics" are repeated until spawning is complete. Eggs should be netted and removed immediately, otherwise the adults will eat them.

Tadpoles have 2 barbels near the mouth and are filter feeders. Provide infusoria, finely-powdered fish flake food, powdered boiled-egg yolk and fish fry food; avoid large particles (filter-feeders can choke) and over-feeding, which pollutes the water. Metamorphosis takes approximately 2.5 months. Similar treatment is required by the Kenyan Clawed Toad (*X. borealis*) and Nigerian Clawed Toad (*X. tropicalis*).

DWARF CLAWED TOAD

Hymenochirus boettgeri. These 1.75in (3.5cm) aquatic frogs from western Africa are often sold in tropical fish outlets rather than by reptile dealers. They are inexpensive and relatively easy to keep, and may be housed in groups of 6–10. The colouring is mainly brown with darker spots and the body is covered in small, spiny tubercles. Albinos are often available. Eyes are not quite as highly placed as in Xenopus species.

Make sure that the tank is covered, or these frogs will climb out. A ventilated cover is necessary (not zinc or aluminium mesh). If heating is required, a thermostatically-controlled aquarium heater is suitable. Some keepers provide a substrate of aquarium gravel, but others prefer a bare tank. Undergravel filtration is optional. If no filtration is used, weekly changing of at least half the water will be needed. Even with filtration, regular partial water changes are advisable.

Males are smaller and slimmer than females and develop a yellow swelling just behind the armpit (the post-axillary gland). Breeding can occur at any time of the year as long as the toads are well fed. Males "buzz" and clasp females around the waist. Recurrent amplexus for 1–2 days may go on for weeks before the actual spawning takes place. Spawning itself is typical of the elaborate underwater "acrobatics" described for Clawed Toads.

The eggs should be removed from the parents' tank for hatching. Tadpoles of this species are carnivorous and initially require a diet of infusoria, which can be cultivated a spare tank (see Foods and Feeding, pages 150–151). They will graduate to eating *Daphnia* and *Cyclops*, bloodworm and tubifex. Once metamorphosed, the young require similar foods to the adults.

Other species requiring similar treatment: *H. curtipes* from the Lower Congo.

SURINAM TOADS

Pipa species. Members of the genus Pipa inhabit South America in similar habitats to the Clawed Toad. The Surinam Toad (*P. pipa*, sometimes called the Star-Fingered or Pipa Toad) is the largest member at 5–6in (13–15cm). *P. carvalhoi* and *P. parva*, dwarf forms measuring around 2–3in (5–8cm), are occasionally available.

Their unusual appearance and breeding habits make Surinam toads fascinating to observe. The body is flat, almost rectangular, with a roughly triangular head. Limbs are typical of the family, but the fingers end in star-shaped sensory organs – the claws are missing. The dorsum is covered in tubercles, as are the lips, sides and belly. Eyes are very small and placed high on the head, like most Pipidae. The colouring is basically grey to brown with lighter underparts. Although Surinam toads do not leave the water, it is always advisable to provide a ventilated cover.

◆ *A female Surinam Toad* (Pipa pipa) *carrying eggs on her back. Most Pipidae have flattened bodies and powerful hind legs, but this species is extreme.*

Females are slightly larger than males. When receptive, they develop a swollen ring around the cloaca and the dorsum starts to swell. Males make a clicking sound. Although the mating ritual is similar to Clawed Toads, the eggs are produced via an extensible tube (ovipositor) which protrudes from the female's cloaca when the pair reach the surface. The male fertilizes the eggs and distributes them over the female's dorsal surface, which enfolds the eggs in tiny individual chambers where they hatch. In both dwarf species, the tadpoles emerge before metamorphosis and finish developing in the water; in *P. pipa*, fully formed toadlets emerge, taking some 12–20 weeks from the time of spawning.

Captive breeding of Surinam toads is not common at present; they are not likely to breed in a small aquarium. You are more likely to be successful with either of the the dwarf species. Tadpoles and toadlets must be netted and removed to their own tank, or the adults will eat them. They are filter feeders (as in Clawed Toads) and can be raised communally. The toadlets will need food similar to the adults' but smaller.

Aquarium Conditions
Surinam Toads

AQUARIUM SIZE
P. pipa Min 48x18x18in (122x45x45cm) for a pair or trio, with water 17in (43cm) deep
P. carvalhoi and *P. parva*   Min 24x12x15in (60x30x38cm) for 2–3 pairs, with water 11in (28cm) deep.

HABITAT	Bogwood for hides. Dim lighting.
SUBSTRATE	Gravel
TEMPERATURE	Water
P. pipa	25.5–26.5°C (78–80°F)
P. carvalhoi and *P. parva*	23–25.5°C (74–78°F)

BREEDING CONDITIONING   Reduce temperatures by 2–5°C (5–8°F) for 7 days, then restore to normal. If this is unsuccessful, reduce the temperature again and drain off half the water; leave 7 days, then flood to restore the water level and restore normal temperatures 2–3 days later.

FEEDING   Earthworms, tubifex, bloodworm, aquatic crustaceans, aquatic insects.

HATCHING   2–3 annual clutches of up to 200 eggs, hatched by the female on her back. Remove new tadpoles to a separate rearing tank.

● *How many clawed toads can be kept together?*

... Clawed Toads are best kept as a single pair. An extra male may stimulate spawning but should be removed when spawning begins. 7–8 Dwarf Clawed Toads may be kept together, but it is advisable to remove any that are not spawning; they may eat the others' eggs. Surinam toads may be kept in pairs or trios.

● *Is a power filter suitable for the aquarium?*

Yes, but turbulence must be avoided. The filter must be switched off for spawning until the eggs are collected to prevent eggs from being drained into the filter.

● *Should an undergravel filter be switched off for spawning?*

No. Undergravel filters rely on a constant flow of water to sustain beneficial bacteria, which process the waste. Switching off kills the bacteria and produces toxins.

● *How often should clawed toads be fed?*

All clawed toads should be fed daily at all stages of their lives. They are voracious feeders and will eat almost any living thing they can fit into their mouths.

● *How long do clawed toads live?*

Given proper care, the larger species may live as long as 15 years; the smaller ones, not quite so long.

● *Will Dwarf Clawed tadpoles eat each other?*

As spawning can last several weeks, well-developed tadpoles will eat eggs and smaller tadpoles. Different age groups must be separated to prevent this.

● *How long does metamorphosis of Dwarf Pipa tadpoles take?*

It varies with temperature: at around 26°C (80°F) it should take 12 weeks. They will then take live foods. Growth will be slow if the tadpoles are overcrowded. (This applies to other tadpoles also). Maturity is reached at about 2 years.

● *What is the best sex ratio for Surinam toads?*

2 males to 1 female, but it is advisable to remove the surplus male once the pair is in amplexus to prevent him preying on the eggs.

● *Is it possible to have plants with Surinam toads?*

Not really. The strong movements of the swimming toads would soon uproot any plants.

Mantellas FAMILY: MANTELLIDAE

THESE ATTRACTIVE DIURNAL FROGS FROM Madagascar have become very popular. They are mainly terrestrial, although at least 1 species, *Mantella laevigata*, climbs trees. They are quite small, only measuring 0.75–1.25in (18–31mm) long as adults. Only a few species have been captive-bred. The best-known of these is the Golden Mantella *(M. aurantiaca)*; most of the others have no common name, and keepers tend to use the species name: *M. cowani*, *M. laevigata*, *M. expectata*, *M. pulchra*, and so on. The taxonomy is unresolved, complicated by colour variations.

Although the conditions given here are suitable for keeping most mantellas, some of the recently discovered species (such as *M. "loppei"* and *M. bernhardi*) need more research. Madagascar has several distinct climate zones, and altitude influences fluctuations in temperature. Avoid extremes; specimens in the wild have more environmental resources to help them adapt than

in captivity. Maintaining suitably low temperatures can be difficult in high ambient temperatures, especially for cooling prior to breeding.

Mantellas are sociable and can be kept together in groups of 6 or so. Males wrestle with each other but do not fight; no damage occurs. It is possible to breed from a pair, but communal breeding (up to 4 males per female) usually produces better results. Females are slightly larger and plumper than males – the most obvious indicator of sex is the distended throat pouch of a calling male. Species with a pale belly (such as *M. aurantiaca*) can be sexed by placing them in a small, clear container with a drop of water. As they press against the sides, 2 white lines may be visible under the belly skin; this denotes a male.

◆ *The Golden Mantella* (Mantella aurantiaca) *is frequently imported. Its bright colours suggest toxicity. It is not known whether this decreases in captivity.*

Burrows for Spawning

Spawning occurs in little burrows made in moss, usually under the hide. Alternatively, you can use 1in (2.5cm) diameter plastic pipes, angled with an end in the water. Moss placed around the pipe prevents rolling. Humidity must be kept high at spawning time. If the eggs are laid in a pipe without matting, tadpoles will wriggle down into the water; or the pipe and eggs can be repositioned in a separate container. Captive frogs lay considerably fewer eggs than those in the wild. Net the tadpoles carefully 3 days after hatching and remove them to prepared rearing tanks with 3in (8cm) of water at 20–21°C (68–70°F). Replace half the water every 3–4 days with aged water at the same temperature. Aquarium plants help to maintain the water quality. Tadpoles must not be overcrowded; 10 tadpoles to a 10x8x8in (25x20x20cm) tank is adequate. For feeding, see Arrow-poison Frogs, pages 168–169.

Metamorphosis takes 5–6 weeks. Froglets need to leave the water quickly as soon as the front legs appear. Provide small rafts or ramps as hindlimbs begin to develop. A ventilated lid prevents escapes. Rehouse froglets in a vivarium similar to the adults' and feed them on tiny live foods.

▶ Mantella expectata, *from the relatively dry southwest of Madagascar, has no widely used common name. It is stimulated to breed by a short rainy season.*

● *Are mantellas toxic?*

The bright coloration suggests so, though little research has been done. The skin of *M. madagascariensis* contains alkaloids similar to those of some poison frog (*Dendrobates*) species. Birds reject *Mantella* species, so they must have an unpleasant taste. Other frog species kept with wild-caught mantellas have died, possibly poisoned. It is not known whether mantellas' toxicity decreases in captivity.

● *Are mantellas suitable for beginners?*

Not really. Although not too difficult to keep (except to breed), they are expensive, and most species are only available as wild-caught. There is little documentation except for *M. aurantiaca* and *M. madagascariensis*, the most commonly available. Beginners would be better to start with fire-bellied toads or tree frogs.

Vivarium Conditions

VIVARIUM SIZE 36x15x15in (90x38x38cm) for 6–8 terrestrial specimens. Water area or container 6x10x0.5in (15x25x1.25cm). *M. laevigata* and other arboreal species require a taller vivarium, at least 30in (75cm), to allow climbing.

SUBSTRATE Moisture-retentive with a moss layer

HABITAT Plants optional. Small cork bark caves or other hides near the water's edge.

TEMPERATURE Use low-percentage, full-spectrum (UVB) light and avoid raising the temperature. Photoperiod: 12–14 hours.

M. laevigata Max 26.5°C (80°F) during day; min 21°C (70°F) at night.

Others 20–24°C (68–75°F) during day; 13–15°C (55–60°F) at night.

HUMIDITY 85%. Good ventilation essential.

BREEDING CONDITIONING Reduce temperature to 20°C (68°F) and humidity to about 55% for 6–8 weeks; reduce photoperiod to 10 hours. Then spray lightly for 2 weeks, followed by heavy spraying and restoration of lighting to stimulate breeding. Siphon extra water off the substrate.

FEEDING Small dusted insects

HATCHING Remove eggs and a portion of the substrate to a small container with sufficient water so that it almost touches the egg mass. Keep for 10–14 days in water at the same temperature as the normal vivarium.

M. laevigata 2–3 annual clutches of up to 10 eggs

Others 2–3 annual clutches of 20–60 eggs

Foam-nesting Treefrog and Flying Frog

FAMILY: RHACOPHORIDAE

MEMBERS OF THIS FAMILY ARE NOTABLE for their unusual method of breeding, although some *Rhacophorus* species are also well-known for gliding – they are often called flying frogs. Relatively few species are seen in the pet trade.

FOAM-NESTING TREEFROG

Chiromantis xerampelina. This arboreal species is found across southern and eastern Africa. The largest specimens may be up to 3.5in (9cm) long. The long, slender limbs possess adhesive discs on the digits; opposable inner fingers enable the frogs to grasp branches. The dorsum is grey or light brown with variable, darker markings, providing excellent camouflage on trees. Rapid colour changes from dark grey to almost white occur in the daytime, especially in hot weather. The belly is pink; the throat and skin fold across the neck are white, often with dark spots. Foam-nesting Treefrogs are adapted to hot, dry conditions and spend hours basking in strong sunlight.

Males are much smaller than females and have white nuptial pads on the first and second fingers. Spawning usually occurs at night. Pairs in amplexus find a suitable branch, usually overhanging the water. The female produces a secretion from her oviducts and beats it into a white foam using her hindlegs. After about 15 minutes, egg-laying begins and the eggs are churned into the foam. In between sessions of "nesting" the female may leave the site and enter the water to rehydrate. Females may nest together, 2 or more producing a single large nest. On the second night they add another layer of foam. The outer surface hardens, preventing desiccation. Several days later the crust starts to disintegrate; in subsequent simulated rainfall, the tadpoles drop into the water to complete their development. Spray the foam mass to help this process.

The tadpoles should be removed to a prepared tank for rearing (see Breeding, pages 154–155). Metamorphosis will take about 10 weeks. The

Vivarium Conditions
Foam-nesting Treefrog and Flying Frog

VIVARIUM SIZE	
Foam-nesting Treefrog 24x24x36in (60x60x90cm) for 2 pairs with a water area 24x10x3in (60x25x 8cm); can be permanent or only for breeding.	
Flying Frog Min 60x36x48in (150x90x120cm) for 1–2 pairs, with a permanent water area min 24x18x3in (60x45x8cm).	
SUBSTRATE Moisture-retentive	
HABITAT Branches and plants, some overhanging the water area; hides placed on substrate. Foam-nesting Treefrogs need a small water bowl.	
TEMPERATURE	
Foam-nesting Treefrog 25.5–26.5°C (78–80°F) during day; 23°C (74°F) at night. Full-spectrum (UVB) light and a basking lamp. Photoperiod: 14 hours.	
Flying Frog 26.5°C (80°F) during day; 24.5°C (76°F) at night. Low-percentage, full-spectrum (UVB) light. Photoperiod: 14 hours.	

HUMIDITY	90–95%. Spray daily.
BREEDING CONDITIONING	
Foam-nesting Treefrog Maintain normal temperatures but withhold spraying for 6–8 weeks to dry out the vivarium; then spray heavily to fill the pool again. Photoperiod: 12–14 hours.	
Flying Frog Maintain normal temperatures and withhold spraying for 6–7 days, then spray heavily. Photoperiod: 12–14 hours.	
FEEDING	Dusted insects
HATCHING	
Foam-Nesting Treefrog 2–3 annual clutches of up to 200 eggs. Spray egg mass to stimulate hatching, then keep for 4–6 days in water with the the same air temperatures as the adult vivarium.	
Flying Frog 2–3 annual clutches of 30–80 eggs. Keep for 4–6 days in water with the same air temperatures as the adult vivarium.	

froglets should be maintained in a vivarium similar to that of the adults, preferably with slightly moister conditions. Other species requiring similar conditions are *C. petersii* and *C. rufescens*.

FLYING FROG

Rhacophorus nigropalmatus. This attractive 4in (10cm) tropical frog from Thailand, Malaysia and Sumatra is typical of the family; there are 4 or 5 subspecies. Extensive dark webbing on the digits enables these frogs to glide. The dorsum is green, often with white spots. Flying Frogs have hearty appetites and eat smaller frogs and even lizards. They should not be kept unless spacious housing is available; injuries can easily occur during gliding. An adapted greenhouse is ideal.

Males are smaller than females and develop nuptial pads on the thumbs during the breeding season, which can be protracted. Like Foam-nesters, Flying Frogs produce a foam nest among the branches overhanging the water. For general care of tadpoles and froglets, see Breeding, pages 154–155. Other species requiring similar treatment are *Polypedates leucomystax* (formerly in *Rhacophorus* and often known as the Asian Flying Frog, though it does not glide) and *R. reinwardtii*. The latter does less well in captivity.

▶ *Flying Frogs* (Rhacophorus nigropalmatus) *are the largest* Rhacophorus *species. They have hearty appetites and are known to eat small lizards and other frogs. Do not house them with smaller companions.*

● *Why do my Foam-Nesting Treefrogs appear to sweat in high temperatures?*

This is an adaptation to hot, dry conditions; "sweating" cools them by evaporation. Normally moisture loss through their skin is low. Their faeces contain very little fluid, conserving moisture.

● *Should surplus males be removed at spawning time?*

This is not necessary. In the wild, surplus males join in communal spawning, and they may actually fertilize some of the eggs.

● *Would a rain chamber be useful for breeding Foam-nesters?*

They are not generally used for Foam-nesters – the prolonged dry period, followed by spraying and raising the humidity, usually stimulates breeding. However, a rain chamber might be useful for *Rhacophorus* species if normal stimuli fail; see Breeding, pages 154–155, for instructions for making a chamber.

● *How far can* Rhacophorus *species glide?*

Some are said to cover as much as 49ft (15m) in a single glide – this depends on vertical as well as horizontal space. Space is essential so that the frogs may exercise their gliding ability without risking injury.

● *Is a basking lamp necessary for* Rhacophorus?

These species do not bask like *Chiromantis* and would become desiccated if too near a spotlamp. However, if a basking lamp is used as a heat source (beamed through the cover glass), then it should not harm them. (See Heating, Lighting and Humidity, pages 144–145.)

Reed and Running Frogs

FAMILY: HYPEROLIIDAE

REED FROGS AND RUNNING FROGS BELONG to this large family found in sub-Saharan Africa. Both are easy to keep. Many reed frogs are poorly known, though some have been imported for years. Only 3 of the 20 or so species of *Kassina* (running frogs) are commonly seen in the trade.

MARBLED REED FROG

Hyperolius marmoratus. Also called the Painted Reed Frog, this is probably the best-known of the reed frog species. Adults measure only about 1in (2.5cm) (from 6–7 months old) and may be spotted or striped in white, beige, green, red or yellow, with red upper thighs and feet. Juveniles are a uniform colour and some adult males are brown. Long, slender limbs with adhesive discs make these frogs agile climbers. They are crepuscular to nocturnal and not particularly toxic.

● *Are Marbled Reed Frogs a good choice for a beginner?*

... Yes. They thrive equally well in a planted arboreal vivarium or in a fairly small, clinical set-up. Juveniles are a better choice than adults – they require similar conditions, and you can be assured of a longer lifespan.

● *Does the rearing tank need a filter?*

Yes – use an undergravel filter. Other types will suck in eggs or tadpoles unless the intake is screened.

● *What care do* Hyperolius *and* Kassina *tadpoles need?*

Keep in 25.5°C (78°F) water, changed often, using day-old dechlorinated water at the same temperature. Feed on algae, powdered fish flake food and aquarium plants. *Hyperolius* metamorphose at about 2 months, *Kassina* at 5 months. Cover the tank and provide rafts or ramps for froglets to climb onto.

Vivarium Conditions
Marbled Reed Frog and Red-Legged Kassina Frog

VIVARIUM SIZE	
Marbled Reed Frog 24x15x24in (60x38x60cm) for 6 specimens, divided with a water area 6x6x 2in (15x15x5cm).	
Red-Legged Kassina Frog 24x24x24in (60x60x 60cm) for a pair, divided with a water area 8x6x2in (20x15x5cm).	
SUBSTRATE Moisture-retentive, topped with a layer of moss for the land area.	
HABITAT Moist tropical set-up with branches, cork bark for climbing, decorative plants. A few strands of aquarium plants in the water area.	
TEMPERATURE Low-percentage, full-spectrum (UVB) light, especially if planted.	
Marbled Reed Frog 23–28°C (74–82°F) during day; 20°C (68°F) at night. Photoperiod: 12–14 hours.	
Red-Legged Kassina Frog 21–27°C (70–80°F) during day; 21°C (70°F) at night. Photoperiod: 12–14 hours.	

HUMIDITY	Spray daily.
Marbled Reed Frog	90%
Red-Legged Kassina Frog	60–65%

BREEDING CONDITIONING	
Marbled Reed Frog Reduce humidity to 80% for just 1–2 weeks. Maintain normal daytime temperatures and photoperiod.	
Red-Legged Kassina Frog Move frogs to a rain chamber 36x12x12in (90x30x30cm), with water 4–5in (10–13cm) deep. Maintain normal temperatures and photoperiod. Alternatively, spray heavily in vivarium to increase humidity to 90–95%.	

FEEDING	Small dusted insects
HATCHING Remove to a rearing tank with plants and keep for 3–5 days at 24°C (75°F). Siphon off any infertile eggs that start to rot or develop fungus.	
Marbled Reed Frog Up to 7 annual clutches of 200 eggs.	
Red-Legged Kassina Frog 2–3 annual clutches of up to 300 eggs.	

Males have a gular disc which tends to be grey, in some cases with orange spots. Newly imported specimens may breed in the northern Winter – November to March – but captive-bred specimens may breed at any time. Males tend to be territorial and competition for favoured calling sites occurs, but this does not lead to combat. After amplexus, the pair enter the water, where the eggs are scattered or laid in clusters on plants. Remove the eggs and replace the water container for further spawnings. Tadpoles may be raised communally and fed on finely powdered fish flake food, chopped tubifex and algae.

RED-LEGGED KASSINA FROG

Kassina maculata. This southern African species, also known as the Red-legged Running Frog, is often classified as *Hylambates maculata* because it possesses adhesive discs and is arboreal (most running frogs are terrestrial). Measuring up to 3in (8cm) long, it is very attractive. The dorsum is brown with large dark spots, each with a pale border. The inner thighs and the groin are bright red, and the pale belly is grainy textured. They are usually nocturnal but may come out to feed during the day. Often they huddle in corners.

The sexes are of similar size. Males can be identified by a gular disc over the deflated throat pouch. The disc may be yellow, and a black pigmentation of the throat pouch is usually visible. Females in breeding condition develop papillae (small swellings) around the cloaca. The rain chamber should have facilities for climbing out of the water and hiding – an island of stones at one end with cork bark caves and driftwood. The "rain" should last from late evening to early morning. Males compete vigorously for calling stations. Aquarium plants assist in egg collection; fresh plants are needed for subsequent spawnings. Other species requiring similar treatment are *K. senegalensis* and *K. wealii*, which are both terrestrial and need hides on the substrate.

Newts and Salamanders

NEWTS AND SALAMANDERS REQUIRE ONLY basic housing, which makes them popular with many hobbyists. Most species are secretive, nocturnal and drably coloured, but some diurnal ones are attractive. High Summer temperatures can be a problem if cooling equipment is not available. In hot, dry conditions these amphibians seek hiding places and aestivate (become less active). Occasional high temperatures (around 80°F/ 26.5°C) do no harm if not prolonged.

RED-SPOTTED NEWT

Notophthalmus viridescens. Sometimes called the Eastern Newt, this mostly aquatic species from eastern North America is well known in the hobby. There are 3 or 4 subspecies. Red-spotted Newts are notable for the juvenile "red eft" stage, which follows metamorphosis. Juveniles can vary from orange to red with small black circular dots that change to red spots as they grow. Adults, at a maximum of 4in (10cm), are olive to brown, with varying numbers of black dots and red spots usually encircled by a black ring. The ventral surface is yellow to orange with fine black dots. The hindlegs are large and strong.

Breeding males have nuptial pads on the hindlegs and a slightly raised crest along the tail; females have a plump body. The cloaca is hemispherical in males, more conical and projecting farther in females. Spawning occurs after amplexus. Eggs must be hatched away from adults.

At metamorphosis, 2–3 months later, larvae need to leave the water. Reduce the depth and provide rafts or ramps, or move the larvae to a terrestrial nursery comprising a moisture-retentive substrate covered with moss. The new red efts should be fed on tiny live foods. This stage lasts for up to 3 years, but can be bypassed by keeping the larvae aquatic.

Other species requiring similar treatment are the Mexican or Black-spotted Newt (*N. meridionalis*) and the Striped Newt (*N. perstriatus*). They will tolerate slightly higher temperatures.

A juvenile Red-spotted Newt (Notophthalmus viridescens) *spends up to 3 years as a red eft – a distinctively coloured, totally terrestrial specimen.*

● *What is the difference between a newt and a salamander?*

... From a strictly scientific point of view there is no difference. In common usage, species that mate and lay their eggs in the water, and whose larvae develop in the water, are called newts; those that are more terrestrial are called salamanders. The names are often interchangeable.

● *Are newts sociable?*

Several specimens can be kept together in a large vivarium with adequate supplies of food; the most compatible living arrangement is a pair. Subspecies should not be mixed; nor should adults and eggs or tadpoles be mixed, as adults are highly cannibalistic.

● *Some of my Red-spotted Newts have lost their legs – is this harmful?*

Aquatic newts tend to snap at anything that moves, and their limbs may be bitten off by companions. They eventually regenerate, normally without any problems.

● *Will Fire-bellied Newts eat pellet foods?*

Aquatic species will only take pellets in the water. Try giving them, but not all species will accept them.

FIRE-BELLIED NEWT

Cynops pyrrhogaster. Sometimes referred to as the Japanese Fire-bellied Newt, this species from Japan and eastern China is dark brown with pale red to bright carmine belly covered in variable dark spots. The tail is laterally compressed. Fire-bellies are quite hardy and long-lived, and will breed easily. Although their lifestyle is predominantly aquatic, they will leave the water voluntarily at the end of their breeding season. The vivarium can be moved outside during Summer, or the newts put in an outdoor enclosure with a pool. Like all aquatic newts, feeding them is easier when they are in the water; on land they will take only moving foods. Young Fire-bellies may be reared in a damp terrestrial environment, but they return to a fully aquatic setup from 4–5 months of age; they are mature at about 2 years. Young newts are expert climbers even on smooth surfaces; their vivarium must have a secure cover.

Fire-bellied Newts (Cynops pyrrhogaster), *like all aquatic newts, are easier to feed in the water, where insects cannot hide as they do in the substrate.*

The total adult length of this species is 4–5in (10–12cm). Males develop a wider tail crest and a blue sheen along the sides and tail. Courtship behaviour is complex, involving a "dance" that leads to the female picking up a packet of sperm that the male has deposited. Eggs are laid a day or so after mating and are stuck to the leaves of aquatic plants, which are folded over the eggs. The easiest way to remove the eggs is to remove the entire plant and replace it.

Other species requiring similar conditions are the Dwarf Fire-bellied Newt (*C. orientalis*), the Japanese Marbled Newt (*C. ensicauda*) and Paddle-tailed or Hong Kong Newts (*Paramesotriton hongkongensis*).

RIBBED NEWT

Pleurodeles waltl. This species from Iberia and northern Morocco is the largest European salamandrid, with an average length of 10–11in (25–28cm). The dorsum is a drab brown to olive with darker mottling. Yellow to orange marks along the sides contain poison cells; the ribs push through these cells to deliver the poison. Rib

ends may be visible in some specimens. In spite of this, Ribbed Newts are relatively harmless if they are handled gently. Young children should not be allowed to touch them, however.

Males in breeding condition are slimmer than females, have a swollen cloaca, thicker limbs, often a red tinge to the dorsum, a slightly longer tail and dark nuptial pads on the insides of their forelegs. Breeding can occur at any time of year, often following a short, cool period or a slight drying out. Bright light also seems to act as a breeding stimulus, but it must not raise temperatures. The newts should be sprayed heavily and breeding pairs removed to quarters with deeper water and aquatic plants. When the external gills of the larvae begin to regress, the water level should be reduced and a land area supplied to enable the young to crawl out. Metamorphosis occurs some 10–16 weeks after hatching.

Species requiring similar treatment: *P. poireti*, a smaller relative from southern Morocco.

ALPINE NEWT

Triturus alpestris. This species is widely distributed throughout Europe and is a favourite with European and British keepers. Paedomorphosis – the retention of juvenile characteristics by sexually mature individuals – is common in populations from higher altitudes. Extremely hardy

Vivarium Conditions
Red-spotted, Fire-bellied, Ribbed and Alpine Newts

VIVARIUM SIZE

Red-spotted, Fire-bellied and Alpine Newts 36x12x 12in (90x30x30cm) for 6 specimens.

Ribbed Newt Min36x15x18in (90x38x45cm) for a pair of adults.

SUBSTRATE Land area: loamy soil topped with moss. Water area: layer of aquarium gravel.

HABITAT Vivarium should be divided to provide a water area 4in (10cm) deep, with some aquatic plants. Plants in land area are optional. Cork bark hides on the land area.

TEMPERATURE 17–22°C (65–72°F) during day; 15°C (60°F) at night. Photoperiod: 14 hours. Low-percentage, full-spectrum (UVB) light will benefit plants. Do not use if it raises temperature too much.

BREEDING CONDITIONING Normal daylight hours

Red-spotted, Fire-bellied and Alpine Newts 3–6 weeks at 10–12°C (50–55°F) for southern species. Others: 6–8 weeks at min 7°C (45°F).

Ribbed Newt Reduce temperature to 7–10°C (44–50°F) for 3–6 weeks, then gradually increase to 20°C (68°F). Spray heavily, then remove pair to a similar chamber with water area 10in (25cm) deep.

FEEDING Slugs, earthworms, dusted crickets.

HATCHING

Red-spotted, Fire-bellied and Alpine Newts 1 annual clutch of up to 200 eggs over several weeks. Remove to a prepared rearing tank and keep for 20–35 days in water at 17°C (65°F).

Ribbed Newt 1 annual clutch of 350–1000 eggs. Remove to a prepared rearing tank and keep for 3–10 days in water at 17°C (65°F).

The Emperor Salamander (Tylototriton verrucosus) thrives in a well-planted vivarium at slightly higher temperatures than other salamanders.

newts, Alpines Newts can often be kept in a permanently aquatic set-up and do well in outside enclosures with a suitable pond. They are one of the most attractive members of the genus. The males' colours intensify during the breeding season: grey to black-blue above, with dark marbling apparent when in water. The lower part of the sides is white to light blue. Legs, flanks, face and tail have contrasting dark spots, and a low black and white banded crest develops in Spring. Females are a uniform brown above, with faint spots along the sides and on the tail. Both sexes have a yellow to orange underside.

Other *Triturus* species require similar conditions, though the Marbled Newt (*T. marmoratus*) will need some form of winter protection. Note: The Great Crested Newt (*T. cristatus*) is strictly protected in Britain. You must obtain a licence in order to catch, handle or keep them.

EMPEROR SALAMANDER

Tylototriton verrucosus. This species is also known as the Mandarin Newt, Emperor Newt, and Chinese Newt. Its native region includes western China, Burma, Thailand, Nepal and India. Although widely imported, its habitat and taxonomy are not well documented. Most specimens are brown with raised orange glands on the head, along the dorsum and as spots on the sides.

Although Emperors were once thought to need cool conditions, they have thrived and bred in Britain at Summer room temperatures. Their tank should be thickly planted with Indian fern (*Ceratopteris thalictroides*) and *Cardamine lyrata*, which grow in and out of the water. Pruning is needed to keep some open spaces in both areas, as Emperor Salamanders like to climb among the Indian fern. Although they may be active in the daytime, they do not need full-spectrum light, but overhead light may be needed for the plants. During Winter the salamanders are less active and do not eat as much.

Breeding Emperor Salamanders is not straightforward. Hibernation itself is not sufficient stimulus. If the first season is unsuccessful, in the following season try conditioning at slightly higher temperatures. A small circulatory pump with a watering-can rose fitted to the outlet hose may be placed in the pool and operated for 5–6 days to simulate rain. Males may be seen waving their tails even if mating is not observed. Eggs are deposited on leaves up to 5in (12–13cm) above the water, and it is worth looking underwater as well. Larvae have thrived at 29°C (84°F) in the day, 21°C (70°F) overnight. They may feed only at night, hiding among plants during the day. At temperatures below 17°C (65°F) the larvae may stop feeding and die. Metamorphosis typically occurs 10–12 weeks after hatching.

TIGER SALAMANDER

Ambystoma tigrinum. These popular salamanders have a widespread distribution in North America from Canada to Mexico. They are protected in some American states but are still available in the trade. With an adult length of 12in (30cm), Tiger Salamanders are the largest terrestrial salamanders. Their colouring – with yellow patches, bars or spots on a dark background – is highly variable, even within any one subspecies; there may be as many as 12. Tiger Salamanders are secretive, crepuscular to nocturnal creatures, but they can become tame enough to accept food from forceps, and will keep watch for anyone coming to feed them. They are voracious feeders, so they also defecate copiously; the substrate must be cleaned and replaced frequently. If you wish to install additional lighting for observation, it must be low-power lighting that does not raise the temperature inside the vivarium.

▼ *Tiger Salamanders* (Ambystoma tigrinum) *have huge appetites. As a result, the substrate quickly becomes soiled and must be replaced frequently.*

Vivarium Conditions
Emperor, Tiger and European Fire Salamanders

VIVARIUM SIZE With mesh cover for ventilation

Emperor Salamander 36x12x15in (90x30x38cm) for 6 specimens.

Tiger Salamander 36x12x12in (90x30x30cm) for a pair.

European Fire Salamander 36x12x12in (90x30x30cm) for 6 specimens.

SUBSTRATE Moisture-retentive, covered with moss.

HABITAT

Emperor Salamander As for Tiger Salamander but omit bowl and add pool 3in (8cm) deep, planted with Indian fern (*Certopteris thalictroides*) and *Cardamine lyrata*, in and out of the water. Prune plants.

Tiger Salamander Cork bark hides placed on substrate, plants optional; water bowl 9–10in (23–25cm) diameter 1in (2.5cm) deep; spray regularly.

European Fire Salamander As for Tiger Salamander but omit bowl and add pool 1.5in (3.5cm) deep with a ramp or stone for access.

TEMPERATURE

Tiger and European Fire Salamander 20–22°C (68–72°F) during day; min 10°C (50°F) at night.

Emperor Salamander 24–26.5°C (75–78°F) during day; 15°C (60°F) at night.

HUMIDITY

Emperor Salamander	85%
Tiger and European Fire Salamander	70%

BREEDING CONDITIONING

Emperor Salamander 15–17°C (60–65°F) during day; 12.5–15°C (55–60°F) at night for 8–12 weeks. Photoperiod: 10 hours.

Tiger Salamander Hibernate for 9–10 weeks at 3°C (37°F). Photoperiod: normal daylight hours.

European Fire Salamander Northern and central species: hibernate for 12–16 weeks at 5–8°C (41–47°F). Photoperiod: normal daylight hours. Specimens from southern areas may not hibernate but become sluggish for a few weeks.

FEEDING

Emperor and European Fire Salamander Earthworms, slugs, dusted crickets.

Tiger Salamander Earthworms, small snails, some slugs, dusted insects, pink mice (for larger specimens).

HATCHING

Emperor Salamander Egg-layer. 3 annual clutches of 20 eggs. Keep for 30 days in individual small containers with aged water at 24°C (78°F).

Tiger Salamander Egg-layer. 1–2 annual clutches of 350–1400 eggs. Remove to a separate tank and keep for 2–10 days in water at 8–10°C (45–50°F).

European Fire Salamander Livebearer. 1–2 annual litters of up to 70 advanced larvae. Keep in small individual containers with aged water at 20°C (68°F) till metamorphosis occurs, about 12 weeks.

Tiger Salamanders are aquatic only in the breeding season. A slight rise in temperature usually brings them out of hibernation. Northern and mountain populations breed from March–June, in the south December–February, and July–August in the southwest. It may be possible to adapt them to northern Winters so that they hibernate when live food is scarce. Breeding males have a swollen cloaca, and the females usually grow plumper. They can be placed in an aquatic set-up or a half land, half water vivarium. The water should be at least 6in (15cm) but even deeper is better, and furnished with plenty of aquatic plants. Eggs are stuck individually or in clumps to pebbles, plants etc. They should be transferred to a prepared rearing tank. Because they are cannibalistic, the larvae are better raised individually when they

● *Can Emperor Salamanders be kept in a tropical aquarium?*

... Although often displayed in this manner at pet shops, they should not be kept in a full-fledged aquarium; they are semi-aquatic and need only shallow water when breeding.

● *Are Emperor Salamanders toxic?*

Like many amphibians they produce skin toxins when attacked. It is thought that the ribs can protrude through the poison glands on the sides, as in Ribbed Newts. Observe the usual precautions and do not allow young children to touch them at all.

● *Can I speed up hatching and metamorphosis for Tiger Salamanders?*

Higher temperatures will shorten these times, but the larvae do not thrive. It is better to leave the temperature as recommended and wait.

begin to grow. Their first foods can be infusoria, followed by *Daphnia, Cyclops* and bloodworms, progressing to earthworms as they grow larger. Other species requiring similar treatment are other *Ambystoma* species.

EUROPEAN FIRE SALAMANDER

Salamandra salamandra. With its vivid black and yellow colouring, this species has long been popular with hobbyists in Europe. It is found throughout Europe (except Britain), the Middle East and northern Africa in moist shady areas, often near streams, at altitudes up to 5000ft (1600m). It is noted for its longevity and hardiness. The colouring denotes toxic skin secretions. There is also a black and orange form. Fire Salamanders require simple accommodation. Normal temperatures and daylight are satisfactory; above 25°C (77°F) they will show signs of distress, and their food intake usually decreases during warmer weather. Low temperatures, on the other hand, do not necessarily prevent feeding; offer food in all but the coldest weather.

◄ *The European Fire Salamander* (Salamandra salamandra) *is hardy and can be kept outdoors in a large enclosure. Ensure shade and frost protection.*

Female European Fire Salamanders are usually slightly longer and more heavily built than males. Breeding males exhibit a swollen cloaca. Mating can occur throughout most of the year, with gestation often taking several months. Slightly drier conditions during the hibernation period followed by spraying in the Spring often induce breeding. Females lie in the water to give birth, producing advanced larvae with 4 limbs and feathery external gills. Specimens from high altitudes may produce fully metamorphosed young. The larvae should be raised individually in small containers to prevent cannibalism. They will usually require larger food than infusoria (see Foods and Feeding, pages 150–151). Metamorphosis may take up to 3 months, and sexual maturity about 3–4 years. Metamorphosed young should be transferred to a small, moist vivarium without a water area.

AXOLOTL

Ambystoma mexicanum. These hardy aquatic salamanders are very popular with hobbyists. They are endangered in their native Mexico but are widely bred for the trade. Growing to 12in (30cm), Axolotls' colouring is dark grey to black on the dorsum, with a light grey venter. The skin has the texture of velvet, and the tail is broad and finlike. Several colour mutations such as piebald, gold, black and albino are often available. There are 4 relatively weak limbs and 3 fringelike gill branches either side of the head. Axolotls are neotenic – the adults retain larval characteristics (external gills, in this case).

Sexual maturity can occur at 1 year. The males have enlarged folds of skin either side of the cloaca, which swells during the breeding season. Mating often extends from November to June. Adult specimens should be separated over Winter and placed together again in Spring. Fertilization is external, using a spermatophore (sperm capsule) dropped by the male.

Eggs are laid within a few hours of fertilization and adhere to plants or lie on the substrate. Remove them to smaller containers with shallow water. Regular partial water changes are essential to avoid pollution and bacterial buildup. Small live foods are needed as for other salamander and newt larvae.

Species requiring similar treatment but needing larger tanks: Lesser Sirens (*Siren intermedia*), Two-toed Amphiumas (*Amphiuma means*) and Mudpuppies (*Necturus maculosus*).

Aquarium Conditions Axolotl	
Aquarium size 24x12x12in (60x30x30cm) glass aquarium for a pair.	
Substrate	Aquarium gravel
Habitat	Aquatic plants
Temperature Max 20°C (68°F) during day; min 10°C (50°F) at night.	
Breeding conditioning 5°C (41°F) for 8–12 weeks	
Feeding Earthworms, mosquito larvae, small fishes, aquatic insects, crickets, occasional pieces of raw, lean beef.	
Hatching 1 annual clutch of up to 600 eggs. Remove to a smaller container with 3in (8cm) aged water, max 20°C and keep for 14–15 days.	

A leucistic Axolotl (Ambystoma mexicanum) *is prized for its black eyes, unlike the red or pink eyes of the true albino. This form is not often available.*

Q&A

● *Is it true that Fire Salamanders can spray toxins?*

... This has been induced under laboratory conditions by using extreme provocation to simulate predator attack. There are no records of keepers being harmed, but minimum handling followed by handwashing to prevent eye or mouth contact is advised. Fire Salamanders should also be kept away from children and pets, and they should not be housed with other species.

● *Are hatchling Axolotls tadpoles or larvae?*

Strictly speaking, tadpoles are the larval stages of frogs and toads only. Hatchling salamanders and newts are properly referred to as larvae.

● *Are young Axolotls cannibalistic?*

Cannibalism does occur when larvae are raised communally. Those showing early growth tend to attack their smaller siblings. They should be removed and reared individually.

● *Is it possible to induce metamorphosis in Axolotls?*

This has been done by administering thyroxine. Very gradual drying out is claimed to be effective also, but may cause fatalities. This species is endangered, so it is best to perpetuate the normal form in any case.

Herptiles and the Law

LAWS CONTROLLING THE KEEPING OF HERPTILES can be complex, particularly if you intend to move a specimen from one country to another. The situation changes frequently, so it is important to check in advance. Ignorance of the law is never a valid defence. Any appropriate licences should have been obtained by the original importer, but if you are buying a specimen listed on CITES Appendix 1 or European Appendix A, you must obtain proof at the time of purchase that it is being sold legally.

The information below is divided into regulations at the international, national and local levels. Most laws are concerned with three broad issues: preventing smuggling; controlling the removal of wild specimens from their native habitats; and preventing the release of non-native species into an alien ecosystem, which they may upset, as with Cane Toads in Australia (see page 165). Local laws may also address animal welfare and public safety.

Regulations covering the transit of live specimens have been drawn up with the airline governing body IATA (headquartered in Montreal, Canada). Major airlines or specialist freight companies should be able to provide current information on the packing requirements for shipment of live herptiles.

INTERNATIONAL LEGISLATION

The Convention on International Trade in Endangered Species (CITES) was signed in 1975 in Washington DC and is now supported by more than 130 countries. New regulations may be proposed at meetings that take place every two years or so. There are three appendices – lists of species – that provide for more or less strict control of trade, according to their vulnerability.

Appendix 1: Endangered species. Cannot be caught in the wild and traded internationally for commercial purposes. Captive-bred species from this group may be purchased and kept under licence. Buyers must insist on a receiving a copy of the licence when taking any of these animals home.

Appendix 2: Species believed to be threatened by the commercial wildlife trade. Licences are required for their import or export. It is the responsibility of the importer to obtain these. Trade is monitored, and if it appears excessive, further controls such as quotas are introduced on a species-by-species basis.

Appendix 3: Species that may be scarce in one country, but plentiful in another; controls would apply to the former but not the latter, at the discretion of the individual countries involved. Many speces not considered endangered are not listed on CITES and can be freely imported. Imports require a health certificate from the country of origin.

NATIONAL LEGISLATION

Individual countries may introduce additional regulations to protect native species and trade in animals from outside their borders.

EUROPE

Under new European Union regulations introduced on 1 June 1997, all species are divided into four annexes corresponding to the CITES appendices.

Annex A: All CITES Appendix 1 species plus some Appendix 2 species and protected non-CITES species. Wild-caught specimens may not be imported for commercial purposes. Captive-bred ones require licences for any sale or transfer between individuals.

Annex B: All CITES Appendix 2 species plus certain others (including some non-CITES species). The importer must obtain import and export licences.

Annex C: All CITES Appendix 3 species. An export certificate and import notification (to Customs) are required. However, the importing country may decide to treat the species as for Annex D.

Annex D: Any other species that is being imported in such large numbers that monitoring is advised. Import notification (to Customs) is required.

UNITED STATES

The *Endangered Species Act* also protects native species not covered by CITES. You can obtain details from the US Fish and Wildlife Service in the Department of the Interior, Washington DC.

The *Lacey Act* makes it illegal to acquire a herptile (or any other fauna or flora) contrary to the laws of another country. The Lacey Act has also been used in the case of interstate transfer or sale of herptiles.

The *Injurious Wildlife Act* prohibits the release of non-native species into the wild, where they could become established and harm native wildlife.

The *Four-Inch Rule* prohibits interstate trade in turtles with a carapace less than 4in (10cm) long. This is intended to prevent salmonellosis in young children, who may put small turtles in their mouths.

LOCAL REGULATIONS

Local laws are often more directly applicable to individual keepers. Some herptiles – typically crocodilians and venomous snakes – are considered dangerous and may require a special licence to keep them at home. This restriction is incorporated into the *Dangerous Wild Animals Act* in the UK, which is a national law but interpreted at the local level; the licence requirements vary. Although most species will not be affected, you should always investigate before you acquire an animal. A local herpetological society can help. Also, if you rent your home, check your lease for any restrictions.

Glossary

Activated carbon Charcoal material used to remove pollutants from aquarium water.
Aeration A technique for adding oxygen to water by means of a constant stream of fine bubbles.
Aestivation Inactivity or torpidity during hot weather.
Airstone A small porous stone used for the AERATION of water.
Amplexus A mating grip used by frogs, toads, some newts and salamanders.
Aposematic coloration Warning coloration – bright colours that warn a predator that an animal is poisonous, or at least unpleasant to taste.
Arboreal Living in trees or shrubs.
Assisted feeding Placing food in an animal's mouth to stimulate a feeding response.
Autotomy The voluntary shedding of the tail (followed by regeneration) as a defence mechanism.

Basking A form of THERMOREGULATION in which an animal (especially a reptile) exposes itself to the sun to raise its body temperature.
Basking lamp A lamp used primarily as a heat source.
Brille A transparent scale over a snake's eye, sometimes called the spectacle.
Brumation A period of inactivity during cool conditions – not as extreme as HIBERNATION, but some keepers use the terms synonymously.

Captive farming Breeding species in captivity on a large commercial scale in order to sell or export them.
Carapace The upper part of the shell in a CHELONIAN.
Carnivore Meat-eater.
Chelonian A collective term for tortoises, terrapins and turtles.
Chromatophore A pigment-filled cell found mainly in the skin's upper layers.
CITES The Convention on International Trade in Endangered Species: An international agreement to control the trade in animals and plants (and their derivatives) through a licensing system based on how vulnerable a given SPECIES is.
Cloaca The common external opening of the excretory and reproductive systems in reptiles and amphibians.
Clutch A group of eggs laid at the same time by the same mother.
Colour morph A colour form.
Crepuscular Active at dusk.

Diurnal Active during the day.
Dorsum The back or dorsal surface.
Dystocia Egg binding; the retention of eggs in female reptiles.

Ectotherm Formerly known as "cold-blooded" – an animal that relies on external heat sources to raise its body temperature.
Endolymphatic glands The glands behind the ear.

Femoral pores Enlarged pores found along the inside of the thighs on certain lizards.
Force feeding Manipulation of food past the oesophagus of an animal (usually a snake) that will not feed voluntarily. See PINKY PUMP.
Fossorial Characterized by burrowing.
Full-spectrum light Light that includes both visible and ULTRAVIOLET LIGHT – the part of the spectrum between 285nm–750nm. Artificial full-spectrum light is thought to provide the same benefits as natural sunlight.

Gestation period The period from mating to egg-laying or giving birth.
Gravid Pregnant (of reptiles).
Green water Water that contains large numbers of single celled green algae and other INFUSORIA.
Gular Pertaining to the throat.

Hard water Water with relatively high levels of magnesium salts, borates, calcium carbonate and calcium bicarbonate.
Heliotherms Animals that regulate their body temperature by BASKING.
Hemipenes The divided copulatory organ in male reptiles.
Herbivore Plant-eater.
Herpetoculture The science of keeping reptiles and amphibians.
Herpetology The scientific study of reptiles and amphibians.
Herptile Any reptile or amphibian.
Hibernation A period of torpidity during cold weather. See BRUMATION.
Hybrid The offspring of parents from different SPECIES.
Hygrometer A humidity meter.

Incubation The period from the laying of eggs to their hatching.
Infusoria Microscopic organisms (especially protozoans or rotifers) that occur naturally in water containing organic material.
Insectivore Insect-eater.
Intergrade The offspring of parents from different SUBSPECIES.

Jacobson's organ An organ connected with the nasal cavity in most snakes and lizards. It aids the recognition of scent particles picked up by the tongue.

Keel A ridge along the CARAPACE of certain turtles, or a ridge on the scales of certain reptiles.

Lamellae Adhesive pads under the toes of certain lizards.
Larva A fully aquatic stage in amphibians after hatching.
Litter A group of live young born at the same time to the same mother.
Livebearer see VIVIPAROUS or OVIPAROUS

MBD Metabolic Bone Disease.
Metamorphosis The change from LARVA to adult.

Neonate Newborn of a LIVEBEARER.
Neoteny see PAEDOMORPHOSIS.
Nocturnal Active mainly at night.

Omnivore Eating both plants and animals.
Oophages Certain frogs that feed infertile eggs to their tadpoles.
Oviparous Reproduction by eggs that hatch outside the female's body.
Oviposition The laying of eggs.
Ovoviviparous Reproduction by eggs that remain inside the female until they hatch and are not nourished by her.
Ovulation The release of ripe ova from the female's ovaries.

Paedomorphism The retention of larval characteristics (gills etc.) into adulthood.
Papillae Small nipple-like projections.
Parotoid glands A pair of glands on the shoulder, neck or behind the eye in bufonid toads and some salamanders. May be present in other amphibians without being apparent.
Parturition Giving birth.
pH A measure of acidity or alkalinity. The scale ranges from 1 (highly acid) to 14 (highly alkaline); 7 is neutral.
Photoperiod The period during which the vivarium is illuminated. The amount of light this produces is crucial for the health of most reptiles and may affect breeding activity.
Pinky pump A small pump used to macerate a pink mouse for FORCE FEEDING to a snake.
Plastron The lower shell of CHELONIANS.
Poikilotherm see ECTOTHERM
Post-axillary gland A gland located behind the armpit.
Prehensile Capable of grasping; usually used to describe some lizards' tails.
Probiotic A mixture of bacteria, enzymes, electrolytes and vitamins that can be used for rehydration, treatment of stress or restoring gut fauna following antibiotic treatment.
Protozoans Single-celled micro-organisms. Some are harmful.

Red leg disease A severe bacterial infection in frogs, characterized by reddening of the hindlegs.

203

Salmonellosis Poisoning from the bacterial genus *Salmonella*. It can be transmitted by herptiles if proper hygiene is ignored.

Scutes Bony dermal plates that make up the PLASTRON and CARAPACE of a CHELONIAN.

Sexual dichromatism Any difference in colouring between males and females of a SPECIES.

Sexual dimorphism Any difference in physical features between males and females of a SPECIES.

Shoeboxes Small plastic boxes used (primarily in the US) to house herptiles, especially in rack systems.

Spawning The laying of eggs by frogs and toads.

Species A group of animals whose genetic similarities allow them to mate only with each other; the seventh and penultimate major group in the formal classification system of living things (kingdom, phylum, class, order, family, genus, species and SUBSPECIES).

Spermatophore A cone of jelly with a sperm cap deposited by male newts and salamanders.

Spindly leg syndrome A condition

sometimes affecting froglets – the forelegs are thin and useless.

Spot-cleaning The manual removal of individual faeces.

Spotlamp Lightbulb with internal silvered reflector, producing a beam.

Sub-caudal Underneath the tail.

Subspecies Members of a SPECIES that differ in some way from each other.

Substrate Any material used to form the ground layer of a vivarium.

Subtympanic scale A large circular scale located under the ear.

SVL Snout to VENT length – the usual dimensions for measuring herptiles.

Sweater boxes Similar to SHOEBOXES but larger.

Tadpole The LARVA of a frog or toad.

Terrestrial Living mainly on the ground.

Thermal gradient The range of temperature across a space, creating a cool end and a hot end.

Thermoregulation The method by which reptiles maintain their body temperature by moving close to and away from heat sources.

Thigmotherm A reptile that raises its body temperature by absorbing heat

through physical contact with its surroundings, such as the substrate.

TSD Temperature-regulated sex determination – a technique for producing a greater number of one sex by adjusting incubation temperatures.

Ultraviolet (UV) light A component of natural light, consisting of wavelength between 285–400nm, just below the threshold of visible light. It has three components: UVA (400–320nm) and UVB (320–260nm) are essential for reptile health; UVC (200–260nm) is dangerous to all living things.

Undergravel filtration Purification of water by drawing it through a bed of gravel over filter plates.

Unken reflex A defensive posture in some amphibians that involves arching the body and lifting the head and tail.

Vent See CLOACA.

Venter The underside or belly.

Vermiculite Expanded mica used in horticulture and for incubating eggs. It is sterile and water-retentive.

Viviparous Giving birth to live young that develop inside and are nourished by the mother.

Further Reading

Arnold, E.N. and Burton, J.A. *A Field Guide to the Reptiles and Amphibians of Britain and Europe* (Collins, London, 1996)

Bishop, S. *Handbook of Salamanders* (Cornell University Press, Ithaca, 1994)

Branch, B. *Field Guide to the Snakes and other Reptiles of Southern Africa* (New Holland Ltd, 1988)

Cogger, H. *Reptiles and Amphibians of Australia* (Revised Ed.) (Reed, 1992)

Conant, R. and Collins, J. *Field Guide to the Reptiles and Amphibians of Eastern and Central North America* (Houghton Mifflin, Boston, 1991)

Ernest, C.H. and Barbour, R.W. *Turtles of the World* (Smithsonian Institute Press, Washington DC, 1989)

Frye, F.L. *Reptile Care – An Atlas of Diseases and Treatments Vols I and II* (TFH, 1991)

Frye, F.L. and Williams, D.L. *Self-Assessment Colour Review of Reptiles and Amphibians* (Manson Publishing/The Veterinary Press, 1995)

Glaw, F. and Vences, M. *Field Guide to Amphibians and Reptiles of Madagascar* (2nd Ed.) (Published privately; available from reptile dealers or from M. Vences, Klosterstr. 124, 50931 Kôln, Germany.)

Highfield, A.C. *Practical Encyclopedia of Keeping and Breeding Tortoises and Freshwater Turtles* (Carapace Press, 1996)

Levell, J. *A Field Guide to Reptiles and the Law,* by (Serpent's Tale Books, 1995; reprinted 1997)

Markel, R.G. *Kingsnakes and Milksnakes* (TFH, 1989)

Mattison, C. *Encyclopedia of Snakes* (Blandford, London, 1995; Facts on File, New York, 1995)

Passmore, N.I. and Carruthers, V.C. *South African Frogs* (Southern Book Publishers (Pty) Ltd and Witwatersrand University Press, 1995)

Ross, R.A. and Marzec, G. *The Reproductive Husbandry of Pythons and Boas* (The Institute for Herpetological Research, Santa Barbara)

Schleich, X *et al Amphibians and Reptiles of North Africa* (Koeltz)

Stebbins, R.C. *Field Guide to the Western Reptiles and Amphibians* (Houghton Mifflin, Boston, 1985)

Walls, J. (ed.) *Jewels of the Rainforest* (Dendrobatidae) (TFH)

World Weather Guide (Times Books)

We also recommend the various titles of the Herpetocultural Library, published by Advanced Vivarium Systems, Lakeside, California, US, and those published by Perfect Python Publications, Nottingham, UK. Check your local library or contact these publishers directly for more information about specific titles and species.

Useful Addresses

UNITED KINGDOM AND EUROPE

British Herpetological Society c/o Zoological Society of London, Regent's Park, London NW1 4RY, UK

International Herpetological Society Secretary: Mr. K. J. Hingley, 22 Busheyfields Rd., Russells Hall, Dudley, West Midlands DY1 2LP, UK

B.M. Tortoise Trust London WC1N 3XX, UK

British Chelonia Group P.O. Box 235, Lincoln LN6 8AX, UK

A.S.R.A. (Association for the Study of Reptiles and Amphibians) c/o Cotswold Wildlife Park, Burford, Oxfordshire, UK

Herpetological Society of Ireland c/o 8 Mulberry, Fairfield Avenue, Commons Road, Cork, Eire

European Snake Society Jan-Cor Jacobs, W.A. Bultostraat 62, N.L. – 3523 TX, Utrecht, Netherlands

D.G.H.T (Deutsche Gesellschaft für Herpetologie und Terrarienkunde) Postfach 1421, D-53351 Rheinbach, Germany

UNITED STATES OF AMERICA

A.F.H. (American Federation of Herpetoculturists) P.O. Box 300067, Escondido CA 92030-0067

International Hylid Society c/o Amphibian Research and Conservation Centre, 2607 Thomas Road, Valparaiso IN 46383

National Turtle and Tortoise Society P.O. Box 66935, Phoenix AZ 85082-6935

American Dendrobatid Group c/o Charles Powell II, 2932 Sunburst Drive, San José CA 95111-2264

Chameleon Information Network 412 West E St., Encinitas CA 92024

International Gecko Society P.O. Box 370423, San Diego CA 92137

SSAR (Society for the Study of Amphibians and Reptiles) P.O. Box 626, Hayes KS 67601-0626

National Herpetological Alliance (Legal matters) Membership Secretary, P.O. Box 5143 Chicago IL 60680-5143

Acknowledgments

ABBREVIATIONS

AOL	Andromeda Oxford Ltd
BL	Bill Love/Blue Chameleon Ventures
DA	D. Allison
DMD	David M. Dennis
FLPA	Frank Lane Picture Agency Ltd
JM	Joe McSharry
M&PF	Michael & Patricia Fogden
OSF	Oxford Scientific Films Ltd
PF	Paul Freed
R&VD	Robert & Valerie Davies

Title page BL; 4 BL; 6-7 AOL; 7 BL; 8 R&VD; 9 BL; 11 JM; 12 R&VD; 13 JM; 14 AOL; 16 DA; 18t Bush Herpetological Supply; 18b AOL; 19 AOL; 21l AOL; 21r Bush Herpetological Supply; 22-3 AOL; 24 DA; 25 AOL; 26 DA; 27 DMD; 28 PF; 29 R&VD; 30 E. & D. Hosking/FLPA; 32 AOL; 33 PF; 35t R&VD; 35b BL; 36 James Robinson/OSF; 38-9 DMD; 40 PF; 42 Zig Leszczynski/Animals Animals/ OSF; 43l Courtesy of A. Meredith/S. Redrobe; 43r Stephen J. Divers; 44t PF; 44b Courtesy of A. Meredith/S. Redrobe; 45 Stephen J. Divers; 47 S. Maslowski/FLPA; 48 Rafi Ben-Shahar/OSF; 50 BL; 51 BL; 52 Dave Travis; 53 Dave Travis; 54 DA; 57 Jonathan Plant; 58 Tom Ulrich/OSF; 59 BL; 61t Steve Turner/OSF; 61b Zig Leszczynski/Animals Animals/ OSF; 62-3 R&VD; 63 PF; 64 PF; 66 BL; 67 Zig Leszczynski/Animals Animals/OSF; 68 BL; 69 BL; 70 BL; 71 PF; 73 DMD; 74 BL; 75 BL; 77 Michael Leach/OSF; 79 DA; 80 Zig Leszczynski/Animals Animals/OSF; 81 K.G. Preston-Mafham/Premaphotos Wildlife; 82-3 BL; 84 Susan C.L. Fogden/M&PF; 85 DMD; 86-7 M&PF; 89 Zig Leszczynski/ Earth Scenes/OSF; 90 PF; 91 DA; 92 PF; 93 DA; 94 DA;

95 R.A. Preston-Mafham/Premaphotos Wildlife; 97 PF; 98 K.G. Preston-Mafham/Premaphotos Wildlife; 100 BL; 101 PF; 102 PF; 103 BL; 104 Danté Fenolio; 106 BL; 108-9 BL; 110 JM; 111 BL; 113 JM; 114 BL; 115c BL; 115b BL; 117 BL; 118 BL; 119 DMD; 120 M&PF; 121 DMD; 122 R&VD; 123 DMD; 125 DMD; 126 Jonathan Plant; 127 R&VD; 129 DMD; 131 DMD; 132 BL; 135 PF; 136 DMD; 137 DMD; 139 Heather Angel/Biofotos; 140 BL; 141 JM; 143 DA; 144 DA; 145 Bush Herpetological Supply; 146 Jonathan Plant; 147 Mike Linley/OSF; 148 DA; 152 B. Borrell/FLPA; 153 DMD; 155 R&VD; 156 PF; 158 PF; 159 R&VD; 161 PF; 162 PF; 163 FLPA; 165 DMD; 166 M&PF; 167 M&PF; 168 John Netherton/OSF; 169 M&PF; 170-1 JM; 172 R&VD; 173 M&PF; 174 DMD; 175 BL; 176 BL; 177 PF; 179r BL; 179b DMD; 180 JM; 182 G. Synatzschke/OSF; 183 Danté Fenolio; 185 Heather Angel/ Biofotos; 186 PF; 188 PF; 189 Dave Travis; 191 Zig Leszczynski/Animals Animals/OSF; 193t M&PF; 193r BL; 194 DMD; 195 Chris Mattison/FLPA; 196-7 BL; 198 DMD; 200 M&PF; 201 Michael Fogden/OSF

Artwork by Julian Baker and Richard Lewington

The authors and publishers would like to thank Gordon and Mandy Bloomfield of The Pet Shop (Faringdon, UK); also, John and Jackie Forsythe, Paul Hoskisson, Dr. Charles Pain, Dr. Stephen Bloye, Dr. Steven Garvie, Bob Worthington, Birdquest International (Bolton, UK), Central Reptiles (Dudley, UK), Lakeland Wildlife Oasis (Milnthorpe, UK) and MC Tropicals (Widnes, UK).

Index

Major treatment of a subject is indicated by **bold** page numbers. References to illustration captions and annotations are *italic* page numbers.